21st Century Essays

DAVID LAZAR AND PATRICK MADDEN, SERIES EDITORS

Wagner

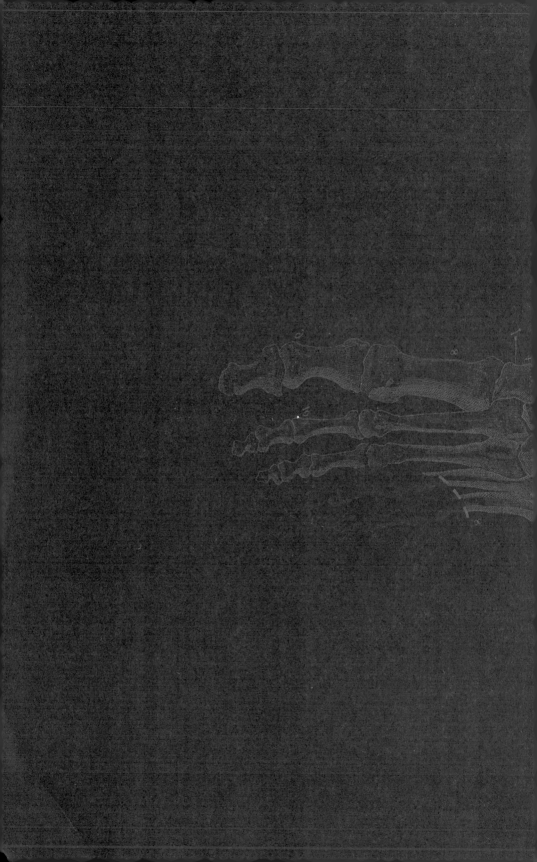

LINA MARÍA FERREIRA CABEZA-VANEGAS

Don't Come Back

Mad River Books, an imprint of
The Ohio State University Press | Columbus

Copyright © 2017 by The Ohio State University.
All rights reserved.
Mad River Books, an imprint of The Ohio State University Press.

Library of Congress Cataloging-in-Publication Data
Names: Ferreira Cabeza-Vanegas, Lina Maria, author.
Title: Don't come back / Lina Maria Ferreira Cabeza-Vanegas.
Other titles: 21st century essays.
Description: Columbus : Mad River Books, an imprint of The Ohio State University
    Press, [2017] | Series: 21st century essays
Identifiers: LCCN 2016039256 | ISBN 9780814253953 (cloth ; alk. paper) | ISBN 0814253954
    (cloth ; alk. paper)
Classification: LCC PR9312.9.F43 D66 2017 | DDC 814/.6—dc23
LC record available at https://lccn.loc.gov/2016039256

Cover design by Nathan Putens
Text design by click! Publishing Services
Type set in Palatino and Gill Sans

9 8 7 6 5 4 3 2 1

PARA MIS PADRES
&
FOR THE DROWNED QUEEN AT THE BOTTOM OF THE LAKE

CONTENTS

ACKNOWLEDGMENTS

For my mother, who tried furiously to keep me from another concussion but never forbade me from climbing trees. For my father and his pathological faith in me.

For nights and nights of almost-workshops, the Canada House Collective: MHK, CC, LM, A(S)P-W, IV, KR, & AL.

For KR, who always has my back. KH, who kept me from self-indulgence. KG, for intermittently trying to poison me and keep me alive. And for KER, who told me when I'd gone too far and made things too dark.

For SV, RV, and IV. For talking me down from ledges, offering me a place to stay, and countering entropy.

For BG and OG, for paying my rent, giving me a job, and helping me bury dead cats in the middle of the night.

For EM, who gave another book a home so that this one could exist.

For Dr. M, who told me to put the aphorisms back, stole me away from fiction in the first place, and pulled this book out of the abyss.

For David Lazar, who schemed with Patrick Madden on my behalf.

For the tireless and generous Mad River Books team: Tara Cyphers, Laurie Avery, Juliet Williams, and Meredith Nini.

For my kind and critical thesis committees: Aron Aji, Honor Moore, and Maureen Roberts and John D'Agata, Russell Valentino, and David Hamilton.

For Graciela, Yaneth, María, Kelly, and all the Colombian women who tell me their stories and let me write them down.

For my grandmother, who giftwrapped hell for me, and for the colonel, who slit the heavens open with his plane.

For my aunt, who asked me to come back, and for all the gods of all the sacred lakes for giving me a country to which I could go back.

DEAD MOUSE PRELUDE

The hamsters were dead.

My sister still insists that I am to blame, and I may still wonder. Because this is certainly likely.

If you drop and throw a thing enough times, parts will eventually come loose inside it. Even if you name your hamster Little She-Rambo. Even if you slip on little bandoliers, and smear its face with mud, and drop it in a backyard-jungle obstacle course of dandelions and broken glass. Especially if you try to tie a miniature bandana around its head.

Words and reenactment are insufficient alchemy.

Tiny skulls need only tiny cracks for tiny swells and leaks to end tiny lives.

Regardless, it wasn't me. (Probably.)

More likely it was the cold slipping in from under the door with a half-rotten board nailed to it. I remember, because I was there the night my father drove in the nails.

I held my green plastic hammer as he swung his, and I kept watch for the things I thought my father meant to keep out with wooden planks and bent nails. A board over a slit between the metal door and tile floor, wood like tape over rust-covered lips. And I turned my green hammer in my hands and waited—for the devil in the backyard, for the god of rats in the oven, for the men with rifles deep inside the mountains. For all of them to kick in the board, rip off the tape, and slip in through the crack beneath the door.

Mostly, however, "rats." My father insisted, "Big rats, Lina."

So, "Yes, Dad," I said, "rats." Except I said, "*Si,*" and I said, "*Si, Papi,*" because I was five and I didn't speak English then and words are still insufficient alchemy—but here I am. "Yes, Dad, *ratas.*" And I spun my green hammer in my hands and planned on killing myself a rat. A good fat one, "*Una ratisima ratota.*"

Just for practice, just for when the others slipped in.

A brown-fur devil I saw peeking behind the tamarillo tree in the back-yard one night, or the men in the news carrying AK-47s, or even the soldiers they shot at who stacked bricks of cocaine in front of the screen and seemed to me, back then, to be no different one from the other. Or, rather, the three-tailed god of rats my aunt Chiqui swears she saw once in the yard, covered in purple-black feathers and yellow spikes, running on two legs and leaping into the oven as it howled.

So I imagined it. Turned my hammer in my hands and heard the coconut skull crack of many heads beneath my swing. Just like my father did when the rats squeezed under the thin slit, swinging tiny feet and shaking black fur heads until they were inside and their little claws made *plick-plack* noises on the tile floor. Then he'd swing precisely and finally. A broomstick like a spear or a hammer like a sling. Swift and sure, down like a paperweight atop a flattened, soggy head while tails and feet twitched as if a mad wind were trying to blow the whole thing away.

So in went the nails. To keep some things in and others out. Because some are pets and some are not, it's hard to tie a leash around a tamarillo tree devil and ill-advised to let the men from the mountain in and lure the rat god out.

Though, of course, they all make it inside eventually. And I carry them with me all my life.

But not yet. Right there, right then, my father had a plan.

Hammer, wood, nails.

Out rats, in hamsters.

Out the conflict, in his children.

A man crouching beside a hamster cage swinging a hammer, driving in nails and keeping out rats.

"Because rats eat hamsters, too," my mother explained. "They eat everything." As she scrunched up her nose as if there were whiskers under her skin trying to sprout through her pores. "Disgusting." And I turned my hammer again and again, picturing rats sitting cross-legged in a circle, pulling on hamster bodies like they were trying to fold bed sheets. One on each end, tug-tug-tugging until hamsters came apart and all went down rat hatches—legs, fur, whiskers, and bellies.

It was not the rats, however. It was the cold.

That's what killed them. Because a wooden plank can only hold back so much.

So this is what we found on a cold Chía morning in Colombia: a stiff pair of hamsters buried in wood shavings inside a painted wire pen.

And it stopped making sense immediately. To keep them in a cage. So my older sister and I ran around the house looking for shoeboxes and old socks my father wouldn't miss. But my mother had a plan.

There is only one way to really know anything. What is inside explains what is out.

So she pulled out the hamsters and took them out to the cement bench in front of our house. "Wait here," she said and disappeared into the house while I poked my dead pet with my index finger. A stiff and gummy thing beneath a cold-licked layer of fur, it was so like life and so unlike it, I poked it again. "Here we are." *Listo.* My mother returned with an orange box cutter and a small assortment of bent metal tools. "Let's see now." *Vamos a ver.*

And this won't be the only time.

My mother aims to slice the world open and have us know it. She'll find dead things in bushes and yards, and half the time she will yield and let us play mortuary and death parade directors, but the other half she will insist. There is truth buried in their chests, and she will slice down the middle, cutting and reciting. Anatomy like poetry and a dead mouse, dead bird, dead Vicky and Little She-Rambo like open books on an altar. My mother unraveled them as if they were full of secret strings you could follow back to the beginning of the universe.

"Damn it," she said, rocking the blade on the dead hamster's body as if trying to cut rope with a spoon. "Damn-damn dead mouse." Not a warm belly that blooms ripe-red beneath the touch of my biologist mother's blade, but a body like a rusted can of baked beans, and little more than a bent nail to pry it open. So she said, "*Maldita sea*," and "Open-open . . . !" and "*Aquí empieza Cristo a Padecer.*" As she always does and likely always will. As all my family always has, as all the world has been handed down to me in little refrains and cyphered rhymes. Footnote aphorism, legends on a map. Because, my grandmother told me, there is nothing in the present that can't be explained with the past. Gift horses, mighty pens, what fortune favors when in Rome, and all the stone throwers living in all those glass houses. "Here begins Christ to suffer." Meaning, "Here pain begins," or, "Here the hard part," or "Here the stiff hamster," as she broke off a piece of the blade, and then another and another, until she had to admit defeat at the curled paws of our dead pets.

Two dead hamsters on a concrete bench. My older sister cried for a pincushion rodent, my mother lamented the dullness of blades, and I stared down at little rolled-up-map bodies, while they stared up at a blank blue sky.

This is the same sky the Muisca priests used to look up to, too.

The myth of myths is that there is always reason and explanation, a divine and tangled thread running through the navel of every breathing-buried thing. A story like a hamster's body, like an origami crane. Something that you can unfold and understand from the creases on the paper and the skin.

Hundreds of years ago, before the white sail ships and foreign crowns, before conquests and concrete, and before us, when deer leapt through the fields now rife with European rats, Chía was a holy city of princes and priests and star-gazers. In the night sky, they explained, lived Chía, and in the day lived Sué. Mist rose from the savannah, men and women crossed their legs, and children gathered, holding dead things they'd found in the bushes, to hear the priests untangle divine string in carful whispers.

"Sué," they said, "is like Bochica, Nemqueteba." They drew circles with their fingers in the dirt as they retold the stories of the great civilizing god of order, mercy, and patriarchy. Then, "Chía," they said, pointing up at a rising September moon, "is like Bachué, Huitaca." Wiping the dirt-drawn sun and replacing it with waxing, waning, and weeping moons, as they retold the stories of the goddess of chaos, matriarchy, and reckless, violent fun.

One god to keep things out, and another to bring them in. One for the men in the mountain in black rubber boots, and one for the men in army-issued boots. One for the tamarillo devil, cold and hungry in the yard, and another for the child inside who knows for what the devil hungers.

And when they told these stories, and threw their heads back to watch Chía and Sué walk across the sky in the perfectly measured steps of equatorial rotations, they knew who they were, and where they belonged, and how to come back if they should ever get lost. Because, the priests explained, the universe's belly is full of strings you can follow back to the beginning. Red tangled yarn and bread-star crumbs. And there is nothing beneath that was not first above.

"Listen," my mother said. "Listen." Because there is truth in the stiffness of their bellies, too. "Rigor Mortis." She spoke carefully. Like *Abracadabra*, or *Open Sesame*, like Paula's crying was a problem to be fixed with precision of language. The myth of language is transmission, translation, transliteration, communication. Where we say what we mean and know what we mean to say and the means are enough to say it completely. "Look. Paula, just look." Flicking a stiff little leg with the blade, "This is the reason. That's why your Vicky's legs stick out like they do, see?" Putting a hand on Paula's shoulder and saying it again, slowly. *R-i-g-o-r.* "Now Lina, you too. Come see." *M-o-r-t-i-s.* Before I learn English, before I take off. Before they look around at the tall weeds and the ticking bombs and decide all efforts should be made to give my sisters and me a chance to leave Colombia, and *Dios quiera*, not come back. "It's Latin," she said, waving at me so I'd come close so I might see Little She-Rambo's claws clutched around an invisible rope ladder. "You can say it, too. It means you get stiff when you die. *Rigor. Mortis.*"

Don't Come Back

CHIMINIGAGUA

In the beginning there was Chiminigagua and the darkness.

Only that, and only him.

Blind darkness wrapped around the great first god as he lay at the black bottom of a dark universe, sleeping. Or, rather, sleeping and waking and sleeping again, barely noticing the difference between one darkness and the other.

He stirred. He turned his body this way and that way. He curled himself into a ball and yawned for a million years before turning right back again and falling into a shallow, interminable sleep. Then Chiminigagua dreamt something he'd never dreamt before. At the beginning of everything, before there was anything, Chiminigagua dreamt he felt a hand being placed on his shoulder as he heard the whisperings of another being stirring in the darkness beside him, so he woke himself trying to kick the darkness off like wet blankets or enormous black snakes, and wondering if he'd really been asleep at all.

He heard his heart beating and in a half-asleep haze he threw out his arms, reached out first in the direction where he thought the hand had come from, and then swung his arms out madly in every other direction around him. Arms out like oars seeking water in black desert, the great first god flailing wildly in search for things that were not yet made.

And he had not moved in such a very long time that he felt it immediately. A sore god out of breath at the very beginning of time. So he lay back down, flat on his back, looking up at the black vaulted ceiling of the universe, and he decided that it must have been a dream after all. Though what a strange dream. Someone else before the notion of others had even been thought up, and whispered words which Chiminigagua—the first great god, all-understanding and all-remembering—could neither remember nor understand. But then, these are dreams. The meaningless mud-made mirages of a mind like stagnant water. So Chiminigagua cracked his neck and scratched his face. He cleared his throat, and as he crossed his arms to stretch his back, he inadvertently touched the spot where the dream hand had been placed.

Something like longing and urgency. Something that immortal beings hardly ever feel. Chiminigagua in the dark, before the earth was earth and life was life, feeling something yet to be named—a hand, attached to a wrist, to an arm, to another someone awake in the black with something to say that Chiminigagua had not yet said. But that which is hard to describe is easy to dismiss, so the great first god made nothing of it, or didn't let it be anything more than the nothing it surely was.

Instead he continued stretching. He felt the darkness pulling down on his eyelids once more, and he threw legs and arms out like fishing lines and deep sea divers tugging on their oxygen lines. Out and out as far as he could reach—to the very edge of the universe where darkness spills over into infinite abysses of deeper and darker space—until he heard his massive bones snap, heard them creak and crack back into cavernous sockets. Then he wriggled his toes and stretched out his fingers. He felt a fluttering in his chest and the darkness shifting beneath him like sand pulled out from under feet as the tide goes out, and then he let his eyelids slide back down, he let himself begin to drift back into immortal sleep when again he felt something brush up against his leg.

Now he was not so quick to dismiss it.

He sat up instantly. Grabbed his thigh where the thing had touched him and tried to follow its trail, as if the warmth it had left behind were footprints in the swamp. He crawled on hands and knees, intermittently patting the ground and swatting at unseen things while imagining something all-through-the-darkness-seeing dancing full-moon circles around him as he searched.

So Chiminigagua sat back down. He crossed his legs and pursed his lips. He tried to put words to what he was thinking. Because Chiminigagua was the very first, and the only one for a very long time, and it was very difficult to think about that which had never been thought, which had never been. About another when there had been none before, when there had been none but him. And yet where there had been no other there was also suddenly a longing for things that weren't and could not be.

But he was the first and great god, so his mind could conceive of the inconceivable. He closed his eyes and touched his chin to his chest and tried to picture it, the thing shifting in the darkness just beyond his reach. But even a great first mind must go slow, imagine 'another' first, as simply first 'an other.' So chiminigagua saw himself in his mind, out there on the other side of the universe, curled on the ground, asleep and awake and unable to tell the difference. And he felt something like sadness—for this other self, and then for himself. Something like, but not quite. Because until there was another—even just the thought of one—there had been nothing to miss, and no one to fear.

And the first god felt first fear and first longing, and he placed his hand over his chest and felt the only thing more familiar to him than the darkness—the rhythmic-whirling fluttering inside his chest which instantly calmed him.

Then he felt his face with his hands, pressing an index finger to the whites of his eyes to make sure they were open, and he was awake. He looked around as if he could see through the thick darkness, and then he knew what he should do. He pushed against the universe, he straightened his back, then he brought his hands up to his mouth and blew into them. Skin, spit, and spark. He held his breath in his hands, blue and yellow flames slipping between cracks and wrinkles, and he rubbed the tips of his fingers together, peeling thin sheets of shadow as he did, because, inside Chiminigagua, between the endless tunnels of his lungs, there was light. Millions of unborn suns and moons and torches and white blinding mornings, flickering between pharynx and larynx. So, sometimes, when Chiminigagua exhaled, air crackled on his lips and little sparks scorched the edges of a dark universe. So he blew again, bellows to fire, and the flames turned white and sharp. Then he took a very deep breath.

Lungs that pull trees from roots, lungs that shift continents. A breath as long as time and as deep as space, and a darkness thick with invisible worlds rushing into him like clouds of dust and flocks of birds at the eye of a storm, and when Chiminigagua exhaled again, sparks flew out from between his teeth. Silver fish, swift and shimmering, and pyrotechnic spiders weaving webs of pure light. But it was not enough, and Chiminigagua had to watch the darkness snatch up his sparks like a starving dog licks crumbs clean off a plate.

Nothing. Or only enough to see the green hue of a damp darkness, and nothing at all stirring in the short distance. So Chiminigagua stood up and inhaled, deeper and longer than before. He reversed the tide; he emptied space and knocked the wind out of it. He held his breath the way children pull back on rubber bands when they aim their slingshots, and he felt the fluttering inside his chest turn furious and frantic as the darkness became ignited inside his lungs like a forest made of splinters and matches.

Then Chiminigagua exhaled.

A storm of yellow-green light. A waterfall-rush of flashing stars and spit made of broken bits of mirror and polished steel reflecting every beam across the dim universe. Light cutting the darkness down the way an avalanche mows down trees.

And it was so sudden, it hurt. He closed his eyes instinctively though even then he felt the light bleed through shut eyelids, and bury red-pulsing stars inside his black pupils, and still he could not help himself. He opened his eyes again letting the new light singe his sight, and he saw, for just a second, something else in the distance. Something standing still and staring back. A shape not unlike his own, but different, curious and slender. Just as he began to really glimpse it, the darkness snuffed out the lights, and the great first god was left once more in darkness.

Then Chiminigagua was truly determined.

He knew the light would have to travel farther than anything before it ever had, if it were to fill the recondite corners of endless worlds of woven shadow. So he placed a hand on his chest one last time, listened for the flutter, and for a second wondered if it might not be a mistake to test the boundaries of his own omniscience. But by then it was too late; he was too awake and too restless to go back to sleep. So he arched his back, heard the cracking of his enormous spine, like the cracking of great logs in a colossal fire, and for a third time, he inhaled.

Lungs that thwart orbits and swallow galaxies. Deeper than the first god's deepest sleep and longer than men will ever have words to measure. Lungs so full, the entire universe heard them stretch and feared they would burst. And then Chiminigagua holding his breath until he turned deep blue, then dark purple, then matte black until he faded into the darkness completely and imagined himself asleep at the bottom of the dark universe, still and quiet while another god lay down beside him and whispered in his ear things that shaped his dreams. He trembled under the weight of his own lungs and then he opened his eyes and exhaled.

Light like water from a broken dam. From cracked skies and deep rivers. Because he meant to put out the darkness in a single blow. Torrents of unstoppable, spinning light burst out of the first great god into the shadows just like the two previous times. And like the two previous times, light sparkled and flickered and lit the god's immediate vicinity before going back out again, phosphorescent brevity and wet matches. But this time, it was different.

This time from between the flames of new stars emerged two black birds gripping light with their talons and unfurling it like a great banner over the cosmos. Chiminigagua felt them in his chest, in this throat, feathers against the insides of his cheeks and the powerful beating of their wings against his tongue. There was a part of him that wanted to close his mouth and pull them back into his chest, but instead he opened wide to let them out.

Two black pairs of beating wings and two sharp bronze beaks that carried light far across the universe and high above Chiminigagua's head. Slow streams of egg-yolk yellow stars and red pomegranate-seed constellations, light so bright it turned to noise and burst the great first god's eardrums.

And Chiminigagua sat back down beneath the star spackled darkness, half blind, half deaf, and wholly awake. He placed a hand over his chest where once there had been the beating of great black wings, and he wondered what his other self saw from the other side of the universe, and if there were birds still beating their wings inside her chest.

NI TANTO QUE QUEME AL SANTO,
NI TANTO QUE NO LO ALUMBRE

or

Neither so much that burn the saint, nor so much that not him light.

or

Neither so much [so close] that burn the saint [is burnt], nor so much [far] that not him [he is not] light [lit].

or

Strike a match/balance.

or

"So close, and yet."

BOG–MIA–CID

In Miami I sweat. Partly because it's Miami, partly because I have a fever.
I'm asked to step out of the line and go up to a table where officers wait
for people like me, and then they ask, "Why are you sweating?" Partly
this fever, partly this coat I'm wearing. Because it's heavy and my bags are
close to the weight limit.

They ask me to open my bags and take everything out, *please*, so I do.
They don't look at anything, they don't look at me, and I'm so tired of
traveling, I can't stop thinking of things outside of room and moment.
It was the eighties and then the nineties, my parents were young and
Bogotá was always ticking. Every doorman had a mirror at the end of a
stick, every guard a sniffing dog. Everyone knew to check the trunk and
never go near police stations because that's where they liked to park their
cars, tick, tick, boom. In Miami I pull out socks and shirts and little sweet
things my mother has packed for me to find later. The officers stand a few
feet away and occasionally look over their shoulders in my direction.

I imagine they see me, all of me. Short, and dazed, and dressed head
to toe in black, like I'm always on my way to a funeral, or a death-metal
poetry reading. I feel swollen too, discolored, and rank. Like something
left out too long, soaked in gutter water and dried by the sun. I feel it,
know it, and I know they know it, too.

Bogotá was once a city of shattered glass. Repair shops thrived. Bombs
are loud and cities are full of windows. Paula remembers, too. Once she
told me, "Bogotá was the place where bad things happened." I remember
these numbers under photographs on the screen between cartoons and
telenovelas. Ones followed by zeros and zeros and more zeros each new
time. Bounties for information leading to the capture of, of, of, of. . . . New
names and old names and always Pablo Escobar Gaviria, the Rodriguez
Orejuela brothers, and José Santacruz Londoño, alias Chepe. It was the
time of the narco-state, the narco-tapes, the narco terrorists. It was the

eighties in Santafé de Bogotá, and the nineties in Santiago de Cali that convinced my parents to get their three daughters out of there. Because it's not just the bombs that do it.

When there are bombs it's harder to care about the guns, and the knives, and the little sharpened sticks and fists, and the limp bodies of those kids that started showing up all over the country with empty eye sockets. In the news they told us they sold the eyes for transplants, wealthy gringos and Europeans with envelopes of cash and red coolers, but we know better now—no good for transplants.

In 2011 in Miami, I watch from afar as a beautiful black woman tells a beautiful Hispanic woman something I cannot hear, and then I see them look in my direction and nod. "Please pack everything back up now." They glance over my scattered possessions and back out at the screens flashing departures, arrivals, and delays. Mine was the last flight, no one in front of me, and no one behind me either, but they pace like I'm taking up their table and time and space, so I stuff these little things my mother wrapped so carefully into the corners where they're sure to crack, and finally I take off my coat. Cali was full of light, and music, and new currency in the nineties; for a moment I wish these officers could have seen it. The stores were colorful mechanical wonders, everything new and shiny and getting newer and shinier by the minute. People installed marble fountains on their lawns, wore gold chains and fur coats in ninety-degree weather. Kids came to school with bodyguards and chauffeurs, and every week some family member would fly back from Miami with a new little trinket, a new little nothing, new little everything just for them. Cali wasn't like Medellin. Cali didn't want to own the world; it just wanted a fair share. So the Rodriguez Orejuela brothers never declared war on the state like Pablo did. Though this distinction meant little to the Colombian government, and even less to the U.S. government. So the city filled its lungs greedily like a man mid fall, off a cliff and half way down. When falling can still feel like flying, right before that illusion slips away, and I swear you could hear it, the creaking of an overstretched rubber-band façade about to snap, even before I actually heard the helicopters.

After I've packed everything back I'm told to wait, and they motion for me to clear their table. I ask again why I'm being detained, and they say things that make me feel conditioned, because they know exactly what to say, and how to say it, because of course they've practiced and I haven't, so I nod even though I neither understand nor agree. The words get stacked into perfect little towers—*protocol, procedure, only a minute, please wait here, let me check with my supervisor, don't move*—and I nod, then try again, but what was it that 'gave me away'? I should stop trying. They tell me not to wander off, to stay put, to wait. They ask me, "Why are you sweating?" and "Are you on any medication?" I feel like we are dwelling on the matter; I don't know why I'm sweating. Why aren't you?

"What is the weather like in Bogotá?" I tell them it's beautiful, so they ask again, "What is the weather like exactly?" Really great, like autumn all the time, and the rain, you should totally go, and I completely mean it too. Sometimes people refer to Bogotá as the fall city, Medellin as spring. Cali is summer itself. When my family was there we swam every day; my mother drove my sister Paula and me to lessons, and we'd sing little songs about my younger sister, Daniela, on our way back. We sang about that time she had worms and we saw one squirming in her diaper, about her blond curls and round cheeks, about the time she stole and hid all the candied almonds, "just like Chepe with all those millions of dollars he must make *a costillas de los gringos*," and then we sang another song. We were singing the day I heard the helicopters, soldiers sprang up from bushes by the side of the road. People ran through the street—soldiers towards us, people away—and I yelled for my mother to turn on the radio. "It's nothing," she said, "it won't tell us anything." We sped simply away.

There is a little statue my family members always have at home. It's a plump, short, pig-faced man with a million bags around his arms, waist, and neck. He is *El Equeco*, god of abundance, and that's what I look like now holding poorly packed bags and carry-ons and coats—and one little bag with Colombian pastries because, "You might get hungry, you never know." The officers don't tell me if they'll be back; they don't tell me anything and I understand, I do, it's a job, but I'm so tired. I wipe my forehead. I feel like shivering but I've stopped sweating so I tell them, "I've stopped sweating now, can I go?" Mostly to say something, mostly to get them to say something back. I ask them one more time why I'm being detained, if I did something wrong, but they don't answer, they only ask me again, "Why were you sweating?" The day with the helicopters and the soldiers was June 9th, 1995. I know because that's the day they captured Gilberto Rodriguez Orejuela, just a few streets away from where I saw the soldiers popping up like weeds. Gilberto is here in the U.S. now, extradited in 2004. They flew him in through Miami.

The black officer comes back and tells me to put the bag on the table, so I do. She tells me to open it, so I open it, and then she says, "Please unpack it." I stare sort of blankly. Why? "Please unpack the bag." Why, again? What are you looking for? Where are the dogs? Bring them over, I'll let you bring them over, what do you need? But she doesn't answer. Instead, this severe look on her face, she repeats, "Please unpack the bag." I'm suddenly aware that these bags have already been sniffed by dogs, been X-rayed, been searched. I'm far away, I am alone, I am not from here, I have less than twenty dollars in my bank account. Almost everything I own I carry with me, it doesn't take much, so I start again, bit by bit until almost everything I own is on a metal slab. She doesn't look at anything; she doesn't look at me. I lived in Cali for three years and then my parents sold almost everything we owned and bought tickets to the U.S., "Where the middle class lives like our upper class and things aren't so hard."

The second time I know better. I unpack slowly and repack carefully. It's been a few hours now; I'm getting cold but I won't put my coat back on. They come back and say, "Please come with us." They watch me struggle with my bags, and I figure the beautiful black officer must be training the slightly less beautiful Hispanic officer because she tells her what to do. "Now tell her to take off her shoes," and she tells me to take off my shoes. "Now tell her to sit down," and she tells me to sit down. "Tell her to wait here," and I'm left alone a few minutes to rethink my answers so far. For example, what is the right thing to say when asked, "Did you meet anyone while you were there?" Or, "Why was your passport issued in San Francisco?" Or, "Why so many books?" What is 'so many'? Or, because these are the ones that fit? Or, you should see the ones I left behind. Or, you should read this one; it's about the drug war in Colombia.

I leave my bags unattended to be interrogated, and I wonder about these protocols. I wait in a little room, on a little bench and the colors are all wrong. To begin with, there are colors. Worn-out greens and blues, and the paint is peeling off. There is no two-way mirror and no one looking in. I slump, feel the salt of dry sweat on my skin, close my eyes for a second. My family left Colombia in 1995, and it was 1998 when we went back, when things were already getting better, as they've kept getting better since.

When the officers get back the one doing the training tells the other to check my feet.

She tells me, "Spread your toes please," and I don't know what that means but I try anyway. The Hispanic officer feels between my toes. I stare down at the socks Daniela gave me for Christmas, this little owl head smiling at the woman as she presses down on its face, as it stares back and exclaims with the knitted writing across my ankle, *Genius.* "Now stand up against the wall." Somewhere inside the black woman's brain she is making the decision whether or not my cavities will be searched more thoroughly. "Against the wall please, arms out." I put my arms above my head and she repeats, "Arms out, out!" The officers are doing their best, too, and I understand, I do, but I'm so tired. "Not above your head, out like this, like this!" She motions but I'm facing the wall away from her and I can't really see. "By your side, like a plane." She raises her voice, "like a little plane!" So I finally get it and then I stop getting any-thing else. Because I'm against a wall pretending to be a little plane and I've started thinking of Wilson, my high school English teacher. "That's what I used to do," he said, "checked planes for drugs and *Huy!* You can't imagine." He told us he worked in Miami, security, that's how he learnt

English. He used to go through planes after they'd landed, looking for the stuff. Between the seats, under the chairs, along the walls, "You can't imagine." Little white bags, latex glove fingers cut off, stuffed down the side, hung like sausages, swallowed like pills. "If this is the stuff they leave behind, imagine," he said, "just imagine how much gets in."

The Hispanic officer runs her fingers down my back. Between my breasts, as deep inside me as clothes allow and I've stopped asking questions. Then they have a little moment, the two beautiful women, and I'm a mushroom growing on a green bench in an interrogation room in Miami. The officers whisper something and then exchange glances. They decide I'm not a little plane full of cocaine and they are going to let me go. Or maybe they are as tired as I am, or this is just an exercise. I don't know. All the same they've decided to let me go, so I thank them and drag my bags up an escalator. I sit by a Subway restaurant drenched in the smell of disinfectant and meatballs.

I was thinking about my aunt before they pulled me out of the line, and I'm thinking about her now. About how she held me tightly my last night in Bogotá. Her chin on my shoulder, the cigarette smell I love, and her colostomy bag against my hip, warm, like her, warm like Cali. "Come back, Lina. Please, please come back," she cried into the fabric of that heavy coat. She told me I had to see her again, and she nearly crumbled in my arms, my beautiful aunt, decimated by cancer, and lupus, and history, and herself.

The next day my mother held me tightly, too, by the international gate I know better than some apartments I've lived in. She choked but didn't stutter. She pulled me close and told me, "There's nothing here for you, Lina. Don't come back."

DEL ARBOL CAIDO TODO EL MUNDO HACE LEÑA

or

Of tree fallen the whole world makes firewood.

or

Of tree fallen the whole world [*Everyone*] makes [*takes their*] firewood. [*from the fallen tree*].

or

Fallen tree [*or*   *fallen people*   *or*   *man down*   *or*   *shot down*   *or*   *shooting star*] everyone [*or*   *every person*   *or*   *all people*   *or*   *every man*   *or*   *Horace Mann*] firewood [*or*   *kindling*   *or*   *twigs*   *or*   *tinder*   *or*   *tenderly*].

or

"Watch your step."

After the Colonel

The cats were poisoned seven days before the colonel fell from the sky.

Yuri never came back. But Nicky dragged the back of her paws raw against the gravel until she made it back to the colonel's wife's feet. "She came up, like that, dragging her paws," my grandmother told me, every time I asked for a story. "Straight up to me, to my feet like she was going to lie down, and then she opened her mouth. And it was like opening the faucet." Because my grandmother was the colonel's wife, and still is—she tells me she is, all the time, while pointing at one of the dozens of portraits of a man I never met perpetually wearing a Colombian Air Force uniform and colonel's insignia.

And then she tells me about Nicky again. A muzzle like an open faucet. "Red, red, red, red. Everything inside coming out." Enough to wash her feet and soak her socks.

Before the cats, though, it was a cow in the path of a spinning propeller. And before that, the chickens. Suddenly-thin birds that left trails of falling feathers as they dragged their wings and pecked off small white scales growing on their skin. A plague like a man out of a clear blue sky. One died, then another and another. And in between feathers and pestilence the colonel's wife asked desperately if anyone knew what was killing the animals, but no one did. So it went without explanation, seemingly random, as more and more chickens died until no more chickens could die, and then the colonel died, too.

That's how they tell it, at least. How we remember it.

My aunt told me about the chickens first, my grandmother about the cats, and my mother about a suicidal cow running toward a jet's propellers as if she were magnetized.

They kept count, kept track, kept a record. I wasn't sure why, as I listened to the careful running tally of dead animals before, between and after the colonel's death. Except that it sounded important, felt important. So I kept count, too.

Chickens, cow, cats. Yuri, Nicky, and seven others. That is, the kittens Nicky gave birth to before the colonel's death, which stumbled blindly into life, dragging their bodies over the bundle of rags into which Nicky had crawled when she felt them coming. Pink furred, round-bellied kittens chirping and suckling and suddenly flickering out without explanation. One by one like lights on a string.

"Yes," my grandmother told me, "seven little ones, and who knows what tramp had knocked her up. But, yes. Seven *gaticos chiquiticos*." And she held out her cupped hand, as if one were laying there, still curled and purring.

Seven and two make nine. Nine cats, nine lives. Keeping track. Cats, chickens, kittens, cow. One cow, twelve chickens, Yuri, Nicky, seven kittens, and one witch with one prophecy one full month before the colonel's death.

My grandmother has always had a fondness for witches. Cigarette ash, tea leaves, and Spanish decks. Under her bed she kept jars and jars full of yellow jelly bulbous things that stirred in the light of a full moon, and that witches swore would bring those who kept them long lives, deep loves, and even deeper pockets. But only after the colonel died did my grandmother's fondness become devotion, become religion. Until the three daughters the colonel left behind had to lie flat on their bellies trying to catch a glimpse of their mother through the slit beneath her bedroom door, where she sat for endless hours listening to witch after witch after witch tell her, "I can almost reach him. Almost, almost, hear him."

For the witch that came before the colonel's fall, however, there is not fondness.

Josefina de León Tovar in a red dress. My grandmother in her thirties, in scarlet, sitting across from a woman with a hard look on her face. "I see you," she says, and my grandmother leans in. "I see you, in a black dress," and my grandmother leans even closer. "Your husband," she continues, "he's gonna be in an accident." And my grandmother leans back.

"No, no, no," she responds. "You're making a mistake," she tells the witch. "That's already happened." As if clairvoyance were a map and the witch were simply holding it upside down. "That accident," she tells the witch, "that was last month. It's already happened, and nothing really happened. He's fine."

The colonel's wife had not gone that day for her husband anyway, and the witch's insistence annoyed her. So she pushed back the prophecy as if the waitress had mixed up her order. "Not him," she repeated to the witch, "my sister—that's who I need to know about, see? That's what I need, do you understand?" And I imagine she must have held her purse tight over her stomach as if she'd suddenly felt a tug on the strap, because this is what she has always done when 'the help' disappoints her. And I also imagine she must have pressed that witch, and faked a Bogotá accent, and pointed at her pale skin, and finished every sentence with the same frustrated question she uses when she knows the person before her is very stupid. "My sister, do you follow? Is her cancer back, do you see? That's what I need to know. Do you understand? "

But when the witch looked into her bowl, into her glass, into her deck of cards and the depth of her eyelids, she did not see what my grandmother wanted her to see. Only the vertical blur of a man plowing into the horizon.

"Your husband," she repeated, "is going to be in an accident."

I want to hunt down this witch. And I say so out loud. It's not too far, maybe eight hours, twelve on a bus. And witchcraft is a family business. Can't move around too much without risking the loss of repeating clientele. So I pull up a map on my screen and imagine knocking on the door of the only other person to have known the colonel's final moment, besides the colonel himself.

It will be hot, and sweat will collect on my upper lip. I'll walk down dozens of dirt roads in Palanquero and feel sharp stones poke through the worn soles of my sneakers. I'll pull out a map and hear girls snicker as they pass me on their bikes, because I'm wearing a black, long-sleeved shirt and fistfuls of sunscreen. I was built for rainy days, and the sun will already have left track marks on my skin. So I'll turn back to the dozens of little scribbled-in extra roads that locals in shops and gas stations will have added to my map, but they won't be much help unless those same locals were to come with me and scribble in the corresponding map names on the corresponding dirt roads. So I'll begin to fold the map and realize from the greasy thumbprints on the corners of the pages that the sunscreen is melting off my skin. It's easier to navigate these parts of Colombia by ear anyway. Everyone will know everyone else and everyone will want to talk to the novelty stranger fumbling about town, though she'll only seem to care about things that happened too long ago to really matter anymore. "Have you heard . . . Do you know . . . Have you seen . . . Where can I find?" All in all it won't take too long to find her. Not long at all before I'll be sitting in a room full of those yellow jelly jars my grandmother has told me so much about. Luminous jellyfish tumors floating in murky water, filling the shelves and lighting the room, and then a woman with coffee-stained teeth will walk in and ask, "What do you want to know?"

"She's dead," my mother tells me while I sit at her kitchen table making plans and plotting trips.

"What?" I look up; get plucked out of my fantasy by her unexpected certainty.

"Dead," she repeats and shrugs.

"What," I whisper more to myself than anyone else. In my mind I was just sweating into her upholstery and looking for the right question to ask. "What I mean is, when?"

"Not long after." She carries on with little chores as she talks. "Cancer, I think."

"I'm sorry," the witch told my grandmother and continued undeterred. "But I'm not wrong. This is another accident." She put out her cigarette on the edge of her plate. "And from this one," she looked up at the colonel's wife, "he's not coming back."

I wipe my upper lip, half expecting to feel sweat. Half expecting to blink and actually be sitting across from the woman who knew before anyone else. And I think, for an instant, about asking my mother how she knew of the witch's death. But of course, I don't. Because I already know that she tried then what I wish I could try now. Tracking down the only woman to see her father's last moment. To ask her something I haven't yet figured out. Though sometimes, for a second, I think I know what I'd say, "Did you also know of your cancer? Did you know you weren't coming back either?"

All the chickens, one cow, nine cats, one witch. Seven days before, one month before. And one older sister, one year later. Ana Cristina.

Because the colonel's wife should really have kept pressing the witch that day.

Because the cancer had indeed come back, and within a year of the crash my grandmother's eldest sister, who was also the colonel's oldest friend, would be dead.

I've heard the stories, I've read letters. In my mind it is a perpetual play without applause that never closes. Ana Cristina begins to feel something stirring awake inside her, and the more it widens its eyes, the less she can keep hers open. Every day there seems to be less and less of her left. Flesh like a thin sheet over a wooden frame, and yet, somehow she feels unmovable, every bone now filled with lead. She is barely able lift her own hand to reach for the glass of water they've left on her nightstand. Thick-knot swollen joints on floss-thin limbs punish every effort to move. What was once only stirring is now wide awake and it pulls her back into this stiff state of semi-consciousness, while dust settles on the surface of the water and the top of her eyelids. Then the doctors tell her they need to operate. Cut it out from the root and put it away for good this time. And when she concedes with a light nod of her heavy head, they set to work. They lay her flat on a table, mumble through surgical masks, and fumble through a double mastectomy. They peel back the skin like old scotch tape and they take everything. "Really get it all, rip it all out." They carve into her chest, scoop out the muscle and scrape out the rest. And then they pull her skin like plastic wrap over her rib cage. Skin on bone and bookend scars on either side. When my great aunt wakes again, she will take a hand to her flat chest and feel her fingers fall into the ruts of her rib cage, and I will wonder if she already knows that even after all that they didn't get it all.

"They told me," my mother says, "that the skin had turned black by then."

"Black?"

"Yes."

I try to reimagine the scene. Her thin fingers on her bony chest. Purple-black, blue-black, red-black, necrosis-black, gangrene-black, frostbite-black. Scorched-earth and coal-mine black. "Why black?"

My mother shrugs again. She hazards radiotherapy, then chemo, then necrosis. "Don't know." And I picture an overeager doctor enthusiastically scooping meat into his bucket as if it were Halloween candy. "Or maybe they did something wrong." A scalpel like a pickaxe into her chest, a burst of blood like newfound oil, a grid of veins that goes dark, a nerve or two cut off completely. "Or maybe that's just what happens, you know?"

I don't. But I write it all down anyway.

I've read the letter Ana Cristina wrote my grandmother before her wedding day. "Lucho," as she called the colonel, "is the very best of men, and only happiness is left before you." I've read it. Reread it. Tried to picture her writing it, sitting in a study tapping her pen to her lips as she thought of the next sentence to put down.

But I don't know enough about this or about her to really build a scene.

I know she met the colonel in Barranquilla when they were teenagers. When the colonel's uncle took him away from his mother in Mompox without her permission. "More or less kidnapped," my mother once said. "Because there were better schools in Barranquilla."

"So, then, why wouldn't his mother have allowed it?"

"I don't know. He was her only son for a long time. She had him when she was . . . fifteen, I guess. They were very close, the colonel and his mother. Did I ever tell you that she breastfed him until he was four?"

What I do know is that that illegitimate children couldn't join the Colombian armed forces back then, and I know the colonel and Ana Cristina were alike in this way. Both "natural," as they sometimes say in Spanish. *Hijos naturales.* Fatherless children as natural phenomena. Rain, mist, moss, and men abandoning their offspring. Ana and the colonel left with only one parent and one last name in a culture that demanded two.

"She was her mother's only daughter for a long time too, she was . . . hm, I don't even know how old she was when she had her." Ana Cristina was my grandmother's half-sister, an uncalled-for and unclaimed child dragged in shame and haste by her mother from Venezuela to Colombia in search of a man who would never acknowledge her as his own.

So this is what the colonel's oldest friend was raised to do: to endure the snickering, the taunting, the shame of the single maternal last name. And to never, ever speak of it.

They were not alike in this way. "I'm a natural son," he said to his then bride-to-be, and my now-grandmother, before their wedding, with his hands on his hips and his hair slicked back. "That's what I am, and that's how it is. And if you've got a problem with that, then we'll call the whole thing off." He didn't endure, he wasn't ashamed, and in the end he got his father's last name and joined the Colombian Air Force.

Though sometimes I think if she ever spoke of it, she must have spoken to the boy who would become the colonel. Sitting on a hill watching the sky while he mirrored the planes with his hands, nose-diving and pirouetting as if short bombers and spitfires were attached to his wrist. Maybe, after all, she guessed who her father really was. Spotted him one day at the market, used her own features to retrace her way back to him like footprints in the snow. As if there was salvation and resurrection in a last name, as if there were anything at all in trying to decipher these men so long after they'd gone for good. "I think I know who he is." She may have told him, and maybe she made him promise to never say a word to anyone about it. "Promise, promise me you won't." And maybe he nodded, and maybe kept his word, and maybe this is part of it.

"Lucho is the very best of men, and nothing but happiness lays before you." My mother's fatherless father and his fatherless friend.

But then, I hear, in my mind, the sound of the doctor's metal spoon scratching against the bone-bowl bottom of her hollowed chest, and the image fades.

"And after all that," my mother tells me with a quiver in her voice, "after all that . . ."

For all their overeager digging, they couldn't have gone deep enough. The cancer had tunneled deep inside her veins and between her organs, as if it had heard the doctors coming. A terrified-rat cancer which dug through the wet cardboard of my great aunt's innards while she clutched what was left of her abdomen and begged God to make it stop.

Maybe witches have a cancer blind spot. I don't know.

"I see you both in black," she said, when the colonel's wife insisted that she'd gotten the accidents mixed up. "Your sister, the one you keep asking about, and you. Both in black at his funeral."

When my grandmother tells the story, she moves her hands in dramatic, well-rehearsed motions. "That day," she tells me, always pausing for effect, "that day the blood right up and dried inside me." She leans back, closes her eyes, and takes both hands to her chest as if to feel the beating of her own heart. "I walked out and as I did I saw myself in the mirror and . . . *Huy!*"

"'*Huy*'?"

"Yes."

"'*Huy*' what?"

"White." She runs the index finger of her right hand from the top of her left shoulder to the tip of her left hand's index finger and then repeats the motion on the opposite arm. "All, all, all of me. White as death." And she nods to her own story, as if to attest to its veracity. "I saw it. Myself white." Red dress, pale face, and visions of black—black cloth and black skin draped over a scratched rib cages.

"But have I told you about the cow yet?"

The cow is new. Or sort of new. "What cow?"

Since I can remember I've known about the cats. "Come here, Lina," I can still hear my grandmother call, "you need to hear about this witch who told me about the crash before the crash." I can still see her decked in gold, and smell the acrylic paints with which she'd color the heaps of porcelain families adorning the mantelpieces beneath the colonel's portraits. "But before I tell you about that," my grandmother said, "you need to hear about the cats."

The cow, however, is brand new to me. Something I did not count until an email from my mother a few days ago, a recently rediscovered memory, a dim recollection in a room of brilliant ones that suddenly lights up for no reason beyond wanting to be counted with the others.

My mother, age seven. She walks through the wet warmth of a Colombian jungle air base. School is out and the sun stokes the dirt like a fire. But she is accustomed to it, walking from under the shade of one tree to the shade of another like a game of hot-coal hopscotch. She kicks the stones, picks up a stick, and drags it across the barbwire fence feeling through her fingertips how rusted metal peels back bark. Then she strikes the poles between the wires with her stick and counts the tadpoles squirming in the puddles, leaping back when she spots a white snake curled beside a patch of wild grass. But soon she recognizes the trans-lucent shed skin outline of a bygone snake. So she steps on it, digs her heels into it, feels it crinkle underfoot. It's nothing new but the image lingers, the tangible shape of something that was and then wasn't. Then the two-tone song of a cuckoo bird while long ribbons of black butter-flies fly through her yard and gather in clusters on her windowsill. Black rice-paper wings and the song of a red-eyed bird, and before she's really noticed she's walking through the front door of her army barracks home and standing stiffly still at the strange sight of a man on her parent's bed.

It's the same. The outline of something familiar made momentarily unfamiliar, present absence and absent presence. The man on the bed is the renowned air force pilot El Coronel Cabeza. Or rather, it is her father whom she rarely sees, barely ever in the middle of the day, and almost never simply resting.

So she walks to the edge of the bed tentatively and before noticing her mother sitting beside him she sees a slab of melting meat lying flat over his eye and dripping red down his face. Back then the colonel led the strike against what would become the jewel of the guerilla movement in Colombia, the F.A.R.C., bombing daily what they called "The Free Republic of Marquetalia." The little girl doesn't consider the possibility of a black Holstein cow running a suicidal sprint toward the spinning blades of his propellers during liftoff. It does not occur to her to picture her father scrambling for control and driving his plane into a nearby ditch to avoid slicing into the animal as he might have sliced into the steak now chilling his black eye. And for a moment she may want to climb on the bed and lie down beside him, but that's not how things are between them, and she's too afraid to ask. So she walks out and doesn't come back in until dark.

"If I could count the times I spoke with my father," she wrote me once in bright green letters. "I would only need one hand." *Five.* I scribble on a piece of paper. I should have written *fewer than five*, if I am to take it literally. *Four, three, two? But, do you remember any of those conversations? Any particular one? Any one?* "Hm. Well, you can count the cow among the deaths, at least." *One. Cow.*

Nine cats, one cow. One month, seven days. A witch, a friend. Every living chicken.

On my last birthday, my mother wrote an email she did not sign: "There are two details about the cats' death that you should know." The email is a four-paragraph list of two memories in a light blue font. Her first memory colors what she's already told me: my grandmother sits in the patio, crying over a dying animal on her lap, then the animal stirs under her hand, empties itself through its mouth and paints her feet red.

The second memory is something I've never heard before. The soldier assigned to guard the colonel's home takes the dead cat from my grandmother's lap and lays it over a mess of newspapers. Then he places two stones over the cat's ribcage and wraps it all in the newspapers like a fish in an open market, crinkling the corners around the contour of her limp body until the newspaper is damp and soft where the blood begins to pool. Then the soldier drops it all into the Magdalena River.

"Why?" I type into a chat window.

"Well"—I watch the cursor blink—"so he wouldn't find it, I imagine."

"Who?"

"The colonel," she writes back. "It was his favorite cat, see? He named them both. Did I tell you that already?"

"Yes. One after Nikita Khrushchev and the other after Yuri Gagarin."

"Right. Yes. And Nicky was his favorite cat."

"So the soldier, he didn't want the colonel to see it?"

"I think so."

His favorite cat on his wife's lap, bleeding through her skirt and dripping down her legs.

"But the soldier," my mother concludes, "was an idiot."

Because she remembers it perfectly. Leaning over a fence at seven years of age to watch a soldier with a bundle walk to the edge of a bridge and forget the importance of string. Paper, stone, and blood, a cat between, and all of it coming undone before so much as striking the water. The stones are gulped down first, then the cat twirls about, *one second, two,* in a little brown and red whirlpool while some loose sheets float down into the river, *three seconds, four,* then the newspaper follows, *five seconds, six,* no string, and a tiny red mark lingering on the surface, *nine seconds, ten.*

After the colonel's death, he was replaced by a sub-commander who scattered bombs over the rebel's stronghold, like marbles in a playground. "How many do you think?" I asked once. "Too many to count."

The colonel's wife and his three daughters were replaced by the *sub comandante's* wife and his three daughters. A colonel for a commander. A colonel's wife for the commander's wife, three little girls for three little others, and indistinguishable uninterrupted laundry being tossed over taut string in their backyard. Perhaps they had cats, too, angry ones and friendly ones, and little ones that tumbled over one another looking for their mother's teat. And maybe in the sleight-of-hand shuffle of hard numbers and hard men, hardly anyone noticed the loss. A house hardly empty before it was full again.

But that's not it; we have to keep count.

Because we're sure there is something in it. All these coincidences must add up to something.

"What happened next happened because it was too much alike," my grandmother told me once. As if it were some sort of affront to the fates to replace things too neatly. Or else as if death were nearsighted and forgetful—and stupid at that—and it was on us to be different enough from one another to avoid being mistaken for those marked and those spared.

Maybe it's a numbers thing.

There are fifty chapters in the book of Genesis, and the last line of the last chapter reads, "So Joseph died . . . and he was put in a coffin . . ."

In Judaism fifty years marked the end of the seven cycles of the Shmita, the Jubilee when slaves were freed, debts pardoned, and God's mercies manifested. Seven cycles, seven cats, seven days, seven years of bad luck.

Fifty is the percentage that separates optimists from pessimists.

And fifty is the number of days after the colonel's death when all of his closest military friends boarded a helicopter and set off for a picnic.

I've seen the newspaper clippings. Yellow pages thinned by touch, laid neatly in little plastic bags my mother keeps in white boxes. It's not much to go on, but I'm certain there were pressure cookers wrapped in blankets and old mayonnaise jars filled with fresh juice—a piece of torn plastic between the lid and the glass to keep it from spilling—and all the smells of steamed meat and grilled corn.

There was likely a woman in a red dress, too, and maybe another in a yellow one. Patterns and styles taken from foreign magazines and black-and-white TV shows. The men wore freshly pressed uniforms and helped their wives into the helicopter. Then they patted each other on the shoulder as they prepared for liftoff. The base commander, the chaplain, and the sub-commander all yelled over the cacophony of spinning metal and mad winds. The women leaned over and looked out the window as the helicopter rose off the ground. They crossed themselves and fearlessly mumbled the habitual prayers. They were safe and they knew it. This is what their husbands did, this is what they did, this is what happened every day, and out there in the distance they spotted a perfect hill for their picnic.

So one of them pointed out the window at a clearing on a hill, and then another joined in, and another and another until it was hard to tell who thought of it first. They all nodded and smiled, and held pots and jars and baskets on their laps while one of them piloted the chopper toward a flat patch of grass. But this was fifty days after the colonel fell, after seven cats died, after a witch prophesied. Numbers must mean something and the chopper must not be allowed to land. A gust of wind like a pack of wild dogs and a helicopter like a child tossed and torn between them. The aircraft suddenly began to pivot and the pilot lost control. The blades twisted and bent in the wind like paper pinwheels, and they felt the helicopter begin to crumple around them as jars flew out of the their hands and they tried desperately to hold on for dear life and hold on to the moment just before this one, when their only worry was juice spilling and the rice getting soggy.

Then, gravity. Sped up and slowed down. Every light on the dashboard flashing, every hinge bending, every joint giving, everything so loud it approached silence, and everyone bracing for the moment to pass as if the next could be any better. And maybe in that instant the subcommander could barely distinguish his wife's screams from any of the others. The beeping of the dashboard from the singing of the cuckoo, the beating of his heart from the rumbling of the aircraft. His own last moment from that of his friend's, the colonel, who fifty days earlier, wrapped in metal and noise, traversed the same sky to reached the same conclusion.

"We heard it from a few farmers who said they'd seen it." My mother tells me.

"The crash?"

"Yes. They said they saw it go down, and then they said they saw the man climb out."

"Wait," I interrupt her. "You mean . . . someone survived?"

She shakes her head, "Not really," and exhales. "Not for long."

"Who?"

"The base commander." She takes the newspaper clipping and looks it over as if making sure the bill adds up. "That's what the farmers said, anyway." And she shakes her head.

"That they saw this man crawl out of the wreck?"

"Hm," she nods. "Yelling."

"Yelling?"

At the top of smoke-filled lungs, dragging shattered limbs out of fire and bent metal, a scorched-earth, brittle-black man yelling: "I killed them, I killed them, I killed them!"

"Because . . ." I stumble over the image, flesh peeled back by fire, black-ash lungs and a man screaming through the flames. "Because, I guess he was flying the helicopter?"

"I figured the same thing." My mother shrugs. "That's what the farmers said anyhow. Though it seems unlikely, doesn't it?" She furrows her brow. "That he could crawl so far on a body so burnt." Pauses in the same spot every time. "Left behind thirteen children." *Thirteen.* "There's another number for you, I guess. Bad luck, too. Like the singing of the cuckoo."

Cow, chickens, cats, colonel, sister, successor, friends. Seven days, thirty days, thirteen children. A biblical wiping out of all that touched the colonel.

When I was a kid I used to sit in the middle of my room, put on the colonel's old helmet, and try to hold myself up against its weight for as long as I could. I teetered and tottered and felt my neck give on one side and then another like a rope worn down by friction, until eventually it knocked me down. Sometimes face up, sometimes face down. Forehead into cheap carpet and a visor cut on the bridge of my nose. Or else, a leather-padded blow to the back of the head and a six-year-old girl with arms and legs outstretched as if she were waiting for someone to draw her outline with chalk.

Then I stopped breathing. I strapped on the disconnected rubber oxygen mask to the helmet and felt it hermetically seal itself around my face.

It is very quiet inside a fighter pilot's helmet. Quiet and heavy. You can feel it, even lying down, like Lilliputian ropes around your head. A paralyzing weight and the washing machine swish of a heart beating out of sync with stilled lungs. The pulsing of a dead-end pumping, thick blood being pushed into the tips of my fingers and the top of my head, and I'd imagine my grandfather flying farther and higher than he ever did on that last day. I would hold my breath and with it hold his plane together. I would abstain from air like holy men abstain from food, and I would imagine that every moment I stayed under he remained above.

One, two. The colonel pulls back on the control wheel as if he can anticipate the plane wanting to buck. *Three, four.* His jet skips over the treetops and nearly sets them ablaze with turbine fire and sheer friction. *Five, six.* The colonel smiles inside a helmet inside a cockpit inside a marvelous Atlas machine pushing up against the corners of the sky, *seven, eight,* while he wrestles gravity with levers and buttons. *Nine, ten.* Then a rumbling and a clanging. *Eleven, twelve.* A plane like a jar of nails tumbling down a staircase. *Thirteen.* The machine spirals downward and the metal around him rattles. The man does his best to keep his nerve, his hands steady while the entire cockpit shakes, and I'd begin to turn blue and shake inside his helmet too.

Then I would press on the metal button at the end of the hose and would feel air rush back into me like water into a cracked hull.

Deep breaths. *One, two,* while I looked up at the ceiling through a tinted visor imagining my grandfather as a kid looking up at the planes soaring over him. *Three, four.* Then, as a man, looking down as the earth rose up to meet him, and tear him apart.

And then I'd let go of the metal button, feel rubber edges dig into my cheeks and seal around my face once more, and I'd start all over again.

But there is more and less to it than that.

The colonel struck the ground on a Sunday but was not found until Monday.

He went to mass that last morning with his family and made his hands rise and fall and pirouette around one another like he always did when he forgot anyone was looking. Then he put on his flight suit and watched his wife hang dozens of little medals from zippers and pockets while retracing the sign of the cross over him more times than he could count.

Then he walked out one last time, maybe wondering about Ana, maybe thinking he should write her when he got back—because he didn't need a witch to tell him that the cancer could come back and he'd been worried for days. Regardless, he walked the length of the Palanquero base and the width of the runway. He climbed the ladder and atop a machine he'd flown so many times before, he felt as if it had been built around him.

This is the last image: a colonel disappearing into a cockpit, into the sky, into the jungle, into the dirt. And he wouldn't be found until the following morning. After the base commander sent out helicopter after helicopter to fly over the trees and try to pick out, from all the possible shades of green, a man dressed to blend in. And his family sat up in the dark listening to the overlapping beating of spinning helicopter blades. No one really slept, but the children were, nevertheless, sent to school the next morning. Because, "What else was I gonna do?" My grandmother more or less explains, more or less dismisses my question. Because, witches are simpler than the simple path of a man falling and his family following. And she tells me again about how she heard the plane fall: "Like a single metal pen falling on a marvel floor. It was Sunday, I remember." And she would rather tell me about the hour she spent looking for that pen, wondering why her husband hadn't yet come home, than tell me about her three girls trying to hear lessons over the search helicopters and the whispering of friends.

In the morning light the search was made easier, and they found him between the trees still strapped to his seat. They marked it on the map and men were sent to retrieve the body. They walked through a chirping jungle and found a white parachute like a mosquito net tangled in the branches and a colonel lying on the dirt on his left side, crushed on his left side, with his right, remaining hand still firmly on a lever.

"We were in class," my mother tells me while I sit at the foot of my aunt Chiqui's bed, where she lays mostly confined since the doctors told her the cancer was back.

"Right. Then that giraffe woman came to get us." My aunt picks up where my mother leaves off.

"Yes, the very tall one. *Toda una dama.* I think her name was Ligia, very strict but . . ." my mother pauses for a second. "But she was very kind that day." And I notice my mother speaks more softly than I've ever known her to. Not like she did when I was a kid and she used to take my older sister and me to Catholic churches so she could point at passing Benedictine nuns and explain in whispers how truly terrible they all were as teachers. Soft but decided, like the practiced stroke of an artist's sketch. *Specially the Spanish ones, those are the worst.* But now, it's something even smaller than that. "I remember," she says to my aunt, "she was very kind to us that day." And I see her almost tremble, "She pulled you out first, and then me, and when she brought us together, she told us that they'd found him. Then you, or maybe me, I can't remember, someone said, 'And we loved him so.'" *Tanto que lo queríamos.*

"I don't remember that." My aunt doesn't miss a beat. "That giraffe was a total bitch as far as I can recall." And she looks at me as she chuckles, so I chuckle, too. "She was." She insists, but my mother doesn't seem to hear her or notice us.

"Yes, that's when we found out."

"And from there, a whirlwind." My aunt chuckles again, though less lightheartedly than before.

"Yes." They both pause for a moment, and I have to prod them to continue. *What do you mean? How so? What whirlwind?* "Well. They flew us out in . . ." my mother hesitates. "A Fokker, I think."

"Yes. Definitely a Fokker, and we had to sit in those awful little benches on either side. Remember?" My mother nods and I know what she is thinking because she's told me so many times before. That my aunt Chiqui's memory is their communal hard drive and that when she dies more than half their memories will die with her. "Straight to the wake from there," my aunt continues, "and then that was it."

My mother nods and then sits down on an old swivel chair that creaks at the lightest pressure. And she seems to me somehow faded, as if she herself had only been lightly sketched on the pad and clumsy thumbprints were threatening to erase her completely. "We could see, from the window, the other planes." She looks up as if they were right there before her. "We could see the funeral planes, flying above and ahead of us. The guard flanking us and the one that held him heading up the front. And . . ." She pauses again and looks briefly in the direction of my grandmother's room. "I remember my mother looking out, too, at those planes, then saying, 'I wish this one would fall down too, get this all over with already.'" And my mother gets quiet for a moment while my aunt rattles off her usual speech. How they really basically raised themselves, what a miracle it was that they'd survived my grandmother at all, and how nowadays no one would allow it. How my grandmother buried herself deeper than the colonel ever was, going three times a day to visit his grave and meeting every which witch in between.

"Like some sort of addict."

But my mother doesn't say a word, and maybe doesn't hear one either. She simply sits quietly and then repeats, "Then that was it."

And for a moment I'm caught between my aunt's nonchalance and my mother's heartbreak. Because I feel them both like the weight of a helmet pulling me forward and back. A girl like a coin spinning in the air, like a falling man deciding which side of his body he will crush against the earth. Nothing but chance between landing forward or landing back, on the left or on the right. And neither letting go nor holding on seem all that different to me. Neither one more a virtue than the other is a vice.

Like once when I was six and sat on my bedroom floor hugging the colonel's helmet with my arms and legs while my mother showed me a glossy black and white photograph of a lab rat doing weightless cartwheels in the air in one of the colonel's old books. And she told me about zero gravity and about Yuri Gagarin, and Laika the soviet space dog, and what it must be like to be completely weightless and untethered. And then she pointed back at the white rat and then up at the sky, and said that that's what happened—if you went far enough into the blue, it turned black. And it made me want to hold on to that helmet forever, and it made me want to let go immediately too.

"But . . . wait," I say, shaking my head while scribbling names and dates on loose sheets. "What do you mean, 'That was it'?"

"Well," my aunt replies, "it was." She fiddles with this pencil and then that remote control the way she used to fiddle with her lighter before a cigarette.

"For us. For life as it was," my mother replies, and then trudges on. "We didn't go to the funeral."

"You and Lulu didn't," my aunt adds, only hinting at what I already know. That she alone went with my grandmother to the colonel's funeral. And she alone stayed with her through the burial, the two exhumations, the twice-a-day visits to the cemetery, and everything else that followed. Everything and more, to this day. Paying the bills and hiring maids and fighting the everyday fights of domestic life. Living with my grandmother still, all her life in the shadow and place of a father she barely knew.

"Yes," my mother whispers, "Chiqui did go. We stayed alone in our grandparents' Bogotá apartment that day, and *that* was it."

Once more she repeats it, but this time I think I get it. "You mean," I say, "you never went back to Palanquero?"

"Right."

"You were in school one day. Had a father and friends and pets, and then."

"That was it."

"Then, it was . . . what? Four days."

"Yes."

Three hundred and sixty five, fifty, thirty, four.

A year for Ana Cristina, a month for the witch, fifty days for his friends, and four for his children.

On Saturday they ride their bikes at full speed into the river. They crash into the Magdalena, gripping their handlebars and holding their breath. On Sunday the colonel falls from the sky. On Monday all that is left of him is found, and as much as can be recovered is placed into a coffin. On Tuesday he is flown into the capital, into Bogotá, and all his children are allowed to go to his wake, but not to the Wednesday funeral where only his eldest, Mirtha—my aunt Chiqui—weeps uncontrollably and inconsolably as her own mother plunges into the arms of family and strangers alike, beating her chest, calling out prayers and wailing for the man inside the box.

The colonel's three girls will never return to the base and are left with their grandparents in their three-bedroom apartment while their mother manages the move and storage of the colonel's possessions.

Lulu, the youngest, will sleep in a crib in the master bedroom, which her grandparents will give up so that the widow might have more room to grieve. The two eldest girls, on the other hand, will have no beds or rooms of their own, so they will take turns sleeping in their mother's bed one night, and their grandparents' the next for the span of a year while they wait for the state to process the colonel's widow's request for a pension.

The middle girl, my mother, however, will be too afraid to sleep most nights. She might lie on her back, or on her side, or on her stomach and it would make no difference. Sleep will not come. Though of course she barely moves, barely breathes. She lays still and stiff and cold as if there were hungry things in the darkness trying to sniff her out. And she will feel truly untethered for the first time in her life. And maybe it's something between realization and suffocation. Or something like a heightened sense of scale and frailty. Or maybe this is what zero gravity actually feels like. Though, really, it will be like nothing else she can name. For that moment, she will only know that when the lights go out and she can't see her grandparents anymore, she will doubt their very existence. Perhaps they go out with lights, into the walls, through the floorboards and into cables and beyond the dirt. So all night long, she will stare into the red light of her grandfather's cigarette, as if she could navigate back to shore by its flickering light and she prays it won't go out.

A year for a widow's pension. A year for Ana Cristina. Thirteen children left behind.

I was nearly thirteen years old when I first met my paternal grandfather, the engineer. And if my father had not taken me to his home for that express and exclusive purpose, I can't imagine I would have even recognized him on the street. *Bueno, entonces adentro.* "Well then, you might as well come in." It didn't become habit to visit and from that day I can only recall the image of a white-haired, broad shoulder man with the gait of someone who used to throw his weight around. "Go on then." He said shaking my hand. "Sit." Before picking up his drink and lighting up a cigarette.

When my older sister was born, the engineer hadn't spoken to my father in years.

His sister, my only paternal aunt, however, pled with him to take the baby to see their father, "Please, Jaime, please." So my father took his firstborn daughter into his arms as if she were something precious he had found in the forest, nearly forgotten and covered in moss, and he told his sister, "No." Because my father is not a sentimental man, not a nostalgic man. Not a man to ever look back at salt pillar cities. He would not hold on to a faded-insignia helmet and he does not visit graves. Not his mother's, not anyone's, not ever.

"People think children are new beginnings," he told me, "and that the future can undo the past." Explaining why he had not wanted to take his firstborn to the father who once tried to knock down his bedroom door, to knock him about, like he did my father's mother. "It doesn't work like that."

"It looks healthy," the engineer said, gazing at the baby my paternal aunt had taken to him behind my father's back. "But it's got nothing to do with me."

And maybe it's as simple as that, and nothing to do with numbers at all.

A grandfather in a glass case who doesn't get to say what does and doesn't have something to do with him.

And I begin to lose count.

"Lina. Lina!" My aunt calls my name as if she were tugging on a string. "Lina." And she flashes the sort of smile I know precedes something she thinks will make me laugh. "Do you want to see the dead man's coffer?"

There is an old trunk in my grandmother's apartment that the colonel's daughters call *El Baúl del Muerto.* "The dead man's coffer." And though on its side there is a half-peeled I.D. tag addressed to an apartment in Quito, where the colonel's youngest daughter used to live, the trunk has never left Colombia. And even now it hardly ever leaves the space beneath my grandmother's bed.

As far as I know it's only been opened twice. Once to pack it all in. And once more to check it was all still there.

"Yes," my mother chimes in, standing up from her squeaky swivel chair. "That's what we should do, while we still have Lina here."

Inside it are the last remaining objects of the once great *Coronel Cabeza*, which my aunt and mother want me to see. "Because," they say, "you've been asking all these questions." And, "Because," they continue in sync, "who else will ever see it?"

So the trunk is hauled out and set on a table. My grandmother's nurse and I do most of the heavy lifting, and I worry I might break something, but my aunt cheers us on.

Cats, chickens, kittens, cow. Colonel, sister, successor, friends. Fifty, thirty, thirteen, four. It's mechanical now, and I have to make an effort to stop.

"Vilma!" My aunt calls out to my mother as she points at a metal talcum powder container, an orange toothbrush, and a tube of Squibb toothpaste arranged carefully to fit together in a little nook among the other objects in the trunk. "Vilma! Vilma! Look at that, Vilma, just look. Ha! Who'd imagine? Do you remember this?"

"Squibb! Wow . . . wow. Wait, wait. Don't touch anything. We need gloves, maybe masks." And my mother pulls out an odd assortment of winter gloves, construction gloves, and a pair of plastic gloves which either came along with a box of hair dye or bucket of chicken. In the mean time I watch a thin cloud of green dust rise from inside the trunk. "Here, Lina," she gives me the heavy construction gloves, "you take these." My aunt straps on what looks like a black, novelty surgical mask. "Ok, let's start."

"We can do this now, you know?" My aunt motions in the direction of my grandmother's room as she pulls out the silk flag from the top of the trunk. "Or rather, we couldn't have done it before."

"Yes," I say, "right," understanding that she refers to my grandmother's mind, which slips in and out like a chain smoker at a Christmas party.

"Otherwise," she grits her teeth and makes a line with her thumb across her neck. "So let's see." And she begins to pull out boxes of medals attached to faded ribbons that might as well be chocolate coins for all we know of military flare. "Look at this one," she says, holding a white cross set on a golden wreath. "What do you think this one is for?"

When they disinterred the colonel to move him from the expensive *Cementerio Central de Bogotá* to a more affordable and less-sought-after cemetery on the outskirts of the city, they had to stick him right back into the wall like an undercooked ham. Out for a minute, and back in for a year, because he had somehow, *Failed to decompose sufficiently to fit in a standard issue ossuary box.*

Another year to count, if I were still keeping count.

The high cement walls of the *Cementerio Central* are usually reserved for the famous, influential, and freshly dead of the military. And in

Colombia, there are always plenty of freshly dead to push the old dead out. So the undertakers and the cemetery men dig up the old to make room for the new and shuffle them around like guests in an overbooked hotel. Then, when enough has fallen off the bone, they pack up what's left in a metal box and hand it over to whoever comes to claim it.

When it was the colonel's time, however, they didn't find any easy-to-pack skeletal outline or the clean hull of a human skull, instead they found the colonel still the colonel, still in the coffin they'd put him in. Somehow, he continued to resist gravity and rot. *Ahí estaba, ahí no más. Enterito como lo habíamos dejado.* My grandmother told me, "There he was, whole. Just like we'd left him. All of him and nothing missing." While she pinched her own forearm as if I didn't know what humans were made of.

I remember pressing her to tell me more, to explain if she meant that he simply had not decomposed enough, not rotted enough for a man to do the rest with his bare hands—still too much meat around the bone too much wax around the wick. Or, rather, if the colonel had somehow remained frozen in death the man she had known in life. The face from the portraits, the hands that rehearsed maneuvers, the man who carefully packed a razor and a toothbrush in his pilot's overnight bag. But she would not explain further. She only repeated that he was "whole," when they pulled him out, and that his shoes alone showed the passing of time. "Like this," she said, curling her fingers like burnt matches and pressing them up to my face as if I were going blind. "Do you see, Lina? Do you see?" Like she wanted me to read her palm and tell her future.

A body still a body, still recognizable—still a man, a pilot, a father, a colonel. Though only just the body, just pulled out of a wall, just there in a coffin like it'd been built around him. Only Dorian Gray shoes on his feet. "Because leather twists like that with time, and rain, sometimes," my grandmother told me. "That's why I never let my leather jackets get wet. They'd get twisted up, too, just like that, just like this." Pressing still her hands into my face. "Are you looking? Do you understand?" A man in a uniform, in a box, in a wall. Just like the day they stuck him in and said goodbye one last supposed-final time.

And now we're digging him up again.

My mother lays out the medals on a line on the table in a sort of trance, while I count discontinued coins, and my aunt has to sit down to catch her breath.

"*Ay, ay, ay,*" she says as she sits down and places a hand over her colostomy bag. "*Ay, ay,*" Almost under her breath but not quite.

"Are you . . . ok?" Because it's a stupid question to ask, but I don't know what else to do. "Is there . . . anything I can get you?"

"*Ay, ay.*" She leans back and closes her eyes. "No, Linita." *Ahorita se me pasa.* "In a minute it'll pass." She seems almost to brace for the turbulence of pain. And I briefly want to touch her. I want to reach out for her hand and for Ana Cristina's hand too, and hold them for a little while so they might not feel so alone in these moments when you more or less know what must, inevitably, come next. Gravity speeds up and slows down, the sound of metal scraping bone and the earth rising to meet you. But that's not how things are and not quite how I was raised. And I'm stuck only looking and counting and hoping it all adds up to something.

For the first exhumation, the colonel's widow decides to take two daughters. The eldest, my aunt Chiqui, and the middle child, my mother, ages twelve and nine. So the colonel's widow and her two eldest daughters watch as a crowd of men heave, lift, and pull the colonel out of the wall. The eldest girl stands beside her mother, shaking and crying, holding herself and looking constantly down as if God were in the cement beneath her feet. The widow weeps, too. She weeps every day, wears black for years, and right now stands at a little distance from the men prying open her husband's coffin. "Stay here," the widow's brother tells her and trudges off, pushes his way through the crowd so he can stand at the edge of the wooden box to see what death and time do to a body.

The colonel's widow and eldest daughters do not want to see, do not want to know. They don't even want to know that others have seen and others know. But the second born can hardly hold still in her mother's grip. She tries to see beyond the wall of bodies surrounding the coffin, standing on tiptoes and stretching her neck. But it's no use, so she breaks from her mother's grasp and runs through skirts and coats and *ruanas*, pushing herself between fidgeting bodies to catch one final glimpse of her father.

Inside the trunk, between old sheets and kitchen rags, we pull out two blue uniforms and more medals wrapped in newspaper. One folded silk flag, which we assume was once draped over the colonel's coffin, and one small leather travel bag with a rusted zipper, which the colonel packed himself forty-six years ago. It has, likewise, been opened only twice, and only ever by the colonel's widow, so she could check it had not all vanished while she wasn't looking and then repacked it in ritualistic exactitude.

Everything kept as he kept it, left as he left it. As if he had not left, as if he could be kept.

"Look at that, Lina. We should get a camera," my aunt says, placing on the table two containers of Yardley shaving cream and aftershave, a Sulton Deodorant Stick, and one heavy metal razor that has been slowly bleeding green-brown rust for nearly half a century inside the "Dead Man's coffer," beneath my grandmother's bed. "Amazing." My aunt Chiqui seems better already, entranced by the sight. Like it's happening through a screen—voiceover, subtitles, and distance. But my mother has stopped talking, and she holds the flag like an ailing cat too still to be alive still, but still too warm to just discard. "Vilma, do you see this? Do you remember this?" She pulls out the deodorant and the razor. I notice a hat I've seen at least a hundred times in official air force portraits, so I pick it up and examine it closely. "I remember this—do you remember this, Vilma?" My aunt pulls out a wrinkled Disneyland pennant, holding it between her index and thumb like a crinkly strip of molted snake's skin, but I'm barely paying attention now. I run my finger across the leather visor, and across the insignia above it—Colombia's coat of arms encircled by a golden wreath and two outstretched wings—then I tap it gently to shake off the dust, and I put it on.

"Did you?" I ask my mother while she is still holding on to her father's flag and my aunt continues to pull out pieces from the trunk as if she might find a set of instructions to fit them all together into one coherent machine. "Did you get to see him that day they pulled him out of the wall?"

"Sort of," she says and puts the flag down on a pile of newspapers. "I made it to the coffin."

"But . . ." I regret my question immediately, but still want an answer. *Was he whole? Was he magic? Did he seem the same in death as he was in life? How was he in life?*

"But, I only saw his shoes." My mother stares blankly at the open trunk and I see in my mind my grandmother's hands curling up like pages in a fire.

I regret asking, regret counting, regret finally inhaling inside that heavy helmet, and regret ever putting it on.

Then I hear my mother say, "gnarled," and watch her curl her fingers into a familiar pose, "like this." She holds up her hands for me to see. "It's what happens to leather." And I feel the leather strap around the inner rim of the colonel's service cap begin to cut a line across my forehead, because, of course, "Leather shrinks and curls with time."

A year later they pulled the colonel out of the wall one final time. For perhaps obvious reasons, my grandmother never told me this story. So I only have one version heard only one time, and it made my mother's voice crack in such a way that I never asked again. I'm left, then, only with three images. First, long-fingered men reach into the colonel's coffin, they pull out bones and shake off the last bits of the once great man as if they were tapping their spoons after stirring their coffees, before tossing them into a metal box the length of a femur and the width of two skulls. Second, they hand the box over to the colonel's widow. She takes it and runs her hand over the metal case, like Ana ran her hand over her chest, like the colonel flew his invisible planes. Third, the colonel's widow sits in the backseat of a small car between her youngest and her eldest daughters with the box on her lap while she feels the skull strike the case with every speedbump and pothole. And my mother will remember that forever. Sitting in the passenger seat and hearing the sound of bone on metal, the clink and clank of her father's bones striking the box while the reverberation sinks into her mother's thighs.

There is something missing.

One hundred and fifty-seven pictures. Every medal, every button. Every tin of shaving cream and every last wrinkled handkerchief. All laid out on the table, catalogued and photographed. But there is still something missing.

"Wait a minute," my mother told me one day as I played with a bit of folded metal she's always kept on her dresser. "There is something you should see." And I watched her almost disappear into the top drawer. "After he fell, they told us he'd landed on his left side and that the right side was perfect, totally intact." *Intacto, entero,* speaking into scarves and pins and dead batteries rolling around a messy drawer. "The right side though. Nothing left of the right." And she pulled out a little dented metal oval she held up as if she wanted to catch the light with it. "Here," she said, stretching out her hand, "take it." And I put down one piece of metal to pick up another. "It's his wedding band," she said as I turned it around and tried very hard not to picture the impact. "And this," she picked up the scrap I'd set down. "This was part of it." She placed it in her palm as if to weigh it. "Last part left," she said, as if there may be one last number trapped inside, the one to make it all make sense. But I've lost count.

A man hits the ground and there is no poetry left. It is not like eggs, like glass, like empty peanut shells being trampled, being crushed, being ground up into dust. A man, not his body alone, but he himself strikes the ground, and it strikes back. And that's it. Bones splinter, sockets crack, an eyeball bursts, teeth shatter, meat explodes—he is turned red, unrecognizable, shapeless, unwoven. Dirt made anvil, man made hammer. The colonel speeding toward the ground and maybe he thinks of his family, maybe he thinks of his friends, maybe he thinks of his mother in Mompox, of walking up to her as a kid and lifting up her shirt when he was hungry. But maybe not. There is likely very little time for that. And if any thought is more probable than any other it is this one: *I should have let go sooner.* Because this is the thing about letting go and holding on. You can't have a little of both.

"You know, Lina," my mother said to me, still holding the torn piece of her father's aircraft. "If he hadn't tried to save the plane . . . hadn't held out for as long as he did." While I looked down at a wedding band bent into an oval against the jungle floor. "Maybe," watching myself hold it delicately as if earth and gravity had not already tried with all their might to obliterate it. "I don't. Maybe."

There is one last animal. Might as well.

A black cocker spaniel named Ninoska. "I think the colonel chose that name, too." But, unlike the others, my mother wrote, "she was the only one to survive." These are her words. *La única que sobrevivió.* As if she herself had not survived the crash, the cow, the witch, the cats, the chickens, the helicopter. "And our mother brought her to Bogotá, too!" To join the rest of the colonel's family in a cramped apartment in the capital. "Our grandfather put her in the yard, I don't remember why." Though she does remember a black, shaggy dog leaping up with muddy paws, trying to knock her down and lick her clean. "And she lived," she writes, as if she still lives, as if this is some fantastic feat against fate itself. As if her grandfather had not found her by the front wall one day, whimpering and shivering and hacking up red chunks of undigested meat, while she licked her front paws as if they were covered in blisters. As I read her emails I tried to decide between nonchalance and magical melancholy. Because why not kill a dog? They bark, they bite, they smell—and in a large city there are a lot of neighbors with long commutes who need to sleep. Why not kill a dog, after all. Why not?

But then, why should it be killed? Why should all the animals die, and not a single one live? Why should the colonel take them with him and leave none to console disconsolate daughters?

"It was poison. That's what we think anyway." A red slab of meat thrown over a fence and a happy Russian named dog gnawing on it a whole day before it begins to burn through her intestines. But this is not Palanquero. There are fewer witches and more explanations than prophecies, and the girls' grandfather finds the dog and decides he will not let it die. He is a professor, a well-connected man. *Un filósofo, y un escritor.* So he patted her on the head until she stopped whimpering, and he picked her up. He let her vomit on his coat and pee red streaks down his pants as he rushed her to the National University's veterinary hospital, to a man he knows, who will save the dog.

"We could make a box, like a display," my aunt says, holding up a gold-plated medal.

"With velvet and glass," my mother adds. "Put it right here, by the table, so we can all see them." Lifting yet another medal by a tiny strip of moth-eaten silk still attached. "We should find out what they mean, too. They could be important. This one looks important." As my aunt pulls from the bottom of the trunk a bar of old moldy soap still wrapped in brown butcher's paper.

"Ok, now. The masks back on. I mean it, Lina, take a mask."

Of course the dog does not live. This much should have been obvious, even to children, especially to the colonel's three young daughters. "We used to ask our grandfather, how Ninoska was doing, and when we might be able to see her again," especially as time passed, "And he would just smile and tell us how much better she was doing, and all the new tricks they were teaching her in the university." But then their grandfather fell ill as suddenly as the chickens shed their feathers. A jaundiced man sweating and writhing and vomiting into a bedpan, his body curled like pages in the fire. And there was no time for dogs, living or dead. "I just . . . I hadn't thought," and my mother seems legitimately confused by her confusion. A memory sealed with child logic suddenly moldy and brittle in the light, I'm not sure if this death counts. Because my great-grandfather did all he could to strike it out, and who am I to rewrite that?

"Look," my aunt tells me as she laughs and begins peeling back brown paper from the bar of soap like strips of dry skin from her own forearm. "Look what madness and loneliness does to a weak mind." Pale blue, green, orange, and flakes of white on a bar of soap that seems somehow still a bit wet from the shower. "Look what the colonel's wife wouldn't even think of throwing out." Decades of multicolor bacteria still blooming on crumpled brown paper and soap. "Look what the colonel left us, and who he left us with." My aunt, the last person left with any real memories of her father, of the colonel, laughing now through a facemask and holding up a dead man's bar of soap. I look down at the pile of dates and numbers and details I've been scribbling all day long, been keeping for years. "Insane," I hear my aunt mumble and feel myself nod mechanically. *Two cats, seven kittens, all the chickens, one cow.* "All these years, all these things." *Base commander, sub-commander. Friends, wives, chaplain. Ana Cristina.* "You'd have to be mad," she says surveying the rust- and dust-covered final remains of *El Coronel Cabeza*. "As if he were coming right back."

And because my head hurts from the pressure of a shrunken leather rim, and we don't know any carpenters who make display cases, or what any of the medals mean, or what all these numbers add up to, we put it all back just like he left it.

EL QUE TIENE RABO DE PAJA,
NO SE ACERQUE A LA CANDELA

or

He what has tail of hay, no himself brings near to the fire.

or

He ~~what~~ [*who*] has [*a*] tail [*made*] of hay, ~~no~~ [*should not*] ~~himself brings~~ [*go*] near ~~to the~~ fire.

or

Flammable people shouldn't play with fire.

or

"But everything can be made to burn."

Catching Moths

He was saying, "We are all alike," when I nearly ran into him outside a furniture store in Colombia. "Won't you spare something, please? Look how they treat us, may God bless you, you never know where you'll end up, and look how they don't even let us stand over there by the mall anymore. God bless you—we're all alike."

This was just a few years ago, in Bogotá, one of those times between semesters, or grad school programs, when I would buy a discounted ticket and sleep under a bench in the Miami airport. And I came so close to him I could have licked the soup still dripping from his black soot beard. So I jumped back. Dirty rags on a dirtier frame, black sails on a burnt ship. And I came so close I nearly kissed him on the lips. He said, "Look how I'm hungry," and, "Look how they don't even let us go stand by the mall over there anymore." And that's when I laughed. And that's when I knew that was the wrong thing to do.

■

Another man, another time—in Bogotá—came up to me once and showed me every wet, cavity-riddled tooth in his mouth. He was hard to miss, a man made of dust and scab and dirt with black streaks running down his face as if he were sweating engine grease. I watched him kick his way through cars at the intersection, spit on street vendors, and yell at the women selling umbrellas to suck his cock. He covered half the sidewalk with his gait and parted crowds like Moses did seas. All black grease lines and bloodshot eyes and spit and spark. I stood against a wall, and I should've looked away, *because this is what you do,* but I didn't. I met his eyes and he fixed on me like he'd been waiting for me all day long. He crossed the street again, grabbed his penis through his pants and rushed toward me. It wasn't "so fast I didn't know what to do," and I wasn't "just frozen there." I felt my toes inside my shoes, the width of my shoulders, length of my arms, saliva drying on my lips, and I did not move an inch, as if perfect stillness could make me bright and poisonous. Then he set a foot between mine, opened his mouth and swung his head toward my face like a hammer. Two crooked rows of yellow teeth, the dampness of his breath on my lips, a mouth like an open palm. The sight of a wide open mouth coming toward me like a dog for his Frisbee and the memory of running as a child, through hallways and bedrooms, trying to catch little moths and fat flies and long-legged mosquitoes. The pink of his tongue and the sound of him snapping his mouth shut millimeters from my nose, like the moment when I finally caught a moth midflight and opened my hands to find bits of wings and specks of gray blood.

I didn't blink, didn't flinch. I just stood still, as if all human interactions were interchangeable and of equal value, and I watched him walk away, spitting and kicking and groping.

∎

"Little rich whore laugh at me, laugh at me, eh?" He shouted louder and louder, and the louder he shouted, the less people seemed to hear us.

Usaquén is one of those nice places: big open markets, Asian fusion restaurants. It was once an autonomous town, but Bogotá is a disheveled hungry thing that keeps chasing down anything at its periphery and swallowing it whole. Now Usaquén is barely a neighborhood, more of a clean weekend playground for drunk-musician evenings and theme-brunch afternoons, where cops spend all their time escorting the local indigent residents down, away, out of sight and to the outskirts of a nearby mall.

I shifted, tried to get past him, but he paced, set his foot down next to mine, turned, took three or four stomping steps, and came right back as if he were anchored to me.

∎

Once, when I was sixteen, a man followed me down a dark alley. He rose from the shadows, and I thought very briefly he was a shadow come alive. It was late; it was Bogotá. I was alone and too tired to take the long way around. So I headed down this unlit alley because I could see the light of a bar at the end, hear the noise of merengue clashing against *champeta*, and some people huddled by the road as if a bus might arrive any minute. Then this man rose up from a corner like a cloud of dust that something large leaves in its wake. I remember seeing it from the corner of my eye and thinking that I ought not to look directly at it. Instead the sound of his feet hitting the pavement, faint but clear, like the first few drops of rain before a storm. He walked quickly and I only caught a glimpse of the shape of him in motion, streaks of a man with hands in his pockets rising and materializing. And just the two of us in an alley, quiet and dark, so I pulled a glass bottle from my bag and swung it against the metal fence. It was not as loud as I thought it would be and some glass hung off the plastic label limp and unthreatening. But, it was surprisingly easy, this movement of the arm, smooth and relaxed, so much like waving hello, as if it might have been the bottle driving the motion, metal and glass and an easy swing. Then I held it out for him to see and waited for something to let me know it was time to turn around and tear through his neck with glass fangs. But nothing came, and maybe he was too tired for a struggle, or maybe he was rushing to take a leak, and maybe I really meant it when I thought, *I'm going to lose this bottle inside you.*

■

Sometimes I think about teeth on my nose, or on my cheek and neck. A mouth like an open palm catching me, specks and scraps, wings and blood and dust. I imagine a half-torn lip dangling on my chin as my mother pours sugar and *panela* shavings into holes and bite marks. She wraps me up with gauze, tells me, "It'll fill in the hole, you'll see. It won't be bad, hold still." I consider flinching and not flinching, and worse, *I'm going to split you open.* I think of another man I more or less used to know. I sat in his mother's living room not so long ago, while he lay on a bed a room away. He's been there for more than twenty years now, ever since the bullet made a nest inside his spine. If I close my eyes I can see his mother pointing at a spot on her lower back, "Right here, see?" That's where they shot him. "To ruin him." It's like pulling a plug on a blow dryer, on a microwave—all of us contraptions with an off switch. The television fizz of electricity races back up, through feet and knees and thighs, and then the lights go out in your legs or arms or eyes. A twitch, a spark, paralysis.

For a long time I thought it had been the stabbing that had put him in the chair. I had this idea of someone pushing in a knife and twisting it, to ruin him like they'd felt ruined by him. I know better now—"No, no, Lina. It was a bullet, the knifing was another time." But I still have the image, a knife pulled out of a spine like a clog from a drain.

I dream about him too. About the knifing. He runs through the night, through unlit alleys, dripping. Someone's unzipped his abdomen with a blade and he's spilling. He runs and holds himself in like a half-torn fugitive piñata, a belly full of red candy, torn ribbons and string. When he finally reaches a hospital, his socks are soaked; they squish as he stumbles, and he has to kick the doors open. Nurses and doctors stand paralyzed before the sight of a man holding himself together with interlaced fingers until they hear him yell, "Sew me up, *malparidos!*" And they do, because what else are they going to do? And for a moment he's whole again, beautiful and stitched and unconscious on a hospital bed.

Last time I saw him he was soaked only in the blue glow of his television. I peeked through a crack in the door as if he were something to see, something to gawp at or poke with a stick. I didn't think there was enough left of his mind to put noise to face, to recognize me, or even notice me, but then he turned and met my eyes. A second, maybe two, both us as alone in this vestibule, ripped-open piñatas, red ribbons and gray moths, and then he turned away because that is what you do after commercial breaks.

■

"Listen to me you little whore, you listen to me now. I'll tell you a story." Every time the man in Usaquén began to walk away, he'd reach some imaginary edge and get pulled right back around. He smelled of wet smoke, as if he had slept over damp coals. "You laugh, I'll tell you what, I'll tell you. I will." He pointed at the street as if picking it out of a lineup, and said, "These white vans come up, with these kids." He turned his head and then pointed at me. "These kids they come, they set my friends on fire." He shook his head and then let it hang as if someone were slipping on a noose. "They're dead," he mumbled, "burnt-dead." Then I saw him tense from the tip of his toes to the top of his head, something between a guitar and a suspension bridge. "You with them?" He looked me straight in the eye. "You come down when we sleep, set us on fire? Clean up society? Eh?!"

■

The first time I saw snow on a camping trip atop a Utah mountain, I put my feet in the fire. It was colder than I'd ever imagined the world could be and it felt primal and dangerous, all amygdala and chilled blood. Like the sound of something moving carefully in the bushes, or that deep, long, rumbling thunder that echoes inside the belly of the darkened heavens, as if the sky were nothing more than the hungry tunnel of some ancient thing's throat. So I stood in the fire, between two logs, flames licking the edges of my socks into a crisp curl. I couldn't feel my feet, and then I could feel them too much, and nothing in-between seemed right or true. But no one seemed concerned; they were all used to this cold and how sharp and hard ice makes everything, and they themselves seemed suddenly dangerous to me, too. Made dangerous by their familiarity with the sharpness of winter. So I stood in the fire, it seemed the only thing to do and I was surprised only by how easy it was to simply stand there until the hem of my jeans was scorched. My shoes caught fire and coals melted holes into the soles. I put my finger through those holes when they'd cooled off; I wore them out walking through Bogotá. I broke a bottle against a metal fence when I thought a shadow had come alive.

■

I apologized. Because, what else was I going to do? But I said it under my breath when he'd turned for a moment to stare at the sidewalk as if it were about to confess its part in the crimes. I walked around his invisible perimeter while his back was still turned, and I apologized. *Lo siento,* in Spanish—which means "I'm sorry," but not quite. *Lo siento,* "I feel it." Less about responsibility and more about company in grief, in regret, in remorse, in a fire, in a snowstorm, in a wreath of broken glass and torn moth wings. *I'm sorry,* about the laughter and the burns, and whatever look on my face made you think I'd set fire to you too. And I'm sorry I looked, and I'm sorry I hadn't before. I'm sorry for little cans of gasoline poured on sleeping men, for catching moths and long-legged mosquitoes, for standing in the fire and the snow. *Sew me back up, malparidos.*

**DONDE HUBO FUEGO,
CENIZAS QUEDAN**

or

Where there was fire, ashes remain.

or

Where there was fire, ashes remain.

or

_____ ashes _____.

or

"Damned spot."

María, María, María, María

Every purple July, they return. In cars, in buses, and barefoot. From Perú, from Ecuador, from Venezuela. From the capital and from the towns and villages in between, and—once, at least—from Rome. From above mountains and beneath bridges, the pilgrims go back to Colombia's holy city, Chiquinquirá.

Did you see them yourself?

"Hm! Of course."

Did you meet them?

"Hm! Imagine. Of course."

What did they say?

"Hm, hm! So many things."

And what did they look like?

"Head to toe, in purple."

I know this, because María told me. "Sometimes on foot, sometimes in cars—you know the kinda car? Snouty. Like pigs." *Renaults?* "Yes, yes."

And María knows because she saw them, every year, on the ninth of July when processions swept through her hometown, sandals and candles, beer and prayer. They arrived in packs to pay their respects to both Mary and Mary, *María y María—la virgen y la devota,* the saint and her servant.

The Virgin Mary, the first Mary, whose miraculous portrait they carry on their shoulders from one end of the city to the other—like a victorious coach, like a casket, like a tired child at a fair. And while the palanquin poles sink into their shoulders, and wax drips on their shirts and fists, they'll quietly pay homage to the second and less famous María, María Ramos, who four hundred years ago restored the Virgin's holy portrait, and made the city holy in the first place.

María, my grandmother's and mother's former maid, won't tell me about María Ramos. Not because, I don't think, she doesn't know or doesn't want to tell me, but rather because I've hardly ever known her to utter more than a fistful of words at a time, and never any sentence uninterrupted by her own personal phonetic punctuation mark. A "Hm!" sound she produces from somewhere between her throat and nose, which I've learned, more or less translates to, *but the rest goes without saying.* "They come and come, the pilgrims, returning, and hm!" It is as if every spoken phrase demands an enormous effort from her, as if she were perpetually hanging from a metal bar and had to pull herself up to it in order to speak, weight and gravity and syntax constantly pulling her down toward silence. "Hm!"

I ask her about Chiquinquirá, and about her husband, and about her father and her brothers and the pilgrims, and she hangs on that bar and kicks her feet, "Hm!" As if all her stories were an exercise in redundancy. She raises her shoulder and drops them like anchors. "Well there and there, and then and then." Every end before the end. "So, on he went. Hm!"

"He," as in her brother. "There and there," as in Chiquinquirá. "Then and then," when they were still basically kids, "on he went," somewhere else, away forever from their childhood home never to return again. With his face in his hands, I imagine, as if he were weeping, which he must have been, through shattered bones and cuts like ruts on a road where the bicycle chain his father was swinging split his face open.

María knows, because she was there—she told me. After I begged a little and I begged a lot, she told me about Chiquinquirá, and her brother, and her father, and the dead donkey, and the cliff, and the pilgrims—how they always return, every purple July.

Start at the beginning María, at home. What is Chiquinquirá like?
"Hm!"

■

Chiquinquirá is an uneven mixture of processions and corner shops. Red brick streets filled with the greasy smell of *mazamorra, arepa,* and *chorizo.* Matching leftover colonial balconies above neon-sign restaurants and drugstore casinos. The clicking sound of barely audible songs through cheap transistor radios and the clinking of empty beer bottles.

This is where María was born. Not in the tourist-friendly town center with its symmetrical, brick-laid streets, but in the unpaved outskirts of moss and smoke and dust.

■

In the beginning of 1586, the only thing María Ramos knows is that the worn-out cotton canvas before her once held the image of the holy Virgin Mary. This is all she knows, and all she needs to know. She pulls the rather large painting from a dark room in the chapel, where it's been for the last twenty years, between wooden slabs and rotten planks, and she brushes the dust off the way someone brushes hair from a child's face.

She doesn't know much about restoration, or paintings, or art in general. But she knows two things, first, that hidden in the cloth there was once the image of the mother of God, and second, that right now, she really needs to gaze upon something holy.

So she sets the painting down gently on the floor, lightly dabbing it with a white rag dipped in turpentine and alcohol. Trying to divine the lines between Saint Andrew's cape and cross, the dark brown of Saint Anthony's robes and the light brown of his bible. The contentment in the Virgin's face as she holds a plump baby Jesus in her arms from her holy serenity as she gazes into a flat distance. But María Ramos does not know this yet. She does not know Jesus' plumpness and how the Virgin's eyes remain half closed, perpetually unimpressed by the ornate composition around her—the golden cherubs holding a crown above her head, the tipped crescent moon around her feet, and the grotesque homunculi posing atop bibles while men drag heavy crosses behind them like cans on a newlyweds's car. María Ramos has never actually seen the face she is so furiously trying to recover from behind layers of dust and mold and moth-laid eggs, but faith lets the blind see, the deaf hear, the lame walk, the hopeless hope, the untrained restore.

So she mixes in prayers with the alcohol as she dabs, for good measure. "Please, please," as she begs, kneeling beside the painting. "Please, Mary, please." Though maybe her prayers are more specific: "Let there be paint beneath this stain. Don't let the cloth tear. Don't let my eyes go." Though maybe they are less specific: "Mary, Mary, Mary, Mary. Please, please, please." Or maybe the painting is the prayer itself and not what she is praying for: "Please Mary, let me see you. Let me hear you. Let me know what to do." Maybe she cries a little and rushes to wipe her nose with the back of her hand, leaving oily streaks of turpentine soaked dust across her face. "Please, don't let me be alone. Show me something, show me anything." And when her eyes begin to burn, she pulls herself away from the painting, looks away into the street—a cat on the windowsill, a bird on the wire, a sleeping dog beside a lame beggar. "Make that cat land on its back, make the birds blind, the dog howl, the man whole. Anything." Maybe what she did know, what she could see, was nothing she wanted to know or see, or have waiting for her back home. Maybe the painting is penance and not prayer.

Either way, she cries, and she dabs, and she goes home late at night and comes back early in the morning, to cry and dab and go home again even later that night. To continue praying and begging and asking, "Mary, Mary, Mary?" Until the holy Virgin hears, through cloud cover and quilted wings, María's muffled cry, and she decides to answer.

She leaps down from heaven, lands softly on the rain-soaked roof of a Colombian chapel, and walks barefoot along the edge where a line of pigeons perch. Then she looks down at María Ramos washing the turpentine streaks from her face, she hears her own name being called, "*María? María? María?*" and she hears, also, what lies beneath the name—the things María Ramos can't quite put into words, the anxious undercurrents of her troubled mind. And the pigeons begin cooing excitedly, and the cat misjudges a distance, and the beggar kicks the dog, as the canvas seems to burst into a blaze of heatless fire that erupts from every ghost brush stroke. The Virgin has decided to scorch the painting back from the depths of the cloth, and slowly, slowly, St. Anthony reappears, St. Andrew reappears, the Virgin Mary and the child Jesus all reappear, while the fat child atop a Bible reemerges like a sunken city in a drought.

■

She will relent. Eventually. María will clap her hands and shake her head and tell me, "Once a whole bunch of them," pilgrims in purple robes, "came up to me and my brother and they said how they liked me, and how I was pretty and white. And if I wanted something to drink or something to eat in the little shop in the corner, and . . . Hm!" She shrugs, shakes her head, and looks up at me as if I know exactly how the story ends because, of course, *the rest goes without saying.*

María is short, light-skinned, calloused, and about two sizes too small for her cheap, baby blue maid's uniform and matching apron. The rest does not go without saying, *What then?* "Hm!" *What then María, what then?* "What then? Hm. They said they wanted to take me, and then they said they were just gonna take me and would give my brother—who was there, just right there with me—a little something for it."

I picture the pilgrims, worn-out t-shirts and sweatpants under their robes, making their way up a dirt road when they notice a ten-year-old girl walking home with her brother. One of them shifts his weight and taps the other on the shoulder. One of them fixes the elastic on his sweatpants while yet another nods. The girl in the distance is pale and short, but she walks with purpose. She clearly knows the road, the dirt beneath and her way home, just as the men watching her know the path of their appetites, and how to satisfy them. So they approach the brother and sister. Maybe they have to jog a little to catch up and they lift their robes so they won't trip. Maybe they are on the other end and have only to wait for the boy and girl to walk up to them so they can say, "Young man," *Jovencito,* "your sister, she's pretty." They are tired, after all; they've been walking for weeks, or driving for days, or riding the bus for hours. Regardless, they are tired. Tired and bored because they are, clearly, also early. Hours if not days before processions and masses and blessings. So they ask the boy, "Is she thirsty, your sister? Maybe she wants us to buy her a little something. *¿Arepita? ¿Gaseosa? ¿Almojábana?*" And the boy looks at his sister. There is a chance he doesn't understand. What do these men want? Who are they, and why wouldn't they offer him something to drink too? But misunderstanding is unlikely. "Give us her, and we'll give you something for your trouble." *¿Qué le parece?*

"But, no. No, no. My brother wouldn't have it." María shakes her head adamantly, arms crossed, eyes closed, head to the right and then to the left like she's trying to shake off years of dust and mold. "He said that I was a little girl, just too little, and he said no. And no, and no. Hm!" And she laughs. A reached-punchline laugh, as if there were no edge to that story at all, or else the edge had been blunt all along and how silly to ever think that it could do any harm.

∎

It seems fitting that María Ramos would not be the first to see her own miracle. She is weeping, the turpentine burns, and she's been at the chapel for hours and hours, so she stands up, pats the dust off her knees, and props the painting up against a wall in the corner. She can't tell if the burning is caused by the turpentine, the strain or the trouble that makes her so desperate for a miracle, so she simply splashes water on her face when suddenly she hears the scream.

An indigenous woman named Isabel had been walking past the chapel with her three-year-old son when she saw it: a white fire burning so brightly she had to turn away and shield her son's eyes as if there were razors in the splendor, and she yelled, "Fire!"

María Ramos doesn't think the word through. The domino drop of ideas has no time to tumble. There is only adrenaline shooting out in all directions, a practiced fear taking over. "Run!" She knocks over the washbasin as she spins around. The water splashes out as the bowl turns and falls, and María Ramos has run halfway out of the chapel before the porcelain base has burst against the tile. But then she also sees the flash of light behind her, off in the corner, where the painting stands, and then the dominoes begin to fall. "*¡Virgen santa!*" She turns around to face the light, and it's as if one of the sun's scales has peeled off and fallen right atop the canvas. A blinding pain pulls her away but a deeper anguish pulls her towards. She wants to look away but she also wants to see, so she keeps her eyes fixed on that spot in the corner.

The outline of a red-coal finger behind the cloth traces outlines, resurrects color and shape, and in a flash the splendor is gone. The fire puts itself out and leaves behind a painting—Anthony, Andrew, Jesus, and Mary perfectly restored.

∎

María laughs with her whole body. She shakes her head with her whole body, waves and talks as if all her tendons and ligaments became at some point irrevocably entangled and no single string can be pulled without every marionette on the stage twitching and jolting in the same direction.

A nod becomes a bow, a word a full-bodied gesture. She is a single four-foot-nothing blur of unspoken motion constantly sweeping, and vacuuming and wiping away, and it is hard to imagine what could make a woman such as this, if a woman such as this can be made at all.

■

María wakes up in the bed she shares with four other siblings in their home on the outskirts of the holy city. She is five years old and it is five in the morning.

Five? How can you be so sure? It was so long ago. "Hm. Same every day."

It is always five in the morning when María's father's closes his grip around her small arm and shakes her into the waking-working world. She stumbles out a bed and into a kitchen where she wolfs down a breakfast of boiling coffee, scrambled eggs and burnt *arepas*, before feeling her father's grip around her arm once more, as he drags her into the red clay pits.

How does that work, María? The clay pit thing?

"What you do is you tear off all your clothes. I tore them all off." *And then?* "And then I jumped right in with the animals. Ox, donkey, right-right there with them."

So she's five and naked and red. She jumps into the pit. She stomps, jumps, slaps the donkey's rear end to make it go faster, feels the clay slipping between her toes and hopes for an even mixture to later pour into wooden molds and bake into bricks for her father's business.

"Clothes get in the way," she says, "so you have to take them off." And I imagine red ribs and red toes and red knees stopping hard, falling often, mixing dust and mud while the ovens fill the air with smoke. And sometimes I think I can smell smoke too.

I see María's face begin to turn. She purses her lips in a way that pushes out her chin like a pole through a tent, and makes her look much older. She looks off to a corner for a second and makes her sound, "Hm," softer than I've ever heard it, and less certain too. She tells me that behind the ever burning oven fires and the towers of uncooked brick, there was a shack. Though she calls it "the punishment room," and tells me how one way or another, her father would always end up shuffling toward it, gripping a child's arm in one hand and a bottle in the other. "He'd get so angry," she says in the same tone as, "How was your day, *niña* Lina?" and, "Have you eaten yet, *niña* Lina?" Only with this little added sharpness, as if she could see it happening right then, in an ever continuous present-past. Her brother, the same who told the pilgrims they could not take her, is himself taken into that shack behind the curtains of smoke. The hand that had held hers as they walked away from the men in purple robes, turns purple now as their father ties his feet to a beam and blood reverses its flow.

An empty bottle, or a stick, or a leather strap, or a bicycle chain, or whatever is on hand. Swinging, striking, and biting an upside-down body, hung like a cut of meat in a butcher shop, and turning like a tire swing in a yard. Rope and beam and boy creaking with each blow until a father's arm or an upside-down child fall silent and limp.

I've never known María to stand still. She moves so fast, so incorrigibly, she sometimes feels dangerous to me, as if making her stand still were the same as closing your hand around a bottle rocket. If I keep asking questions I may lose my thumbs, I want to look away, but I also want to see. So I wait, I watch her stand shockingly still. Or mostly still, as she shifts her weight from right to left, left to right, and back again, and tells me how her drunken father would kneel beside the swinging body of one of his sons, to pile wet sticks beneath their heads and try to light a match, try to start a fire.

María, María, María? Why, why? To burn them? To kill them?

"No *mi niña* Lina, no, no. The wood was wet, *niña*. Only smoke. Hm." A quiet smoky fire rising up while a man takes drunken swings at the body of a child with red-clay dust still in his hair.

■

The story changes. Sometimes it happens in a day, María Ramos hangs the painting, not knowing what lay beneath while she whispers a prayer, "the prayer of the faithful," and it's like adding milk to instant pudding. A microwavable ready-in-a-minute miracle. Sometimes, however, it takes weeks, cleaning and mending and restoring. She wears holes into her knees and fingertips before the Virgin deems her worthy. Sometimes she is a wealthy pious woman generously volunteering her time, and sometimes an ignorant but kindly maid who stumbles on the painting while cleaning out the closet of a nobleman, or the forgotten shack behind the chapel.

Sometimes the indigenous woman walks alone and sometimes with a child. Sometimes she disappears altogether like silver snakes into sacred lakes, though whenever she *is* mentioned she is always *una mujer indígena llamada,* Isabel. Sometimes the fire burns red, sometimes white. Sometimes the blaze can be seen for miles and people run to the streets half-naked holding buckets of water and sand.

But always, as many times as I've heard it, from as many people as I've asked—and from a "documentary" video playing on loop in the tourist information center of Chiquinquirá—always: María Ramos, tears, prayers, and the Virgin's return. At the end, no matter what, Mary always comes back from behind the stains and prints and cracks, from the ether of wearing and tearing, from the rubbed-out edges of brushstrokes and patina. She returns.

■

María, María. Tell me about the donkey again.
"We were little, like ten and nine, I remember. Ten or nine, because we had the *alpargatas* my mother bought us for our first communions. Me and my brother." I lean in, cross my legs, run my finger along the rubber edge of my sneakers and picture María, in her straw and dry-*fique* sandals running down a hill toward the Basilica. "Yes. Of course." I've worn them once or twice, in school plays and dances, and remember only brief sticky nights of blisters and straw. "Yes, nine-ten. I remember, because it was so much better after." *What was better? What before?* "Hm! Than barefoot, *niña* Lina."

I picture it, her and her brother walking back from town in their new *alpargatas*, avoiding large groups of men, anyone wearing a robe, while they count and recount their first communion money. "All those streets were dirt and pebbles. Back then all that was like that, not paved like here. And my brother and me, we walked back talking just like this, about shoes. Leather ones, wooden ones, real ones, do you see, *niña* Lina?" I nod and lean in closer; I like this story. "Talking about all sorts of things to buy with our money, and walking back with that donkey loaded very, very heavy with all the firewood on its back." María bends over, mimicking the donkey. "Then my aunts, they come out to the road and they do like this." She steps sideways and motions with her hands, "Like this, see?" I nod again, "Like, 'come in, come in.' So we do."
What María doesn't say, she acts out. She paces up and down the kitchen and plays every part. Though, sometimes, it still doesn't make sense to me. *But, María, why? Why go in and risk being late? Wouldn't he beat you? Weren't you afraid?* I can't let go of the punishment room, nor of María's tone when she talks of it. How normal and casual it all sounds, and how extraordinarily pragmatic extraordinary cruelty can be. *Why fire?* "To choke them." *Why hang them?* "Easier to hit 'em." *Why by their feet?* "So they wouldn't run."
I think, in part, it might be the stupid notion behind the impulse to peer into locked rooms, and stare into the barrel of an abyss. As if seeing were knowing, and staring into the cliff were the same as coming apart against it. As if I could actually understand this moment in María's life, if I only think long and hard enough about it.
A man swinging a bicycle chain against a child's face while the room fills with smoke is a great and terrible mystery to me. Not because the

trajectory of the chain or the sound of bursting capillaries is unimaginable, but because there seems to be no purpose in either. The speed of his swing is motivated by neither hunger nor cold, by neither the reproductive imperative nor the gratification of biological and intellectual pleasure. His motivation is something on the periphery of compulsion and panic. He happens like things have happened to him, he occurs and he survives, and he carries on in twisted pragmatism.

Wouldn't your father be mad, with you both gone so long? She shrugs, "They had little things for us to eat, my aunts, little sugary things, you know? *Alfandoques, panelitas,* things like that, so we went inside." *What about the donkey?* "We tied him up outside and we went in and then. And then. Hm!" *María? Then what, María?* "¡Ay, ay, ay!* No, no. *Niña* Lina, no, no." María laughs, she claps her hands together and shakes from head to toe. The story pulls a spring-loaded spine back and farther back like a catapult, until she finally bounces forward with a howl of uncontrolled glee—laughter like water from a broken pipe.

"We tied him too tight!" She shouts, "Do you see *niña* Lina? Just too tight. Hm!" Too tight and too close to the tie rack, so maybe a blind bird flew into the donkey, or a white light blinded it for a second, or more likely it tried to shift its weight from one side to the other and gravity won out in the exchange. *Down went donkey, flat on its side, down all the wood they'd laid on its back, and further down still they both would have rolled, if only it hadn't been for that rope.* Though not a rope anymore, but a noose. "That there, where we tied it, there we found it." She points to a spot in the kitchen floor at which I stare dutifully. "Feet all up to heaven when we came back out, all strangled and by itself."

María stands on the spot at which she was pointing, she extends her arms like Frankensteinian limbs, and then she tosses her head back and opens her mouth like a dead cartoon frog while I picture stiff legs and a big round belly, a grey furry radish with four toothpick legs sticking out.

∎

Chiquinquirá was built by the wife of a Spaniard bored of waiting for him to return from the old continent. She ordered, perhaps accidentally, that her new town be built atop sacred Muisca ground. Bits and pieces still remain from the lonely wife's construction. White adobe, uneven stones, an empty fountain in the middle of a square. Though Chiquinquirá is also full of corner markets, anything-you-need drugstores and neon signs advertising big portions and cheap alcohol from small, colonial-style doorways.

The epicenter of the town, however, remains nostalgically preserved. Or at least this is what it is meant to look like to tourists and purple-robed pilgrims. The municipal government paints the balconies, keeps the facades, patches up the adobe walls, and, when the original chapel burnt down years ago, they built a better basilica to house the sacred painting of the resurrected image of the mother of God. If a tourist were to travel to Chiquinquirá today, for example, she might be fooled by the reconstruction and relocation, and even knowing the story she might have a hard time finding the actual place of the actual miracle.

The much larger basilica is, on the other hand, nearly impossible to miss. It stands enormous and yellow in the middle of a new idealized version of what a colonial plaza should be. It is, as the priest in the visitor center explains, "a better home for the painting and a proper altar for the memory of María." Though he does not clarify which María. Business followed the reconstruction, legions of believers hoping to be restored by the restored painting—to health, to happiness, to sanity, to saintliness—flocked to the fake site of the real miracle. When I last visited, people still lined the sides of the narrow alleys around the basilica with wooden carts full of prayer cards and wax figurines of square houses, rectangular cars and little plump, faceless people to aid the faithful in their prayers. Wanting and worrying made wick and wax, made totem, made prayer prop for the devout to leave below the painting like torn shirts in a seamstress basket. And as I stood between the faithful and the ear-wax idols, I realized I was standing where the men in purple robes must have also stood. In the middle of the fake colonial square, holding fake cars and fake houses while wax and good intentions melted away.

I clenched a fist and turned a wax figure in my hand. Featureless, genderless, nameless, with a tiny wheel-of-cheese belly and the ability to represent every sick son, every distressed daughter, every unemployed father and homeless mother. I looked back at the altar below the painting; it was covered three-rows-high with waxen bodies, buildings and vehicles each representing someone someone knew—someone someone wanted a car for, someone someone wanted a house for, someone someone wanted someone for. I saw a woman carrying a little yellow man between her hands as if it were the last flame left on a windswept earth, and I wondered what a boy hanging by his ankles in a smoke-filled shack might represent to the man who swings the chain.

María, are you going back? Do you miss it?

María fiddles with her apron, tries to stand still long enough to answer my questions.

"Well, there and there, *niña* Lina."

■

Sometimes I dream of dead donkeys. I dream of the rest of the story María told me, and I see her, nine or ten with her communion money in her pocket. She grabs a dead donkey's leg; her aunts and brother each grab another. They pull the dead thing uphill on a dirt and gravel road.

They drag it on its side, on its ribs, on its face, an ear gets sort of caught and the cartilage snaps like a carrot, as they scrape parts of the grey fur off, make it smooth down one side, like a spent lottery ticket.

You dragged it? But, why María? What for? "Hm!" I hear her and see a little girl covered in dust and sweat, "Hm, what else to do? Take him up hill." They start to wear out their new *alpargatas* as they push the animal to the edge of the cliff. *What then, María? What then?* "Hm! What else *niña* Lina, what else to do?" They are all very, very tired, because donkeys are animals built to carry and not to be carried, and least of all dragged uphill. Donkeys are big and heavy, and María and her brother and her aunts are all so tired, but they take a deep breath and finish dragging it up, right up to the edge. Then they push it off the side of the cliff. It slides down on the dirt, slowly at first, then faster and faster until it hits a big rock and a tangle of roots, and it snags. For a moment they worry it might get stuck, but then the roots give out and it slips silently into a free fall. Legs and broken ear and tail appearing suspended in the whirlpool of gravity until it finally hits—a wet, quiet, distant crack. *Why, María, why?* "So he wouldn't beat us. Hm. To say, 'isn't it terrible it got stolen just like that?' And 'who would do that?' Do you see *niña* Lina?" *I do. I think I do. Did it work?* "No," Oh. "But it wasn't so bad as other times." *How so?* "He mostly just took all our com-munion money, and bought himself a new donkey. Didn't beat us so bad."

■

I tried to see the painting, I really did. I tried to push my way through the crowd and see what María Ramos wanted so desperately to make visible on the canvas, but a woman holding a wax baby pushed me out of the way so she could place her figurine on the altar and kneel beside it in prayer.

Perhaps the crowd was too large to fight, or else it had too much to fight for and I too little. Perhaps there needs to be a bigger selection of wax figures to encompass all our prayers. All the same, I stepped out of the basilica. I walked the length of the town until I found the site of the first chapel where María Ramos peeled back the heavens with turpentine.

Inside the white adobe replica there was silence. I stared at poorly drawn images on the walls of Franciscan monks landing on yellow shores and handing bibles and two-dimensional doves to half-naked brown-skinned people, and then a man jumped up from behind a desk, eager to explain the myriad miracles of God's mercies. He leapt to his feet and slipped seamlessly into a recitation of the story of María Ramos while pointing with large exaggerated gestures toward an empty corner as if fire might have erupted at any moment and burnt portraits of St. Matthew onto my forehead.

I stood still and half listened while running my index finger through the knife-made grooves of names, hearts, initials, and swastikas carved onto a wooden railing leading to some underground room beside the pulpit. "Ah, and there," the man pointed at the railing, "we still have, from before the fire, the well." I didn't know about the well, so I followed the railing down as the man told us to be careful because the steps were steep and very old.

"Pilgrims come yearly from all over the world to be cured by the holy waters of our well." It wasn't very far down, but the steps were steep and the well was deep and the *plick-plick* of a constantly falling drop echoed up sharply. "They come from Venezuela and Perú, from all over the world. Pope John Paul himself came once, from Rome." The well was locked, and I assumed remained so until pilgrim, leper, or pope justified digging through a messy drawer for the key.

∎

"What do you want to know, *niña Lina? Hm?*"
I'm not sure, it's complicated.
"You go on then, hm! Ask and one will see if it can be answered."
Tell me, María, what really happened.
"When?"
After you pushed the donkey off the cliff, he bought a new one. And then?
"My dad, he was, hm!"
What? What was he?
"Bad!"

María laughs and with nothing to clean she begins picking up random things, turning them around and setting them back down in the exact same spot. *I'm sorry.* "Less so with us girls, but with the boys, hm!" *I'm sorry, María.* "Us girls only got hit until we bled. The boy got hung."

María's hands are thick with callouses, and she used to wrap them around me when I left for the airport, for the States—because I was only seventeen then, "*Solo una niña,*" and "Too young to go alone, just like that. No, no." She said, "So far away."

I imagine her hands, small and strong, and I wonder if they are anything like her father's hands. I try to picture them wrapping rope and tying feet. Did he use a pulley system? Was he as tall as María is short? Did he hoist them up in a single motion with some sort of perverted grace? Had he passed out from drink or exhaustion the day one of his sons squirmed out of the knot, fell to the ground, and rose back up to pick up the chain laying still in his father's grip?

María's brother was small back then, "Only a kid." Small enough to slip out of the rope, but big enough to pick up the chain. María doesn't laugh when she tells me this story. Doesn't move, doesn't fidget, doesn't weep either. She says only what needs to be said, pauses only when she needs a breath, and then stops. So I don't ask any question, I just listen and picture a small boy swinging like a pendulum above a pillar of smoke.

What does one do, I wonder, upside down all night while rope burns and father snores? On the night of the worst beating, while blood ran from his chin, across his face and into the dirt, did he get bored? Had he learnt to sleep like a bat, to swing like a hammock? Had he slipped out before? Taught himself how to loosen the creaking knots, to climb down gently, and simply walk out of that room as if it were any other meaningless room in the world? Or, was that night the first, and so, also, the very last? Did, perhaps, María's father realize right away what that metal taste was, or did his son have to swing it multiple times before it was clear? Did he recognize the feeling of a burst lip and chipped teeth and blood springing like a geyser? Is it perhaps familiar because it is familiarly inherited, is this shack built on the ashes of another? Is it full of wax and simulacrum, or is this single punishment room his one creative contribution to the world?

"He didn't kill 'em," María clarifies with a shrug while I picture a small boy swinging a chain like a pick ax, like he is loosening the earth and digging up the corner stone of an old cathedral. *He didn't kill him,* I repeat, thinking of a chain like heavenly fire and vertical scars like brushstrokes on a canvas. *Didn't.* Though it's hard to imagine he did not at least consider it. Maybe he meant to, maybe he stopped when the chain cut the skin, or maybe only when his father begged with a gargled whimper. Maybe he had simply been upside down for too long that night and he could only manage so many swings before he began seeing red and white stars. Maybe that's when he decided to run—with his face in his hands and the beginnings of scars that would last forever.

■

María? María? Why did you stay? Why didn't you leave, María? "I did, *niña* Lina. Hm! I did. When I was nine I left." *Where did you go?* "Bogotá, right here to Bogotá?" *Where?* "I first came to an aunt's, but she said, 'You can't stay here, nothing's free in life.' Hm! Life isn't free." *Then where?* "To work. Life isn't free, *niña* Lina. So I went as a maid and looked after the children." *But . . . how old were you?* "Hm! Nine, ten. I did the cooking, the cleaning. The *Doña*, she showed me with the rice, and the laundry. You learn, there and there, then and then. In the job, you learn." *María, María. Did they pay you well, María? Were you ok, María?* "Hm! Imagine that! When I finally told them I was leaving, the *Doña*, she gave me a little clothes, a little money. Almost nothing." *María, María. . . .* "But. She did give me shoes."

And then? "Then I was sixteen, then back to *mi tierra*. Chiquinquirá, Hm! When one has nowhere to go, one goes home."

■

María Ramos is never mentioned again in the story. The holy fire makes the painting; the unholy one takes the chapel. The Vatican sends its commission of priests, briefcases, and interpreters. The miracle is examined to determine if it meets the church's quotas, it is charted, counted, and finally it is certified.

In 1919, during a procession to the capital where the painting is carried miraculous mile after miraculous mile, the then-president, Marco Fidel Suarez, crowns the painted María queen and patron saint of Colombia. The crowd cheers and roars, *María, María, María, María!* María Ramos is barely a footnote.

Fire, procession, crown, and crowd. María Ramos walks out of the chapel and story having, maybe, seen what she wanted to see, heard what she needed to hear, or knowing, finally, what she wanted to know. And then she never walks back again.

In my mind she wears *alpargatas* and walks with purpose up a hill to a small adobe home. It's cool, as colonial constructions tend to be, and she keeps it as neat as is possible under clouds of smoke and red dust. Maybe she lies down beside her sleeping husband and runs her hand down his back. Maybe she plants a kiss between his shoulder blades and whispers, "It'll be alright now." Or maybe she plants a knife instead. Takes a deep breath, buries it deep into him like a seed or a secret, and whispers, "It'll be all right now."

Whatever she does after, wherever she goes next, she has earned a miracle and she alone knows its true meaning. Perhaps she is cured and has no reason to return, perhaps that is what it means to see the face of God. Or else, perhaps she isn't cured, it was just a painting meaninglessly-miraculously restored before her eyes, and perhaps that's what it means to see the face of God.

■

María didn't return to Chiquinquirá after that, but when her father fell ill, he did return to her. "When you have nowhere else to go, you go home."

It's been years since I last saw her, and even though I have the story secondhand I know María, and I don't need to see to believe. After years and years in silence, a brick maker from Chiquinquirá called his daughter in the capital. He coughed through red-dust storm clouds gathering inside his lungs and he told her what the doctors had told him, that he was dying and should not be left alone. I do wonder, however, about what María thought then. Did she think of her brother, of falling donkeys, of purple pilgrimages, and a barefooted Virgin Mary kicking sleeping pigeons off a ledge? Or else did she see, suddenly before her, great pillars of smoke rising from the ever burning fires inside red chimneys and hidden shacks? Did María feel the weight of a broken bicycle chain in her hands and the burden of a violent legacy on her shoulders? Is she her father's daughter, her brother's sister, her namesake's heir? Is this what it is to see the face of God? And is it weakness, habit, or an honest miracle when she offers him a bed, cares for him for the five long years it takes him to finally die? And isn't this, at the very least, much more mysterious than the brutal swings of a drunk man in the dark?

"Hm! *Niña* Lina. Hm!"

CADA CUAL ES LIBRE DE HACER
DE SU TRASERO UN CANDELERO

or

Each which is free to make of his rear end a candlestick.

or

~~Each which~~ [*Everyone*] is free to make of his [*own*] rear end a candlestick.

or

Whatever lights your candle.

or

"But let there be fire."

El Coco

I was standing at a Walmart, looking for grapes, when I decided to pick up a coconut—there was no real thought behind it, no plan, no premeditation beyond, "I may buy a coconut today."

But I was only able to hold it for a few seconds before both my hands hot-potato-tossed it back into the pile, and I felt myself recoiling. A thud and a knock and a woman by the strawberries glaring as a miniature coconut avalanche spilled over apples and oranges, and these yellow-jelly memory jars cracked inside my head, leaking the clear vision of a giant, sentient coconut chasing me through the streets of my childhood neighborhood.

Not a memory of something lived but of something believed so deeply and thoroughly, the images played uninterrupted, sharp and rehearsed, as if they might as well have happened. The flimsiness of facts yielding to the concreteness of childhood convictions.

I saw it clearly, as if projected from the back of my skull on to a screen hung across my forehead. An enormous anthropophagite drupe rolls at full speed down the streets of *el conjunto* Santa Helena in Chía, Colombia, where I grew up. A Volkswagen-Beetle-sized coconut rolls faster and closer and faster still, toward me like a boulder in an Indiana Jones film. Nothing specifically monstrous about it, save its size and apparent self-awareness. Nothing really anthropomorphic at all. No eyes, no fangs, no arms, no feet. No claws, no horns, nothing palpitating, nothing growling—nothing to growl with. Just a "normal" coconut. Round but not too round, hard on the outside, soft on the inside, cushioned by brown fiber-fur. Quietly, swiftly rolling toward me and stopping mere centimeters from my face. Mere seconds from crushing me just to crack itself open into toothless mandibles, white viscous gums that would—I knew—inevitably clamp down around my head and pull me in like a bird with a worm.

My head covered in white slime, wedged between coconut jaws while I helplessly pull out tufts of brown vegetable fur like fistfuls of beard. Then it pulls itself back, rotating on its axis, lifting me clean off the ground, inserting me further into its concave center and snapping its jaws back down before I can make any attempt at an escape. My head stuck between its pulpy gums, *pull-snap*, a slightly crushed windpipe, *pull-snap*, torso, hips, thighs, knees. *Pull-snap*, ankles, feet, toes. *Snap, snap*. And a sidewalk like a clean plate.

There are a limited number of people who could have—would have—gifted me with such terror. So I start with the most obvious source.

"Lina, no." My mother. "That's not what that means."

She recognizes the words but not the images. So she puts her hand on her forehead and shakes her head, "Not what it means at all." I've misunderstood from the beginning, apparently, and elaborated fabulously on my mistake. "First," she says, "it wasn't me who told you about him." The pronoun strikes me, and for a second I try to place gender on a rolling, furry sphere. Frame by frame, it—*he*—rolls forward, striking the ground with a padded thud, spinning forward in the frames between the thuds while widening its jaws *a la* Pac-Man. He, apparently. "Second," she continues, "*he* does not eat—he steals. And third," she holds up three fingers, "it is El Coco not un Coco." *The Coco*, not *a coco*, not a coco-nut.

The problem is that *he* has too many names. Or the Spanish speaking world has given him too many. *Satanás, el Diablo, el Demonio, el Patas, el Putas, el Puto Erizo, el Uñas, el Uñon, el Diantre, el Pollo del aire, el Macho Cabrío, el Chucho, el Cucuy, el Cuco. El Coco*—literally "The Coconut." Except not. *El Coco* is the devil, or at least a devil—because the business of damnation lends itself to outsourcing. *El Diantre*, for example, is the devil of the poor—a lazy, clumsy, stuttering thing neither his victims nor coworkers can ever quite take seriously. *El Patas*, on the other hand, is the devil of convents and monasteries—a comfortable glutton loosing crumbs and memories between belly folds and hangovers. While the thin, "man" wearing counterfeit cufflinks and a fake-Rolex while illegally downloading the last season of a show he doesn't even watch, goes by *El Uñas*—Nails—the devil of hypocrites and forgers, and that's only three. There are so many in so many shapes—chubby fingered, clawed, sweaty palmed and hooved—they wouldn't fit in a police lineup even if you could keep all their names and proclivities straight.

El Coco, however—I'd pick him out.

He is the devil of children. A long man made of shadow, wire, and teeth waiting just outside, just behind, just there if you go too far, yell too loud, stay too long, cost too much. He carries a burlap sack or a black heavy-duty plastic bag. We all know him, and we've all known about him for a long time, too. There is a 1799 drawing by Goya in the Madrid Prado museum titled "Here Comes *El Coco*." It is simple and dark. Two children and their mother cower under the shadow of a cloaked figure. The woman appears to recognize the thing beneath the mantle, or at least its intent. She is depicted shuddering and seems to plead with her eyes for the shadow to leave her little ones alone, while one of her children wears a face of such exaggerated horror it quickly turns comical. The child is frozen in sketch, reaching out with her arms and pushing off with her legs in a Bugs Bunny proto sprint. She knows this thing before her; she's known it for a while. And above all, she's known that it would come for her eventually, and now it has.

I know, because I knew it would come for me, too.

The cloaked shape is long and long-feared. It has history and meat, corroborating evidence, and a list of witnesses as long as the devil's toenails. A man, dark with roadside dust, a burlap sack full of children. Simple and terrifying and always the same for the children before I was a child, before their parents were children, before their parents' parents' parents were children, and long, long, long before that, too. Always the same shape traced by our mothers and grandmothers and great-grandmothers in shadow and resolve. A quiet, unblinking man dragging a heavy sack down an unlit street.

I contemplate the Goya print. Pull it up; print it out. At an angle the mother appears to be almost smiling at the looming stranger—maybe not such a stranger, maybe not entirely strange either. I picked up my five-year-old niece not long ago and tossed her as far up as I could, catching her on her way back down. She screamed and smiled and shrieked at the possibility of my arms failing her, of cracking sunny-side-up against a warm California sidewalk. And then she asked me to do it again.

Twenty or thirty times later my arms were dead at my sides, weighed down with sympathy for devils dragging bagfuls of heavy children on a hot day's evening. Has anyone told him about the comfort of hiking back-packs with aluminum frames? *Walmart coconut avalanche.* Maybe now he carries a pocketful of little airport combination locks and does his carpal tunnel exercises before walking out of hell in the morning, rolling luggage in tow.

Occasionally—I've been told—he does in fact eat children. Some even believe the word *Coco* comes from the Latin *coquus*, meaning "cook." The Children's Chef, spilling eyeball batter on the remote control as he tries to deep-fry toes and chop tongue tips, while pausing Julia Child on the screen to find a pen that works. Maybe he finds Julia Child's name a bit misleading.

But this scene is rare. Children are a sometimes food. In the stories, the devouring is more a rare sighting than a defining characteristic. Maybe something that only happens when he's forgotten to pack a lunch or he feels his blood sugar dropping—kids are so loud and hell so far, and he'd rather be sitting in a convent, or the back of a stoner's van, or the shoulder of a politician, and maybe he was just very unlucky on the day the satanic lottery was drawn.

"Not a coconut then?"

"Definitely not."

"Does everyone know this?"

"I think so."

"Then, where did I get coconut?"

"I don't know. What else do you remember?"

My maternal grandmother. Always. The source of most of my specters.

She stands at the doorway, pointing at a homeless man across the street while five-year-old me pours water into a red washbasin full of snails. My grandmother tells my older sister, Paula, and me to look up, "Up-up and over there," at that man wiping his nose with the back of his hand. "Do you see him? Yes?" The one pulling wrappers and orange peels from ripped plastic bags and sticky trashcans. "That one." Paula and I hold stones and snails, because we are making snail islands on a washbasin sea, and my grandmother points again. "That over there, that's The Man with the Sack." *El Coco.* The homeless man tosses the orange peels and wrappers inside the bag and then the bag over his shoulder. "*El hombre del costal.*" She repeats it, like someone might point up and call out "sky," or out in front and call out, "Sea, earth, fire, brimstone." Permanent, perennial, perpetual. That man was not any of many, but a single always-man, like a single always-earth and a single always-sky. The Man with the Sack, come to take you away, to never come back.

We drop the stones; maybe we drop some snails, too. We know who he is now and we won't forget. Our grandmother has told us, and cracked-shelled snails lie at our feet.

But she only half told us, and this confusion is going to haunt me more than The Man with the Sack ever will.

"Yes," my mother agrees. "That sounds like her; I think she told me something like that too. All children are told."

"Same person then? *El Coco* and 'The Man with the Sack'?"

"Yes."

"Then why didn't she just say that?"

"I don't know. Forgot?"

There is something irresponsible in this shared memory of ours. "The Man with the Sack" is such a clumsy title—even potentially vulgar. To which one must add that children already have such limited vocabularies, why quibble? *El Coco* is a far better stage name—alliterative, succinct. To which one might also add that "The Man with the Sack" is clearly a *man*, but *El Coco* is not necessarily anything. Necessarily evil, necessary as evil, but not necessarily anything past the knock-knock of his alliteration. *Co-co. Who's there?* "Who's there, in th' other devil's name? Faith, here's an equivocator that could swear in both the scales against either scale, [. . .] O, come in, equivocator." *A coco is a coco is a coco is a coco,* except when it is the devil.

Whatever my grandmother did or did not mean, I did have a general understanding of the human, and by extension—I believed—the demonic digestive system.

"Paula." It kept me up at night while my older sister slept on the top bunk. "Paula"—Coconuts—"you awake?"—do not have esophagi. "Paula-Paula-Paula." No esophagus, no stomach, no digestive tract, nothing. "I have to ask you something—Paula?"

"What?"

"When *El Coco* eats you."

"Yeah?"

"Where do you go?"

Never a matter of "if" but "when." Sometimes it would take me so long to eat lunch that the sun would set and Paula would go to bed and I was left alone in the dining room with a plate full of boiled cow foot and a threat I never questioned. "Lina," my mother told me, "vomit, and I will spoon-feed it back to you."

And sometimes a girl cannot help climbing higher and higher up a tree and *everything that goes up must come down.* And when she does come down, she comes down hard enough to faint and bleed. Leave a mark on the sidewalk and a speckled-star sky of a scarred skull. It is not the girl's intention to bleed and break, or sit there for hours staring at a plate of cold, gelatinous meat blocks, wondering if her mother would ladle the vomit from the toilet bowl were the girl to make it to the bathroom in time. It is the nature of gravity, poor impulse control, and an overactive gag reflex. And can anyone really say if the Mattel Company did not intend for at least some Ken dolls to be dismembered and lightly roasted over an electrical fire?

"What?"

"He eats you, right? *El Coco.*"

"Yeah."

"If you are bad?"

"Yeah."

"And then?"

"Then that's it."

"Forever?"

"Yes."

"Forever where?"

"There."

"*Where* there?"

"Just *there*, in the middle."

"And when he opens up again?"

"Then, there still."

"And when he eats someone else?"

"There too."

"Forever?"

"Forever."

Hell is other people—stuck forever in a rolling coconut prison.

Or a memory display spilling over into a public display. Older women pushing their shopping carts while they glare and shake their heads at the girl slowly stepping away from the coconuts as if she were negotiating a hostage situation.

Or the images of soot-faced men with their hands deep in trash bags and burlap sacks, hell made hot by ovens replete with minced kid pie and child bourguignon. An enormous drupe opening its jaws to reveal a child standing in the middle, bored and sticky—just *there*, forever-there, like an unflushed toilet. My wonderful-terrible grandmother's certainty that it was time to give her granddaughters the gift of *El Coco*. Maybe that's when she realized it, on the patio with the snails, that left to our mother, precious childhood years could transpire Coco-less while other children went on shivering in unison and whispering his name as we wandered around, fearlessly, and stupidly, and out of the loop.

I was nine years old when I found out that my two-year-old sister had no fear of the dark. A short circuit, a spark, the loud tack of a fuse going out, and Daniela would simply sit there on her bedroom floor holding a plush raccoon and a talking police car just waiting for her pupils to dilate, or electricity to come buzzing back through the wires. And I watched her, sitting there—no crying, no wailing, no metaphor, no monster, nothing— trying to work out what had gone wrong with her. I flicked the lights on and off like scientists prod brains and open bellies, but it was a shallow city darkness. Something always glowing from afar, neon, halogen, reflective, and automatic. So one day I took her by the hand, up from the carpet, out of her bedroom, down the corridor, and into the darkest room in the house. Not a single window, only one light-tight door, and a thick, disorienting darkness. I led her in, turned off the lights, and closed the door behind me. Then I pressed my ear to the wood, thinking it was the quality of the darkness alone that had failed to illicit my sister's screams before. A little girl in absolute-zero darkness, eyes like broken zoom lenses widening and tightening and trying desperately to find focus. And I waited for a scream. A whimper, a sob, a sniffling, anything.

But nothing came. Not a single sound.

I turned the doorknob, opened the door, and shook my head, as in "No, Daniela," as in, "That's not what this means." Like I shook my head when a dog failed to sit on command. She should have known, I thought, and I shouldn't have had to explain it. Jokes, fear, and shame ought not to be explained. *Listen, Adam . . . Eve. You are naked. It's sort of embarrassing for all of us.* Because, I believed in innateness and "original fear." But here she was, untaught and unafraid, confusing darkness with the mere absence of light. An unplugged television, dreamless sleep, nothing more.

When I opened the door she looked only a little sleepy, like a factory chicken responding to its darkened environment. So I sat on the tile floor beside her and told her about the dark. Told her that it was like standing water—full of mosquito eggs—invisibly swollen and slithering with things waiting to hatch and feed on whatever they could lay fang or claw on. That they are really always there, but the darkness is the warmth they need to hatch from their shells and slink into ear canals and under fingernails, or else huff themselves into huge bloated forms. Black malformed lions with enormous heads they have to drag around like metal balls at the end of rusty chains, and bulging hairy bullfrogs with human hands reaching through shadow veils to pull us back into their lairs.

Then, one more time. I turned off the lights and closed the door, and this time I had to hold on to the doorknob as she screamed and wept and tugged, banged her hands against the wood, and begged to be let out.

Sometimes when I start telling this story I will crack up mid-sentence like a twirled-mustache villain and laugh so hard I can't even finish telling it. I can't help it—it pours, it spills, it geysers out of me. I am otherwise, mostly, the picture of perfectly acceptable behavior, except in these strange moments. It's the humor of cruelty, surely, but not wholly that. It is also that I am often a stranger to myself, because when I am asked why I did this or didn't do that, I feel I sometimes have to guess rather than remember. "I'm not sure," I say. "It must have seemed right at the time, I suppose." And I do, suppose. I jumped into a fifteen-foot-deep hole in the ground just because it was there. I hot-glued names onto my forearms squeezing melting silicone atop yellow-red blistering skin. I put a live mouse in my mouth to win a two-dollar bet. I didn't wear shoes for five months. And maybe because none of those things felt like I thought they would or hurt as much as I thought they might, I took a girl by the back of her neck as she tried to slap me, and I swung her into the ground like a pickaxe. I could have done something else, anything else. But I didn't, just because, I suppose. But I'm only guessing.

Maybe the mind is like standing water, idle playgrounds built from detached hands.

I still have scars on my forearms and I dream of concussions. A confused mouse hits the back of my teeth with its nose, and then whiskers tickle the back of my throat, as monstrous black lions watch me sleep—but I do not know the people who did these things. I do not understand them, like them, or even recognize them. We have no kinship. But this nine-year-old guiding her baby sister into a dark bathroom, I understand her. Or, at least, I understand why she thinks it must be done. And I understand my grandmother, too.

Three in the morning at twenty-three, on the deep end of a bout of insomnia, I click on a link to the music video for the song "Frontier Psychiatrist." A man holds a dummy in a suit with a coconut for a head. Red-sclera Muppet eyes have been attached to the top of the husk, and the drupe has been cut across the middle to create a gaping mouth that opens and closes as the man shakes it like a toothless man asleep on a bus.

I know exactly what I thought the first time I saw the featureless head atop a well-dressed body. *Toss it back, Walmart coconut avalanche.* Grey suit, black tie, the shape of a face not quite a face. "Paula? Paula? Paula? You awake?"

In the nineties in Colombia, when things were particularly unsafe, it was decided that it was too dangerous for judges to judge openly. A life sentence for the wrong person could boomerang right back and become a death sentence for the judge. So they tried to deflect with anonymity all the kidnappings attempts, and bullets, and the metal and bone fragments from car bombs and horse bombs and strap-to-what-you-like bombs. They called them the faceless judges in the news: *Jueces Sin Rostro.* And I saw—through a crack in my bedroom door—the photographs of men standing in rows, with white question marks over their black-blurred faces.

"Paula. Paula. Paula."

"What? What!"

"The faceless judges?"

"Yeah?"

"Under the masks."

"Yeah?"

"Do they have faces?"

I pictured coconut ski masks being pulled off, slowly, carefully. Wool-knit fibers sticking to the wet softness of a skinless face, like so many socks I'd pulled off, from so many ankle cuts—blood and pus and cotton and scab. A limited but certain understanding that these faceless images on the screen drained the blood from my parents' faces.

The certainty that beyond the pregnant darkness of imagined shapes—eyelids lined with fangs and cold tongues curling around ankles and necks—something yet remained. Something to practice fear for. Like a match is practice for wildfire, and boys are practice for men, and being knocked unconscious is practice for death. And *El Coco* is practice for all the deep pits hidden by overgrown grass and over eager smiles and one's own overactive, monstrous mind.

"Paula, Paula."
"Hm."
"Paula?"
"What?"
"Can we leave the door open tonight?"
"No."
"Please, can we leave it open?"
"No."
"Please."
"No."
"But . . . what if *El Coco* comes through the window?"
"And what if the masked men come through the open door?"

Goya was critical of the very concept of *El Coco*. His illustration in the Prado museum in Madrid is accompanied by an explanatory note that reads, *A baleful abuse of the first education [. . .] to force him to fear that which does not exist.*

A casual search will yield further elucidation: an accompanying inscription, which explains Goya's theory that *El Coco* was the invention of promiscuous mothers who—I imagine—lacking access to affordable childcare services, left their children in the care a song and of *El Coco*. "Sleep, little child, sleep, sleep, sleep. Lest *El Coco* come, to eat, eat, eat."

A promiscuous woman conceives of the Children's Chef on her way out to meet a clandestine lover. She crawls on all fours looking for an earring to match the one she is already wearing. She reaches under furniture, and between desiccated bits of potatoes and lentils fallen from plates in the restless shuffling of her now-sleeping children. There she finds it, dangling from the half-burnt ear of a rag doll, and just as she slips it on, a child yells out, "*Mamá!*"

She hears herself sigh as she sits by her daughter's bedside and hands her a cup of water. The girl wants to get out of bed, wants a story, wants something to eat, wants so much so often, wants maybe to sleep in her mother's bed rather than her own. But her mother strokes her forehead and invents the devil instead. "*Duérmete niño*," she sings. Sleep little child, "*Duérmete ya . . .*" Sleep little one, "*Que ya viene el Coco y te comerá.*" That the Coco is coming to eat you right up. And she sings the child to sleep or at least into a paralysis akin to sleep. Then she slaps on lipstick, pulls on heels, and rushes out, slamming the door behind her and trotting down the sidewalk as if flames were nipping at her heels.

But *El Coco* far outdates Goya and the likelihood of this particular theory. During Samhain people would often carve turnips into small and grotesque faces, light small flickering candles inside the miniature lantern heads and hang them in the night to ward off malevolent spirits. Light to chase off shadows, surely, but also the devils you know and carve to fend off all the unknown and self-made devils creeping through the darkness. A rosary of glowing turnip grimaces, little coconut avalanches, a crown of skulls and fire. The word *Coco* is colloquially used to refer to one's own skull in Spanish. "*Le partieron el coco,*" they cracked his skull open. Or "*Esta mal del coco,*" he is crazy in the coconut. The new world only offered the old rituals new proxy heads to carve and fill with candle wax and flame, and soon, wide-mouthed, hollow-eyed pumpkins began to cover doorsteps and verandas on All Hallows' Eve. The headless horseman does not carry a bouquet of shrunken turnip heads, but one howling orange husk alit in red flame. Though it is all the same fire leaping between continents and lanterns.

The new world offered old gods to further the cause—the alliterative Mayan god Kukulkán, for example, whose imposing pyramid temple was erected high above the plains of the Chichén Itzá valley around 800 AD. Upon which a zigzag-ziggurat serpent made of shadow descends every equinox like a plumed serpent, arching its back against the horizon. And the gods of the old religion always become the devils of the new. And even Kukulkán is not as new as that; he was given to the Maya by the Olmec, or the Toltec, or any of the many unnamed others that came before. Even these old ruins were built on the even older ruins of even older temples, on the piled bones of even older gods and devils and rituals to keep the darkness at bay or to usher it in. And deep inside the intricately carved and massive stone walls of Kukulkán's temple hides a sacrificial chamber once lined with human tibias.

"Daniela?"
"Hm."
"Daniela?"
"Yeah?"
My younger sister, is eleven, when—while I'm watching something mindless on television—I hear the flush of the toilet accompanied by a short little whimper, so I turn my head to see her running out of the bathroom as if shaking off the cold grip of something hungry and pale. She slams the door behind her in one swift motion and hot-coal hops across the carpet and unto the couch.

"What was that about?"

"What was what?"

"That."

"What?"

"That. The Jumping thing."

Daniela never did learn anything I ever tried to teach her. Not as I meant her to anyway. She had appeared to me to emerge from her childhood and lessons on fear entirely and mysteriously unscathed. At least, I had thought so until the day I saw her shoot out of the bathroom like a proverbial bat out of hell.

From our little excursion into darkness so many years earlier, she had retained only a general and fuzzy fear of the dark while harboring a deep and paralyzing terror of bathrooms and toilets. "A baleful abuse of the first education." Nine-year-old me holding the door shut and feeling through the doorknob how my two-year old sister pulled and turned and tugged and begged me to let her out.

"Lina? Lina, please, please. Lina!"

And when she stopped screaming, she cried, and when she stopped crying, she moaned, and when she stopped moaning, she whimpered, and when she finally stopped whimpering, I let go, and listened. Nothing. I waited. Nothing. So I called out.

"Daniela?"

Still nothing.

"Daniela?" The same stillness as before but nothing like it, so I knocked. *Toc-toc.* Knock, knock. "Daniela?" I opened the door to find her swollen-eyed and dripping, tears and snot and a look of utter certainty— despite having just sat unharmed through the darkness—that her life had just been in unequivocal peril. Which of course it was, and had been. Because she was small and it was the nineties in Colombia, the world is like standing water. And shadow monsters are like training wheels, and real terror like the torturer's wheel, and we all play shadow parts in each other's shadow plays. And we like it, too. Being thrown so high we know that if we are not caught we won't survive, and we use fear to tame fear, brief moment of panic to scare off the undeniable predictability of our own small lives.

Co-Co.

Who's there?

Satan.

Satan wh . . . wait. What?

Santa! I mean Santa!

Contrary to my grandmother's *Coco* policy of relative ambiguity, Christmas was a time of full disclosure. I broke many things on Christmas night. Set many fires, tore many plastic limbs, crashed many bikes, lost nearly every detachable accessory and voided all warranties. But I never believed the child God wrapped, packed, or delivered any bit of it. Not one.

Adults stood around helping with wrapping and tape and toys, while my grandmother sat, front row, directing the scene. "Paula, open that one first. Lina, wait, you are second." We peeled carefully. "Isn't that so pretty, I picked it myself. Don't rip it." We followed directions and learned to appear excited regardless of how unexciting the gift. Because the moment our fingers touched the cardboard of a box, the folded corner of a coat, or—most commonly—the felt of a cheap jewelry box, my grandmother would point and declare, "That!" Like someone might yell out *Bingo!* "I gave that to you!"

She instructed which gift should be opened next, proclaimed its origin, demanded she be thanked properly with a hug and a kiss, and as the presents disappeared from under the tree, a wreath of colorful paper grew around her. There was no mystery, no fear, no magic. No unknown of any kind. Only a required kiss and occasionally feigned delight. My grandmother, the source of most of my specters, most of my Christmas presents, and all the turtle-shaped jewelry I've ever owned and never worn, forever in my mind on a throne of wrapping paper and coconut husks.

When Daniela was born we moved to Cali, however, and she grew up away from our grandmother, who in turn never quite warmed to this young, tan-skinned girl. Never knew or liked her well enough to point at a man across the street and say, "That man is going to steal you and drag you to hell!" Hence, Daniela never believed in *El Coco,* The Man with the Sack, or *El Niño Jesús.*

So, one December day when I was nine and she was two, I took her by the hand, up from the carpet, out of her bedroom, down the corridor and into the darkest room in the house. Not a single window and a glimmering onyx darkness I dispelled with a flick of the lights. "See here," I pointed at a small Santa Claus embroidered on a green towel. "This is Papá Noel." I held her hand and explained as best I could. "He goes 'Ho, Ho, Ho' and brings you presents on Christmas." She stood silently, glancing nervously and intermittently at the door and toilet. "Ho, ho, ho," I repeated, "Ho, ho." A twitchy little girl with tan skin and big cheeks looking at the image of a small round man on a green towel, "'Ho, ho!' Can you say it, Nani? Papá. Noel." And because she never learned any of my lessons the way I meant her too, she sometimes still turns pale at the sound of a flushing toilet, and she called Santa Clause "Papá Ho-Ho" until she was eleven.

ECHAR LEÑA AL FUEGO

or

To throw firewood to the fire.

or

~~To~~ Throw firewood ~~to~~ [into] the fire.

or

Add fuel to the fire.

or

"Some must burn so that others may see."

Tinfoil Astronaut

My mother made me an astronaut helmet out of tinfoil, cardboard, and a leftover pipe from when she'd fixed the leaky toilet. I got a supermarket-brand "NASA Shuttle and Launch Pad Play Set" when I learned to read later that year, too. I tore off the paper and dragged it back to my room like a fresh kill and my mother followed. She knelt beside me, picked up the plastic replica—a blank-mind-white shuttle attached to a threat-level-orange rocket by three plastic latches—and she said, "Look," as she ripped them apart. "Just look," to show me I'd been wrong all along, drawing all those hollow rockets with portholes and all the floating tinfoil men inside. "The rocket is not the shuttle," she told me, "The rocket is just what gets them there, and that's all it is." But it got stuck. Because the plastic was cheap and the latches were brittle, so she had to pull and tug while bits of orange plastic flew off like sparks at takeoff.

It doesn't matter, "Just look."

Grainy footage from the 1980s dubbed in Spanish on our small Sony television. Dust and smoke rising around the shuttle like a million white-foam jellyfish suddenly awakened by the roaring of a rocket plunging into the uncharted depth of a blue sky. The cloud mushroomed up, puffed out, swelled high. It covered the shuttle, the rocket, the platform, a solid curtain of white and noise and a brief moment of incredulity, *Now you see it, now you* . . . "There! There!" Both rocket and shuttle emerging from the cloud, riding a pillar of white flames and brown smoke and noise, and noise, and so much noise. An enormous crushing cacophony as big as the fiery wake was long. And it was incredible, to watch a thing pull on its own bootstraps until it was out of sight and out of orbit. Until it became imaginary and unimaginable. Another invisible thing lost and tangled in the made-up lines of the made-up constellations, the black cobweb thread that makes archers and queens out of specks of traveling light.

"Are you looking?" The shuttle and rocket rose while the people on the screen mumble in the background in a language I'd never heard before. "It's called English." But I was barely listening because the ship was barely visible, and I was wondering what would happen to the bright orange rocket, when it fell, where it fell, if it fell.

■

I found this embroidered insignia patch in a box of my mother's old things once. A crescent moon blade over a faded hammer. I pulled it out and waved it around like a tiny flag I'd plucked right off a cheese platter. Small and tightly knit with a few random strands sticking up like the hair on the back of my neck when my sister and I were children, and my mother would chase us through the house pretending to be a colossal and voracious spider-roach name *Cucaraña*. The flag smelled of damp cardboard and mothballs, and it felt a little heavier than I thought it should have, as if it had been sewn with lead thread and shrapnel. And when my mother saw it she said, "Those were different times."

I wanted to ask where she'd gotten it, or who had given it to her, but instead I simply ran my fingers on the spikey strands, half expecting them to rip my fingertips open like barbed wire bristles.

"Do you still remember any Russian from back then?" my father asked, conjuring up images of my mother riding in buses through Bogotá when she was seventeen. In my mind she sways with the rhythm of the bus, holding a cheap umbrella under her arm and exact change in her pocket as she makes her way to the *Colomborussian* institute for evening classes.

"Shto eto tako'e?"

There has to be a little red book somewhere in the image, I think. Idealism, intellectualism, rage—these things fit; they are likely. Regardless, I know that as she holds fast to the pole of a clattering bus, to the Russian book beneath her arm, and to whatever promise there is in learning that sharp and angular language, the colonel must hold faster still to his secondborn daughter. Her father was a constant presence—the colonel, the air force pilot, the self-made man; the serious man who never smiled for a picture, never missed a chance to fly, never stopped drawing invisible flight plans with his hands during mass. *El Coronel Cabeza*, forever in my mind in uniform and on an air force base patio while a cat jumps up on his lap and another sits at his feet licking its paws. Yuri and Niky, which the colonel—who daily bombed the men who would become the Soviet-inspired leftist guerrilla group known as the FARC—named after Yuri Gagarin and Nikita Khrushchev. "I think he would have sent me there to study," my mother told me once while I drew cold war maps for social studies class. "Eventually, that's what they told me he had planned for me, anyway. And I think he would have," she said, "had he been there."

Meaning: had he lived past her seventh birthday? "Who knows?" Had the plane not malfunctioned, had the parachute opened in time. Had things turned out, worked out, worked at all, somehow, somewhere, differently. "He might have. Who knows."

"What does that mean?" I asked. "'*Shto'a tata . . .*' what?"
"*Shto eto tako'e.*"
"Right, that." She didn't like Lenin, but she loved Trotsky. That much I know, she told me once over breakfast long before I knew what either one of those names meant, but those were different times.
"'What is that?'"

■

I used to stand alone on the concrete bench in front of my childhood home for hours and hours. I tilted my head under the helmet and stared at the tips of my shoes as they inched forward like a flame down a fuse. *10, 9, 8.* My breath fogged up the cellophane visor and the tinfoil crinkled. *7, 6, 5.* I held the helmet with both my hands to keep it from tilting to the side where the piece of flexible pipe looped like an oxygen tube. *4, 3, 2.* And I watched my brown orthopedic shoes reach the edge and pivot, seesawing between trepidation and anticipation, as if I didn't know what would happen next. *1, 0. Liftoff.*

Because I really hoped I didn't. I hoped one day, one moment, one leap would summon my own pillar of fire and foam, and I'd ride it over the purple flower trees and above our next door neighbor's house, and that night I'd sleep with the spiders who wove the night black, swinging thread between columns of light.

■

One day, while I imagined countdowns, ignitions, and torn skies, my mother told me about Laika. I stood barefoot in the doorway holding a rocket in one hand and a shuttle in the other, and my mother told me space was very big and very cold and very empty, and the soviet space program sent a small, curly-tailed dog name Laika into orbit just to see if they could. Like some people kick pebbles into ravines, to count the seconds between the edge and the base, to guess depths and envision falls.

I had not asked about Laika. I had never heard of anything close to it, of anything remotely like it. But she told me all the same.

■

Revolution made sense then, makes sense now. It is trite and true, but never either and always both.

The whole world third-wheeling on a U.S.-Soviet cold war date, and all these countries engaged in their own tangled and violent internal affairs. And not much has changed. It made sense then, makes sense now. The oligarchs, the autocrats, the plutocrats, the corrupt bureaucrats and slithering diplomats. The triggermen and the trigger tyrants inventing bullet-hole constellations on skies of skin and skull.

■

I nearly cracked my own skull open more than once, more than twice, sometimes more than thrice a week leaping off higher and higher benches and trees and fences. I shaved my head once as an adult and found that beneath my dark brown hair there lay a star-map scalp that I suddenly wished I could have unrolled on a table, to run my finger between each skin-stitch and read the future in my past.

Every arid patch where hair refused to grow another leap, another fall, another failed launch, another certain moment of uncertain certainty that in just one more moment I would be barely visible from the ground. So they brought me home unconscious and limp more than once, and twice and thrice a week as I covered my head with bruises and lumps, and my mother covered the bruises and lumps with green dish soap, because someone once told her it helped to make the swelling go down.

"Stay close by this time. Will you?"

So I played with the next door neighbor's kids who had red-eyed rabbits on their red tile patio, and parents who had met in the mountains while they ran a pirate radio station for a local branch of the revolutionary guerilla armed forces.

■

It made some sense, at least. At the time, at least.

The M19 with their books and rifles, the ELN with their Catholic roots, the FARC with the proletariat cry, the waving of machetes and the march of orphaned farmers. In the beginning, at least, when the Soviet Union called for revolution and flipped the bill. Before the car bombs, the child soldiers, the throngs of *secuestrados* chained to the base of jungle trees. Before Reagan said to tear down that wall. Before kidnappings and coca fields replaced Soviet funding. But the means can carry on long after the ends have been severed and forgotten, a resilient and headless atomic insect made of bullet casings and momentum, running from under one piece of furniture to the other while someone chases it around with a broom. There is little revolutionary left in this revolution. Only the shelling and the shell. And most of the sprawling reasons to revolt mostly intact, and mostly the same. Things get better and they get worse and people grow accustomed to growing accustomed, and we export prisoners, brutality, stereotypes, the plotlines for foreign spy films, and white kilos in suitcases, stomachs, and leaky submarines. And maybe sometime in my life time there won't be an official war or the six or seven unofficial ones hidden amidst leaves, and street lamps, and tinted windows, and drawn curtains, and closed doors. But it's hard to imagine.

∎

I didn't know about our neighbors for a long time. If ever it came up during my childhood, they simply spoke in a thin-veil code. Things like, "up in the hills," and "the guys with the rubber boots," and "those were different times."

But then one day I found this patch in a box of my mother's old things, and it seemed quite heavy for something made of only thread and cloth. So my mother took it, held it between her fingers like something delicate but distorted, a large translucent flake of dried skin. And she seemed to me to momentarily wonder why she had kept it all that time. And that's when she told me about the neighbors, and that's when she told me about herself. Red tiles, red eyes, red patches, and books on a red Wednesday morning of improvised revolutions.

∎

Space is very big, and very dark, and very, very cold. But that's not what killed Laika. The official soviet report reads, "During the ground simulation of this flight's conditions, the conclusion was made, that Laika should be lost due to overheating . . ."

For a long time when I was a child, right before I fell asleep I thought I could hear the automated beeps of a soviet satellite in orbit. *Beep. Beep.* While I lay in bed, on the grass, or on a bench. While moon-light streamed through the colored shards of broken bottles stuck atop the wall around our house—the cheap alternative to expensive barbed wire and bullets. *Beep. Beep.* Or under a tree while I watched a tiny, green spi-der weave an almost-invisible web between my index finger and thumb. *Beep.* And under the beeping, I thought I heard Laika's muffled bark.

∎

Laika puts her nose to the hatch door and fogs up the window the way I fogged up my helmet visor. She is not yet panting, panicking, or pass-ing out. Sputnik II punctures the sky in a single uninterrupted motion. It slides into orbit like a missing gear in a clockwork universe, and Laika travels at speeds close to eighteen thousand miles per hour. She encircles the planet, tracing its width. Laika is unleashed for a minute, free and confined all at once with her nose pressed against the porthole, almost up against the stars that tug on the dark embroidery that holds them in place. For a moment, I imagine, she knows beyond her knowing that she has gone farther and seen more than any man, woman, or dog before her. And in less than two hours she has shot across soviet and American skies alike, and she begins a second earth-round bound. She circles the planet again and again and again, as if she were wrapping it with sacred ribbons and secret strings; as if she were tying rope around a witch, around a pole, around stacks of kindling and tinder; and around, around again she goes for a hundred and sixty-two days before burning up in re-entry.

But that's not what kills Laika, either. Sputnik II breaks free of the blue orb's pull but fails to break free of itself. "The rocket is not the shuttle." A part that was meant to come apart has clung and followed Laika into orbit. The "Blok A" core, or booster rocket, does not separate as planned and as a result the thermal control system is shot. The temperature quickly rises to a hundred and four degrees Fahrenheit, and some intelligence analyst in the U.S. intercepts Laika's agitated heartbeat echoing through encrypted radio waves and across space.

I try to think about Laika thinking, too. Try to imagine in dog—wordless, chemical, bright-flash thoughts. "Where am I? What is this? Where-what-how?" Or maybe, simply, "Hot. Tight. Loud. Hungry. Scared." Canine evolution did not prepare Laika for this moment. Predators, hunger, rats, and garbage heaps, yes—but not space, not weightlessness, not a tinfoil ship blindly burning through space. But maybe, I imagine, she understands more than we think. Laika was handpicked from dozens of candidate dogs; it was not chance but choice that put her in orbit. Someone looked at Laika and saw a satellite, a cosmonaut, a curly-tailed meteor spinning farther from earth than any dog or human had ever spun before. Laika earned her place in the sky; Laika is smart. So maybe she understands, or tries to understand. "It's like a big dog snarling, like an open oven door. Like your tail getting stepped on, your head getting kicked. Like falling asleep under an exhaust pipe, like falling out of a moving car. Like falling, like falling, like fire and fire and falling." But maybe it's not so hard to understand after at all. She is going to die; it is nothing new. Every dog before and after Laika has and will. She will die and she knows it.

■

"I didn't know," my mother said as she handed the patch back to me. "Back then, I just didn't know."

I noticed the mistakes of a rushed design, the sickle's blade too short, the hammer's head too thin. "About what?"

"Well." She sighed. *Well.* Squinting like she does when something is either too far or too close to see. "Well. You know." *You know.* The mountain, the manifesto, the boot, the patch, the dog. All of it, none of it. *You know.*

Then she told me how lucky she felt, to have found God and family just in time, and it made sense then, makes sense now. Because I'm glad, too, and I didn't have to say anything, ask anything, just put the patch back into the box and feel glad. Lucky and glad, box and patch and past all packed and latched away and ago. But I asked her anyway.

"To keep you from what?" Maybe because it's hard to imagine she was ever someone who thought things could be made to change. Or maybe just to kick a pebble down a cliff.

"To keep me from joining."

■

On November 6th, 1985, nearly two months after I was born and nearly a decade after my mother found God, the M19 revolutionary armed forces of Colombia sieged the Palace of Justice in Bogotá to change the course of the country's history.

For twenty-eight hours the vastly outnumbered men and women of the M19 held the palace while their nearly three hundred and fifty hostages huddled together in groups as tight and fragile as petals in a bud. No one anticipated a government that had only months prior discussed peace agreements with the *guerrilleros* to flat-out refuse negotiations, to blast the gates with mortar fire and plug the doorways with sharp-heeled soldiers.

Inside the palace, inside my mind, Irma Franco Pineda—a dark haired *guerrillera* in her twenties, roughly my mother's age at the time—grits her teeth, and I imagine she must try to understand. *It's like a hail storm inside a tin-roof house. A fire inside a locked chicken coop.* And as she listens to the *tak-tak-tak* of semi-automatic gunfire, the growling of tanks rolling up the steps, the cracking of wooden desks torn apart and set ablaze, she may even begin to realize—it's nothing new, it's not so hard—she's going to die.

I've seen the footage, read the reports. A bloody Wednesday in November, chipped door frames, broken glass. Hostages in suits and heels, running and crying and holding hands. Smoke and ruin. In 2005 a commission of truth was finally organized, and it was determined that Irma Franco Pineda made it out of the palace alive and well. She hid amidst the hostages as they were moved from the Palace rubble to a nearby museum, smuggling herself out like contraband and avoiding the stone-turning gaze of soldiers and cops and former hostages. And in the museum I imagine her trying to catch her breath, one Lot's-wife look back at the pillars of smoke rising from the palace, one moment to feel the width and breadth of her movement's failure, to feel the contrived narrative of her movement slip away from her, and then to feel lucky, or at least luckier than those left inside, and was it, after all, so hard to imagine walking out of the museum as well? To make it back home before dark, shake off the shrapnel, and wash off the dust? But then the soldiers begin lining up the rescued against the wall and sifting threat from threatened, and I imagine her holding her breath as if it were oxygen alone that made her visible.

By the end of the siege, ninety-eight of the hostages would be declared dead or disappeared, nearly all the random victims of crossfire, the side effect of their own rescue, from the military, from the captors, by the military, by the captors. Stray dogs and stray bullets have a way of finding a warm place to lay themselves down. And I'm not sure what made sense then, what makes sense now; it's all a scattering of disconnected flickering dots across a sea of black.

From the surviving documents—the report states—we can ascertain that "the survivors were indeed moved from the Palace of Justice to nearby military installations." Irma Franco Pineda was moved from the museum to one of these military installations. She did not make it home, not to a prison, not to a jungle, not to a courtroom. Instead it is suspected that she was tortured for hours and later executed on the orders of high-ranking officers.

■

Though as children we were forbidden to watch the news, my sister and I would sometimes catch glimpses through a slit in our bedroom door: soldiers on the screen building towers of confiscated cocaine kilos and kicking over the bodies of dead *guerrilleros* for the camera to get a good look. The images were grainy and my parents very quiet as they watched, shaking their heads and holding their breaths. One day I dressed up as Rambo and told my mother how great it was that the soldiers had gotten all the white stuff back and built such nice neat rows with it. But she said it wasn't real and I shouldn't be glad. "It's just recycled cocaine," she said. "Bags they keep in a closet somewhere and drag out like a prop for the photo op."

■

Fear is in the brain, and when the brain dies, fear must die with it, too. That's what I tell myself. That it was very brief and she barely suffered. That most place her death within a few hours of the launch, some at four, and none beyond six. Which still leaves one hundred and fifty-six days of an orbiting coffin beeping and burning and sending still images of a still dog, still orbiting a still blue planet. Some speculate the last automatically dispensed serving of gelled food was poisoned to spare Laika the confined mixture of panic and boredom. But we can't be sure. So I tell myself, that instinct is its own dark sky, immeasurably deep and meticulously ruled by black vigilant spiders keeping track of every orbit and every blinking star and every stray dog that strays through their sky.

■

I kept my own tinfoil helmet beside the dead colonel's in my bedroom. My fake one beside his real one. I'm not sure why or how I was allowed to play with this precious last object of a grandfather I never met, but I was and I did. And I loved it.

I lifted it with difficulty and often scraped my ears and nose when I let it drop down and encase my head in old leather padding, metal, and fiberglass. I fought the heavy helmet, and it fought back. I tried to keep my neck straight, and it tried to lay me flat on my back. I tried to keep it from sliding down, and it tried to cut a visor shaped trench on the bridge of my nose. When I finally managed a teetering balance, I would try to sit perfectly still and press the colonel's old English aviation books against the visor so I could smell the glossy pages and stare at the photographs of weightless mice in zero gravity. Legs and tails spread wide apart, waiting to fall the way a man waits for a pebble to hit rock-bottom.

When my mother walked by, I pulled back the blue visor, drawing its springs like the string of a bow, the way I imagine the colonel would have after a flight. "*Mamá*," I said and lifted the book so she could see, "what is happening to the mouse?"

■

Laika spun around the planet an estimated two thousand five hundred and seventy times. She traveled roughly a hundred million kilometers, or more than sixty-two million miles. Most of which she covered in the perfect stillness of death.

Reports disclosed by the Institute of Biological Problems in Moscow during the 2002 World Space Congress in Houston finally put speculation to rest. After seven hours in flight the electrodes attached to Laika's body sent back nothing but static.

■

My mother knelt beside me and glanced at the opened book. She pointed at a floating mouse and explained zero gravity and the likelihood of a post-experiment dissection. "To see what it does to them." And then she told me astronauts need to be very good at math, and I was going to have to study a lot harder if I was going to hitch a ride on an orange rocket, so I turned the page and looking at words in a foreign language, I wondered what math had to do with it.

■

I think anoxia, hypoxia, hyperthermia, Sputnik II. I'm a little girl. I put on a makeshift astronaut helmet and I am certain of my fate. I'm going to be an astronaut; I'm going into space. So I climb a tree and prepare to jump, but my orthopedic shoes are large and clunky and they get stuck between the branches like cheap plastic latches on cheap plastic shuttles, and I cannot yank myself free before leaping. I try to push myself off but feel my leg tug back like the string on a kite. So I topple forward and a thin sliver of time grows fat and slow as my brain recognizes the inevitable trajectory. I see my arms swinging, my legs kicking, my helmet slipping off. I see the grey sky of a paved sidewalk growing larger and larger in the slow succession of slide projector images. *Shhhh-clack. Shhhhh-clack.* And it seems for a moment as if I might be falling forever, never landing forever. I think I can taste the ground before I've felt it, the electric surge of a concrete blow to the head, like biting into a sandwich and finding a metal plate between the two slices of Wonder Bread. I close my eyes to try to slip out of consciousness before the whiteout blank of a blackout blow, but the sun shines through my eyelids and tints the world red and imminent, until finally, impact. The black. The passing of time, or the passing through it, and my mother on the other end rubbing green dish soap on my head and yelling at me not to fall asleep.

■

Incalescence, calefaction, calidity, fever—dog days in space. A booster rocket still clinging and sparking, a dog panting and spinning, harder and faster, while hundreds of men and women below look up to see if they can spot Laika tugging on Sirius's leash.

Before Laika was Laika she was just a nameless stray like the colander dots of flashing light in the sky. Then she was rescued and recruited. She wagged her tail and hardly ever showed her teeth, so they called her *Kudryavka,* and *Zhuchka,* and *Limonchik*—Curly, Bug, Lemon, and finally *Laika.* "Barker." Whimpering inside a metal box accompanied only by the intermittent beeps of a rushed construction satellite.

■

Sometimes my mother would let my sister and me pack leftovers in a plastic grocery bag to go to the open fields and feed a beautiful stray dog named Tatu. His coat was heavy with dust and mud, and she told us not to pet him too much, though I'm sure she knew we would regardless of instruction. Because he beat his curly tail against the pavement when he saw us coming—when he saw anyone coming—and when we poured cold rice and sliced potatoes at his feet, he sat perfectly still as if he were bound by otherworldly old-world etiquette. We begged and begged our parents to let us take him home, put a leash around his neck, and wash the light brown patch on his chest until it was white again. But all the other kids begged their parents, too, and I think they must have all silently agreed it was best to share Tatu, to let him run through the unkempt field beyond the fence, to send children with leftovers in plastic bags and wash their hands thoroughly when they returned. "That dog eats better than we do," my father told us. "Trust me. You don't need to worry about him."

Though, of course we should have. It was the nineties and things were ticking and clicking, and some of those things were the sporadic gangs of restless adolescents craving the validation of ritualization. They were invisible in the daytime, like germs and stars, but at night they emerged hollering and screaming and whooping and howling. They kicked the fences until they bent the bars, they broke the windows and scratched the cars, and then they took the animals. At first only scrawny, rabid strays sleeping in ditches and beneath cars. Cats and dogs they'd wring out like dirty rags and toss over a fence like wet things on the clothesline. But soon they ran out of those and began climbing the fences to slit the throats of Dalmatians and poodles right in their own front yards.

They hung our street's friendly Saint Bernard on the driveway door, and they hung Tatu on the front gates of my preschool.

My older sister says that at least I did not hear him. Did not lie awake that night hearing the screech of a truck's tires and a tied-up dog being dragged through unpaved streets until they wore him down to the bone, until he was quiet like only dead things can be quiet, like space is quiet, like too much noise can short-circuit the inner ear and make it seem insufferably quiet.

I didn't hear him, but I did see him the next morning when I lined up outside my preschool gates. Mud and blood. Delicate and distorted. Boneless and limp, the puppet without the hand. Tatu hanging from the top of the fence, hooked through a gash on his throat, his head hanging loosely back at an impossible angle, almost perfectly parallel with his spine, almost painless, nearly painless. Except that my older sister heard him the night before, and sometimes at night, lying in her bed, she says she can still hear him.

■

I used to think a lot about Tatu. I sometimes still do. Though now I think more about the people who took him.

The kids drove him up and down the streets of my childhood neighborhood as if they could erase the roads with his body. "Why?" I think, and, "What for?" As if all things were thought out and thought through before bursting into existence, inevitable and infected with intent. Maybe there's just not that much to do in a small town, maybe boredom is a heavy planet with an inescapable orbit, or maybe they were simply angry, or they had every right to be angry and no one to hold accountable, not a single head against which to press the cold muzzle of their rage—not really. The peasants? The manifesto-writers? The kidnapped sons of oligarchs and plutocrats? The drafted soldiers? The hired guards? The men in the jungle? The jungle? The drug? The men growing the drug? Taking the drug? The children of the men growing the drug sprayed with foreign pesticides which kills everything else they try to grow, for others, for themselves as they scratch toxic rashes raw? The Spaniards who left us a mess? The soviets who left us a mess? The conservatives, the liberals, the *narcotraficantes*, who left us all a mess?

But maybe it's not so hard.

Maybe they simply wanted to be part of something serious and important like a gang or a space program. So they drove all night under a cast net of obsolete constellations, while a dog howled and screeched and whimpered as he was sanded down into nothingness. Now if my sister ever hears about someone hurting a dog, she gets this look on her face like my mother did when I would wake up from a concussion and she wouldn't let me fall back asleep.

And my sister adopted a dog that looks a lot like Laika, a little curly tail and a face made to smile. And this dog used to wheeze like a vacuum cleaner because her previous owner didn't like small dogs and thought if he squeezed her neck hard and long enough she'd finally stop breathing, and then he'd only have big, important-looking dogs around, and maybe that would mean something about him.

■

Every time I leap there is a chance I will fall, and every time I fall there is a chance I will finally crack my head open like a Faberge egg, and luminous black spiders will crawl out to mark the outline of my body with blinking stars and black thread. And there is a very good chance someone will carry me home, delicate, distorted, boneless, and limp—and a stray boy will take my tinfoil helmet.

■

The colonel fell from the sky in 1964. Only three years after Gagarin had followed Laika's wake into the darkened heavens and circled Earth for one hundred and eight celestial minutes. More than twenty years before I was born, before the cold war would officially end and the hot internal Colombian conflict would hit its violent peak. Four years later Gagarin would follow. Another pilot, another more-or-less inexplicable accident. And Gagarin left two daughters behind. The colonel left three, and my mother is the second one.

■

Something is wrong. The colonel already knows it, but he is too stubborn to admit it. He struggles to maintain altitude. The machine bucks and tilts. Something is very wrong. But he loves this plane, loves to fly, and tries desperately to get the machine under control. But it won't work, and maybe he already knows it won't. The airplane has slid into the gravitational pull of a fated collision course, and the colonel sees too late that the machine is intent on extinction. The entire cockpit shakes, and he shakes, his eyes inside his sockets inside his skull inside his helmet shake. But he is a colonel in the Colombian air force; he has trained in San Diego, California, with the very best of the very best, and inside his flight suit, inside his uniform, inside his bones, *he* does not shake.

He pulls on the latch and his seat is ejected into the air, a miniature launch. *10, 9, 8*. Did he wait too long to eject? *7, 6, 5*. Will the parachute open in time? *4, 3, 2*. Is something stuck, something locked and latched? Has something failed to detach?

1, 0.

The colonel falls like a pebble, like a cosmonaut, like an orange rocket, like a child from a tree or a dog from a fence, and the jungle watches him fall from so far up it seems for a moment that he might never hit the ground. Then, the explosion. The machine strikes; the colonel strikes. His wedding band is bent into an oval; the left side of his face is gone; the right side of his body is gone; *he* is gone.

■

"Lina." One day after my mother had been listening to the news on the radio, she stopped seven-year-old me by the staircase. "Listen to me," she said. "Just listen." The sun shone incandescently bright through the window, and my mother seemed glazed with an equally incandescent rage. "No matter what, you hear me? If anything happens." Talking as if this were the conclusion to a long conversation. "Anything at all," she said. "I want you to bite it off." And I think her lip was trembling, though I know her voice was firm. "Do you understand?" she asked. "Do you?"

I'm wearing a cardboard and tinfoil helmet, I'm going to be a Colombian astronaut when I grow up. No, I don't understand, I don't feel the weight of a failed revolution, I don't know what men do to girls in the depth of a jungle or the back of a truck, and that is probably why she repeats it. "Just bite *it* off." But, maybe it is not so hard. If they come, when they come, don't sit still, don't smile, don't volunteer, and don't wag your tail. "Just bite *it* off," whatever vulnerable bit is offered, sink your teeth into it and rip it out. A vein, a hand, a finger, a member. A gushing, writhing, warm, torn thing to spit out before turning and running, wiping your mouth with your sleeve like you've been told a hundred times never to do. So I nodded, a bobble-head cardboard nod, with one of my grandfather's books under my arm and a plan to try zero gravity experiments on my hamster, Lil' She-Rambo.

■

The other night I woke up to the sight a large black spider walking across my bare midriff. I lay perfectly still as if it were pinning me down, as if it were made of lead, shrapnel, and fate. And I watched it walk diagonally across me and stop at my hip, at the edge of me and the bed where the darkness becomes thickest and the fall must have appeared endless. In 1754 an English naturalist and apothecary named John Hill published a book titled *Urania: Or a Complete View of the Heavens*. In it he reconnected the dotted sky to remake it into what he must have thought was a better story and a better set of constellations: a scaly lizard, a bull-frog, a black snail, a series of angular crustaceans, and a large spider named Aranea. This is what we do, impose narratives on the unfurled darkness, try to steer heavens and countries for the greater good and the greater truth. Look back and look forward, look up and look down, look out and look in, and run back and forth between the dots until we've made ruts and grooves the light can fill and we don't have to see anything but the shapes we've drawn for ourselves to see. For a while there were so many reconstellators that the practice became known as "constellation mania." A man Christianized the heavens to purge them of pagan monsters and winged horses, while dozens of others drew royal portraits and attempted to claim part of the sky for France, for England, for Germany. But no reconstellated star map caught on, and these came to be known as the "obsolete constellations."

I held my breath while the spider held its ground at the edge of my hip, until I couldn't hold it any longer. I took a sharp breath and saw the spider stretch out all eight legs across my skin thinking it might be about to leap, but then I saw it raise its two front legs as if worshiping or surrendering. For a few seconds it moved them in delicate circles, as if unraveling penumbral strings or directing celestial traffic, and then it hopped off and disappeared into an unlit corner of the room.

∎

I closed the lid to the box of my mother's old things and felt the sticky dust between my fingertips. "*Mamá*, do you remember how old I was back then, when you told me about Laika?"

"No," she replies. "Not really. Six? Five?"

"But you remember telling me?"

"Certainly, why?"

I pause a moment. "Why did you tell me?"

My mother doesn't hesitate. She remembers and thinks it should be obvious why. "Because it was true."

∎

I left Colombia when I was seventeen because my parents said there was a better future for me somewhere else, or a worse one in Colombia, or else no future at all. Or I'm not really sure anymore what made sense to them then. This was the early 2000s, and the country was just emerging from some of the most violent decades in its recorded history. So they sent my sisters and me away and hoped I might be an intellectual after all. I learned a rounded-edge language, boarded a white plane, and flew eight hours up the spine of a self-destructive continent. Because the colonel fell from the sky, and the soviets lost the cold war, and the guerillas lost their north, but my mother found God and family and she had three daughters and I'm the second one.

Because my mother made me a tinfoil helmet and told me that if I got better at math I could be weightless and part of something undeniable and important, and then she told me about Laika. How even strays can become cosmonauts, and even cosmonauts stray. How Laika died to help us measure an immeasurable sky.

BACHUÉ

The world begins in a lake. Not far from Bogotá, which they say, was once a lake too.

A woman steps out and the world begins with her, Bachué—but there is no one to call her that yet.

She moves in the water and it parts around her, because she is beautiful and perfect and first. And a three-year-old boy follows, gripping her hand like a jaguar's tail or the strings that hold up the stars. They both emerge from the water barefoot and naked, and she kneels down beside him to wipe mud off his cheek and then stands up to build him a house.

Bachué raises the boy, hunts deer for him, catches frogs and plucks off their legs for him. She carves a long-billed bird from a fallen tree for him to balance on his index finger as if it had been caught midflight in an invisible web. And when he is a man, she marries him, gives him children and raises them too. She's carried them inside her from another world. In her womb and in her blood. Every heart and every mind and every disparate part of every disparate woman, man, or child that will ever be is in her, and is hers and hers alone to dream up, to bring out and make flesh. So she gives birth in batches of four and six, and she lives a very long time so she can fill the world with people, but she does not age like the others. Her thighs are strong and she moves softly through the *Páramo*, through the mist, while little frogs sing—*Bachué, Bachué, Bachué*—and tiny green snakes curl around her wrists and ankles. Until one day all the weight of years postponed comes down on her suddenly. Legs and arms and breasts loosen and all at once her ash-green eyes look tired and lost.

Her children gather around her as her husband reaches for her hand one last time, and they walk back to Lake Iguaque together. But she is old now and she has to sit down every so often to catch her breath. She crosses her legs and traces a shape in the dirt—mud, symmetry, and prophecy. She presses her index finger into the wet dirt and traces the shape of the universe as water fills the grooves and worms emerge to kiss the tip of her finger. And she tells her children how to live, how to gather food, how to give birth, and how to worship. Then she tells the women to lean in closer. "Listen now," she says. "Weave, walk, cook, sit together, eat together, talk. Govern while I'm gone." And then she reaches for her companion's hand because she is tired, and she's not sure how she got there, and she thinks she can hear the beating of enormous wings inside her chest, and she wants to go home.

The whole world walks to the edge of the lake with them, but they must go in alone. Some cry, some beg her not to go, telling her it will be too much for them if she does. They say, "Promise us." They beg, "Promise you'll come back." But she does not reply. Maybe she does not hear them, though some will say they saw her nod when they begged and pleaded, before she walked into the water still holding her husband's hand.

Regardless, they all saw them stand, ankle deep, for a few minutes before the water reached out with silver scales that travelled up their legs and spines to the tips of their heads, pulling them tight, thin, long, and suspended between shapes for a fraction of a moment, a slice of a second, a bead of time. A flash of an instant gleaming under the Andean sky before falling into new shapes, brand-new silver-green snakes slithering back into the sacred lake.

The world begins with a woman, ends with a snake.

PONER EL CUERPO

or

Put the body.

or

[above]

[behind]   [beside] **Put the** [between] **body** [*in front*].
    [around]
[beneath]

[across]

or

Put your body on the line.

or

"But don't flinch."

Aurelia

Once a year, every May, we run to our mothers and beg for plastic bags.

We say, "Please, please, please." *Porfa, porfa, porfa.* Pacing like penned bulls and bouncing on tingling feet as we listen to the *plick-plick-plick* of disoriented insects striking windows and doors.

"Please. Please." Plicking back against the sound of shells on glass. "Please." Until our mothers relent. And they hold used shopping bags from every local store up to their lips and huff and puff like fairytale wolves until the wrinkled logos blow up large and smooth and the plastic is tested for holes. *Cafam, Carulla, Los Tres Elefantes, El Éxito.*

Then we are handed our bag and they fetch their brooms, so they can swat the loose thread of black insects back into the swarm, and we can run into it with eyes half-open, holding bags like nets like white flags and plastic sails, above our heads, as we try to catch all the fluttering chaos of just-hatched, black-carapace life blotting out the sun and filling up our lungs.

And their legs get tangled in our eyelashes and wool sweaters. And they crash against our teeth and ear drums. And we have to learn to unclasp their tiny grapple legs without tearing them like petals from a daisy. "*I'll maim him, I'll maim him not.*" Tiny fish from tiny hooks. Tiny tangled legs off from wool-sweater nets. So we hold our breaths and steady our hands, just to have them for an instant, to watch them walk across our palms. Clockwork beetles with black shoe-polish shells which we gently lift to see stained-glass wings and holy geometry.

And then we throw them back into the buzzing tide and spit out mouthfuls of torn wings and cracked shell.

The rest of the year we wait.

Us and them. Children and *chisas*. Before they become *Mayitos*, May beetles, they are thick, white, wrinkled, and underground. Small, black, prickly hairs poking out in irregular patches through their crumpled pupa pallor and in thick black clumps near the hump where a neck might have been and from whence a black beetle head erupts grotesquely. A limbless, miniature Minotaur, a made-up creature of mismatched parts and torpid excess. Built for taxidermy and traveling carnivals.

The rest of the year we do our best to dig them up and kill them.

We smash them with stones and bricks. We run them over with our bicycles and skateboards. We flick them with sticks out of their holes in the earth, too afraid to touch the dirty toothbrush legs we've decided are poisonous. Their hard, black heads move from left to right, seeking the resistance of dirt that might tell them in which direction to crawl, but we flip them onto the sidewalk where they writhe in confusion until one of us lifts a stone and the rest of us follow.

We see the fleshiness of them, the wriggling surplus of meat and setae-stubble and brown-bristle legs, and we bring the stone down against them. Up and down again, up and down again, again. We crush them past the certainty of death because something in their form offends us. Because we don't want to kill them; we want to destroy them. Because they make us scratch our scalps, and behind our necks, and the blank-map spot in the middle of our backs we almost never see and can hardly reach and sometimes think does not actually exist, and sometimes still are sure its erupting with white-flesh *chisa* pupas, bursting out, crawling in, and filling us with white-pulp eggs. So we scratch until there is skin and blood and scalp beneath our fingernails, and we lift red bricks with both hands and let them fall on the squirming things. We touch the spot in the middle of our backs; we lift the bricks and let them fall. We touch our backs, our arms, our necks, our faces, to try to make sure there are no larvae squirming beneath, no black heads pushing out through pores like birth canals. We lift the bricks and let them fall.

We do not want them to stop existing; we want them to have never existed at all. But we want May beetles, too—mist and clouds and whirlwinds of them rising from the ground and falling from the sky. And because we don't understand how the larva grows her wings, we dig them up and smash them to bits.

METIO LA PATA

or

To put in the leg.[1]

or

To put ~~in~~ the leg [*in*].[2]

or

To blow it.[3]

or

"Huy."[4]

---

1. **Pata** *(feminine noun): of animal, table, or chair. Vulgar, 'of a person.'*
2. Where one should not.
3. **It** *(n): everything.*
4. "Poor thing." / "That's terrible." / "God bless her." / "Had it coming."

Rueda

I want to know what happened inside the tent.
"Which tent?"
Twenty years ago.
"The gorilla tent?"
The one I wasn't allowed into.
"Yeah, yeah. I remember this."

It's New Year's Eve in Henderson, Nevada, and everyone's asleep,
everyone but my older sister and me.
"When we lived in Chía, right?" I see the shadow of her extended
arm stretch across the ceiling as she points toward the kitchen, as if past
the crumb-covered counter and plate-filled sink lay our small Colombian
hometown. "I'm like nine and you are like six, right?" The DVD menu
screen flashes between silent explosions and dramatic, slow-motion walking. "The gorilla lady, *La Rueda*. I remember."
Once a year, every year, like Christmas and Holy Week, it arrived in
scattered parts and submerged the whole city in lights, noise, and nausea.
La Rueda, The Wheel, the ramshackle traveling carnival that came to town
in trucks and vans and big rusty Jeeps, packed and wrapped and notice-
ably faded from the constant lashing of an Andean sun. And we watched
the keepers of *La Rueda* chase cows and sheep out of an abandoned field
and replace them with giant metal parts like some enormous, assemblable
god—mechanical joints and vertebrae strewn about leaves of wild grass.
Two days, three—no more than four—and it was up and spinning.
A modest fee, an improvised gate, and a precarious fence around the oil-
dripping bumper cars, centrifuges, and rollercoaster cars in the shape of
grinning insects and lopsided cartoon characters. An undaunted Dumbo
grinning through a half-melted face flew in screeching circles not that
far above our heads, one side a drooping plastic grimace, the other a

fading smile. A long line of people waited to ride *La Rueda's* crowning jewel, an enormous metal hammer lovingly nicknamed "The Kamikaze" after—I was told—a girl a few towns over had fallen out mid-ride.

"Everyone we knew went before us," my sister tells me. "And they gave us so much crap about it, too." I lie across the couch and tap my clavicles with my fingers while she talks, feel the tapping travel through my throat and imagine myself reborn as a percussion instrument. "They were so obnoxious, like 'have you gone yet? When are you gonna go? Are you even gonna go? Are your parents too poor to take you?'" Paula lies on a beanbag, gesturing into the darkness, making accidental shadow puppets gallop across the ceiling. "We always went on the very, very last day, and our mother never came with us. And we couldn't even ride anything good because of your amazing projectile vomiting skills. Do you remember?"

It's both vague and precise, the memory of walking into the mist and turning back to look at our mother waving goodbye from the window.

"I don't know if she didn't come because we couldn't afford for all of us to go, or because she hated all those spinning rides. You're like her, with all the vomiting."

But I love rollercoasters. I like the suspension of logic, the enforced Marshall Law of panic which momentarily moves the seat of my internal government away from my brain and into the black pit of a stomach certain of nothing but the threat of imminent extinction. I loved them then, too, as I tugged on my father's hand and told him about all the things I was going to do when we got to *La Rueda*, as if I did not already know I was too small for half my plans.

"You were impossible." Through the shadows I see my sister shaking her head. "Do you remember? Every time our father came back from a trip, the stacks and stacks of vomit bags he brought back from planes? He used to ask the air attendants for extras. Did you know that? Do you remember?"

I do. A memory on loop, a reel of packed night buses and dilapidated taxis driving from Bogotá to Chía. Then the warmth of vomit pushing its way out, a shaken-soda-can spray of pressurized sick gushing through lips and fingers and shirt sleeves, and my head on my father's shoulder as he carries my limp body home and vomit cools and congeals between my cheek and his white shirt.

I move my hands from my clavicles to my mouth suddenly, as if I were about to wretch, but really I'm trying to hold on to a strong sensation, to some moment anchored in body and time.

I try to hold on to the feeling, the burn of stomach acid in my mouth and the sickly saccharine smell of strawberry car freshener, black coffee, and faint rot. I used to do this a lot but backwards. Try to picture myself in a static elsewhere—in a house, in a field, try to keep the contents of my stomach from leaping out of my throat like rats from a burning building.

A place like this, I imagine. This corner of Henderson, Nevada, is as quiet and early as Las Vegas is loud and late. Paula's voice, a dog's sleepy wheezing, and the sound of me tapping on my collarbones. Nothing more beyond the distant lights of a phosphorescent city convulsing with life. "But," Paula continues, the light softening the geometry of her face, "even when we actually went, it wasn't much better, you know? I mean between your vomiting and no money for popcorn or cotton candy, or anything— it was just basically walking through a field watching other people have fun."

Except this one time. "Well, yes," she concedes. "That time, sort of." *The time with the tent.* "Yes, that one." *Where I wasn't allowed.* "Yes, yes." *So you went alone.* "I know." *And I stayed outside.*

"But that wasn't the problem." The dog wakes up suddenly, and I stroke its back with my foot. "The problem started with the fact that, because of all that other stuff, we obviously got stuck with the 'less frequented attractions.'" The sideshow side of the traveling carnival. Scattered tents and booths, men selling cold food on sticks and in cups surrounded by dozens of worn out tents. The hand-painted signs promise of mindboggling deformities and impossible contortions. "But Chía was already a town of freaks, you know? So we weren't even all that impressed." And I wonder if it's a coincidence that Paula ended up living a stone's throw from Vegas, "The bearded lady was fat. Really more fat than beard," she continues, "and even less of a beard and more of a huge mole on her face. Looked just like the butcher's wife. Remember her?" *Yes,* I lie. I don't remember her. I don't remember anything but the smell of blood dripping from the mouth of an upside-down animal, and how sticky the floor felt of a small town butcher shop. "Yeah. Just like her." A similar woman visited our home once when we were kids and Paula pointed at a small mole on my face and said it was only little because I was little, and as I grew it would grow and cover my entire face and neck and chest and arms, "like the butcher's wife," until Paula would have to sell me to the *Rueda* next time they came through town. "Facial hair on a woman. Not impressed." We grew up surrounded by Colombian matriarchies and the sport of sharpening one's tongue against the edge of friends' and acquaintances' miseries and defects, and listening to Paula takes me back. She makes a face as she describes Chía, the butcher's wife, the taunting kids and their parents bragging of soon-to-be-had trips to Melgar and Miami which we never took. She shrugs and shakes her head as if she's just spotted Chía in a crowd waving a dirty hand enthusiastically across memory, a shrug like an *"I don't know you"* meant to be overheard, and I laugh at the version of herself she plays for me.

"So we're there right, the last, last night of *La Rueda,* and we see this tiny black tent and there wasn't a line yet, so my father and I can go all the way to the front holding on to this mangy velvet rope, and I'm there thinking, 'We have the best seats in the house.' For the first and maybe only time, 'We're at the front of something.'" I remember this part. The sun setting on a mostly empty field while ride operators started up their centrifuges and haunted mansions like rusty lawnmowers. My father went in with Paula, told me not to move an inch and that they'd be right back, *"Quieta Margarita."* I remember begging to be taken along, but there must have been some objection to my age or height, and I was left outside while a man in a dirty vest waved them in with promises of *Magical mystical miraculous marvels inside!* "Biggest fire hazard ever," Paula chuckles, but there's something else, too. "Tiny tent, no visible exit, and stuffed—stuffed—with people, right?" *Then what?* "Darkness, and a voice." She imitates it, something between a film trailer voiceover and an auctioneer mid sale: "'Frooooooooom the miiiiiiiiiiiiiiiiiiissssts of tiiiiiiiiiiimmmmeeeeeeee!' Loud, deep. That's when she comes out, right?" *Who?* "An ugly woman. The bearded lady's cousin, who—unable to grow a full beard—must have been discarded from the act." This is also the point in the story when my father left Paula alone in the tent. "Yeah, off to be responsible he went. You know, probably afraid you'd throw yourself off of something, or something." *Yeah, ok. But then what?*

Enter a woman in a peach bikini with matching veils. "Dressed sort of like a cheap odalisque." Paula stretches in her bean bag and in the shadows I see the contour of my older sister as a scrawny nine-year-old who lived perpetually trying to tuck in her shirt, trying to make her ill-fitting clothes fit, trying to keep her good pair of jeans clean and somehow assuage her paralyzing shyness. "Red lips, dark hair, you know the fashion back then." Then she motions with her fingers, draws a sort of rectangle in the air, "And it's a small tent, with only a tiny stage elevated a little off the ground, and on it, an empty cage." An empty cage the cheap peach odalisque walks right into, with neither pomp nor circumstance, with absolutely no regard for the prestige of an illusion—no waltz, no twirl, no smile—as if she were just about to buy a pack of cigarettes from the corner store. "And all this while the voice explains that she is now going to turn into a gorilla and not to worry because everything is perfectly safe. So she goes in and locks the door behind her." One-two-three, she's in and it starts. "It gets dim. I see something like a mirage, like a shine. I guess there must have been mirrors in there or something. Then it gets blurry and the voice keeps saying something or other, and then." *Then?* "Gorilla."

Like it is that simple. *Just pull the damn rabbit out of the damn hat; that's what they came to see anyway.* A woman walks up to a stage, a voice explains what she intends to do, and then she does it. No patter, no frills, no strings, no twirls, no lies.

"It was sort of amazing, in a really provincial way—except it really did look amazing, I can't explain it. And we all started clapping immediately." Of all the things I regret, few compare to missing this. To not simply running into that black-garbage-bag tent and pressing my face against the bars of the gorilla's cage.

The Nevada desert wind howls outside. It's been raining every other night, Bogotá and Chía weather really, hardly like a North American desert. I know what comes next. "I'm standing there and I think, 'This is amazing and I'm doing it all on my own, and I'm finally in the front row!' And this is a ginormous gorilla." Paula spreads out her arms to show me. "Huge, huge gorilla." I try to correct for our sizes back then. We are not very big now, but we were very small then. "Just freaking huge, right? And it's just a second, it transforms, and I'm in complete awe, and then the voice starts yelling through the speakers." Paula starts waving her hands above her head, as if she were adrift in a raft and a rescue plane flew by. "'Oh no, ladies and gentlemen, the gorilla is aggressive,'" I hear her say it in English, but really I hear her say it in Spanish in English. In one language remembered, in another retold, and the whole while the grammar and diction of one language dripping through the other, like pouring mushroom soup into a cardboard box and hoping for the best. "*¡El Gorila es agresivo!*" *The gorilla is aggressive!* "'Ladies and gentleman, remain calm, the cage is very secure, remain calm!'"

I tap my clavicles—thin, breakable flute bones. I press down on them, feel them bend a little, and I wonder, because it hasn't occurred to me until now, if the voice may have been prerecorded. If maybe it did not run in automated, half-hour loops, which demanded an expedited, nononsense performance from the hairy odalisque. But it seems somehow unlikely now, too high-tech for *La Rueda,* for Chía, for this bit of my shared childhood with Paula. For a place where most houses didn't have landlines and we all went to the colonial rush-job town square to rent a phone booth and pay by the minute. "'Ladies and gentleman,'" Paula gestures in great, exaggerated strokes, as if she's been cast in the silent film adaptation. "'Ladies and gentlemen, the gorilla appears to be aggressive. Please keep away from its reach, as long as it remains within the confines of its cage—oh, no!'" I've began to laugh uncontrollably as Paula continues to narrate the slow-motion explosion. "Ladies and gentlemen, it appears that Stellar Stella did not fully secure the cage. Ladies and gentlemen, run! While you are still able, run, please run!"

Paula sinks back into her beanbag chair still flailing and shaking her head, "Ridiculous, *pueblerinos.*" *Villagers.* She shakes her head again. But she seems almost shaken by it. This is one of my favorite stories; I ask for it every so often. And every time, when she tells me, she says, "The Gorilla." Never, "the gorilla illusion" or "the woman in a gorilla suit." it is always, without fail, "the gorilla" or "the woman who turned into a gorilla." Inherently magical and absolutely terrifying. Like, "What were those *Rueda* people thinking?" Or, "How could she be so careless with the lock?"

Then what happened? This is my favorite part.

Paula doesn't hesitate. "It got me." She tells it with the same matter-of-fact stoicism she uses when she talks about the bus that plowed into her when she was crossing a street in Bogotá, and that time she tried to coax a horse into stepping on a pig. "Because the pig had it coming." Paula nods her head and points at her forearm as if I could see the mark the transformed ape had left there. "It had me pretty tight, but I kept pulling and pulling and pulling until I got free." *Then what?* "What else? I ran."

I remember this part, standing perfectly still in front of the tent as people rushed out screaming and pushing and stumbling and tripping and disappearing into other crowds and lines and rides. The sudden realization that the sun had set and the music vaguely matched the flashing lights around me. Streams of people like two pressurized torrents from a torn hose. People, people, people, and more people. Then nothing, nothing, and nothing. Quiet, the flapping tents in the wind, and finally, finally, my sister, eggshell white and eggshell cracked, trembling and staggering, holding up her forearm where the gorilla had held her, pointing at her untucked shirt. "I was running, running and thinking, 'I don't think the gorilla's left the tent. I don't think it's following me.'" She continues to hold her own forearm out for me to see as she speaks, as if she can slip her own fingers into the grooves the gorilla left behind. *What was it like? Do you remember?* "I don't know," she says. "It was like thick fur, like Paco's fur. You know?" She points up at the staircase, where one of the only remaining objects from our childhood resides inside a linen closet: a nightmarish orange monkey with long, scarflike limbs and cheap, coarse synthetic fur. "And it was like, I don't know, just this one arm reaching out to get me, you know. One attacking arm." I imagine a disembodied limb reaching out for Paula in the dark, and I remember Chía, Colombia. Before my parents saved up enough to buy a small Sony TV, we would go to a store above a store, where a couple would rent out a room, a television, and a video for a few hours for a small fee. Paula leaning back and I leaning forward on knockoff director's chairs while Linda Hamilton performed open-heart surgery on an animatronic King Kong. *Pueblerinos.* Phone booths, stone fountains, and unregulated gangs running through the night killing dogs to prove a point or to prove there was no point to anything at all. Paula awake all night listening to the howling of a tortured dog. And I look around my sister's pristine Henderson home, her own sleeping dogs, her husband, her children. This admirable life in this admirable place, and how my mother never had to tell her, "Don't come back to this country; there's nothing here left for you." And in the blue light of a DVD menu on loop, I know that somewhere in a cupboard there is a blue U.S. citizen's passport with my sister's name on it. "Ladies and gentlemen, behold." Not the Colombian name we shared for most of our lives, not the one she has shed like a sheath of skin, but a shorter, more efficient name to make sure she's never separated from her children the way our mother used to be separated from us in U.S. airports and immigration offices because, "How come you don't have the same last name as them? That doesn't make any sense ma'am, please step aside." And it makes sense to me now, though it didn't then. A name is only a name only a name only a place only a moment anchored in memory and a field of wild grass, and nostalgia is toxic and metaphors empty. Linda Hamilton chainsawing King Kong's chest open to switch out a faulty heart for a shiny new one.

"I thought I was dead. I thought about the news headline, 'Terrible tragedy. Gorilla eats ill-dressed child in crappy local carnival.'" But, she told my parents, she would keep her middle name. Because it's our younger sister's middle name, and all our female cousins' middle names, and my middle name, too. "But the gorilla didn't get me, did it?" She says with a smile, "I got away."

PONER EL DEDO EN LA LLAGA

or

To put the finger on the sore.

or

To ~~put~~ [*place*] ~~the~~ [*a*] finger ~~on~~ [*in*] the ~~sore~~ [*wound*].

or

Salt for sore cries.

or

"Some things should hurt."

Tenjano

This kid, he's from Tenjo. Little nothing town outside of Bogotá. They keep cows there; kill pigs. Friday afternoons, you can hear them half-squeal, half-scream echoing through the valley. Large pink bodies bumping up against each other as they get funneled into smaller and smaller pens. Not much else in Tenjo. Cows, pigs, barbed wire fences, and this stupid experimental school we are all stuck in. So we call this kid *El Tenjano*, since that's where he's from, and that's where we are—though mostly it's because he's short, his school uniform is thin from handwashing, he has a stupid haircut, and there's nothing special enough about him to earn him his own name.

Which should be enough, you know? To keep people where they are, and where they're not supposed to be, or whatever.

But one day he just comes up to me anyway. Walks straight from the door to my table and just sits down. No nothing. None of this pretend politeness, no circling things for an hour with our ears perked up before we finally run into them with our eyes closed and our mouths open, or whatever. Which I kind of know is some sort of learned behavior, like how dogs learn to be afraid of sticks or not afraid of highways. I know, I do. But it's just the way things are, you know? Kid's not even in my grade, anyway. Not in my class, anyway. And his parents aren't in my parents' social class either. But he just comes in, sits down, and says hello.

"Hello." Like that.

And I say "Hello" back. Just because I don't know what else to say.

And then he asks, "So, you know your sister?"

Which is a stupid question, because everyone in this school knows my older sister. So, yeah, I say, "Yeah."

And obviously he knew I'd say that, but it's like this kid's rehearsed the whole thing in his head. Because he doesn't even take a breath, doesn't even blink.

"So, what is she like?" Straight to it. Except not quite, because *"What is she like,"* is really *"What does she like?"* Is really, really, *"Who does she like?"* and *"Could she be persuaded into liking someone like me?"* Because he wants to give her something, I guess. "Something really special, you know?"

By which I think he actually means, "I love her." Or, "I want her." Or some such variation-combination that makes the boys in this school look vaguely stricken and like they think themselves the lead characters in one of those shitty TV shows. But this is new; the look on *El Tenjano's* face is new. Like he actually cares, or he thinks he actually cares. Or worse, like he thinks *she* might care. That sort of *"If she only knew me"* slobbering bullshit. Which is obviously not true, but I don't tell him that. I say, "I don't know." I say, "Stuff." Meaning, *"I really, really don't know."* And, *"Can we talk about something else, now?"* But it doesn't matter because he's only half listening. He's rehearsed this whole thing in his head. He knows what comes next, and he already has what he wants to give her anyway.

"Do you know? Does she like . . . porcelain?" Which is when I realize how strange it is that I actually know exactly how she feels about it. And how I feel about it, too. Because we're the same in this—and that's the strangest part.

But I don't say that either. Instead, "Maybe." And, "I guess that depends." Which, still, doesn't make any difference. He's not even looking at me anymore.

"Because," he presses on, "I have this really beautiful porcelain doll, right? Really delicate and beautiful, right?"

"Ok."

"Expensive stuff. And your sister, she's . . ." He pauses with this really dumb look on his face like he's swishing wine around in his mouth. "Really delicate and beautiful, too, you know?"

"No."

"And I just don't know, right? I don't think the guys she hangs out with really actually tell her that. Do you see what I mean? If she really knows what she really is."

Some guy asked me once if I'd sell him pictures of my sister. He promised twenty thousand pesos apiece, enough for a new CD or bus money for a month. So I told him I'd think about it. Actually, no. I said yes. I had her old passport photo in my wallet, so I thought, why not, right? And I'm sitting right across from him during lunch when he asked me, expecting me to say no—because I guess that was the right thing to say. And he has this dark birthmark on his cheek like someone took a brush and tried to clean off the paint on his face, and it gets stretched out a bit when he fills his mouth with food, and it trembles a little when he hears something unexpected like, "Sure. Why not."

Across from me, I see *El Tenjano* rest his elbows on the table as if he's carefully contemplating the next few minutes. He rocks forward and leans in as close as this half-rotten, plywood chair allows. "It's like this tall," he whispers, holding a flat palm a few inches above the table. His thick black hair sticks up as if objecting in unison to something said or unsaid. "Like really beautifully painted, golden lining, and everything." Brown-black eyes, a hairless chin, and sort of big-headed when I look at him closely. "Not cheap at all. Like, think high-end, right?"

People don't really talk to me here. There's only about a hundred and fifty people in this school, and less than half over the age of ten. It's not exactly easy, to not talk to someone, anyone. So if they want to talk to me about my sister, ok, I guess. Even if it's *El Tenjano*, I guess. Even if I'm better than him, even if it's only by a little and he doesn't quite act like it, but I know he knows and he knows I know he knows. And even if he doesn't really know, even then. Fine.

"So what do you think?" He asks with this confidence that turns my stomach, and I don't know what to tell him.

I think about all the porcelain dolls my older sister and I broke when we were kids. Mostly me, but still. My grandmother sitting inside a cloud of porcelain dust, a hundred expressionless faces waiting for eyes and mouths and pastel patterns. Shelves upon shelves upon shelves. A hundred happy things. Polite geese, gentle mice, playful dogs. Children with fishing rods and balls and grins and birds leaping from their hands. A pink gypsy twirling a teal tambourine, slight ballerinas demurely turning their heads away from each other, a woman in a blue dress pressing her hand against her own cheek as she blushes—as if some off-color joke were assaulting her exquisitely pale sensibilities. Everything incredibly, endlessly, pointlessly, stupidly asinine. Permanent watercolor smiles everywhere, and I wish I'd shattered more of them.

"I don't know," I tell him. "How should I know?"

"Well, maybe you can . . . find out." And I think maybe we've gone off script for a moment because he's looking straight at me again. "Maybe you ask her. Find out for me and then tell me, right?" Or maybe not. Maybe this is exactly where we were meant to be.

"I don't know."

"Please." His confidence sickens me, but his sincerity catches me off guard. It seems almost vulgar. Reckless and strangely pragmatic. As if you could just draw a line between point A and point B. As if he would ever be point A in any diagram.

"I'm . . ." I should say no. "I'm not sure."

"Please. You'll do it, right? You'll do it and tell me."

And then he walks away. Really. Just stands up, smiles and walks out. Like he actually rehearsed it, and it would be almost impressive if it weren't also totally disconcerting. And now I guess I have to ask.

I don't know how many porcelain dolls are scattered about our apartment. But I do know I don't want there to be any more than there already are, not even a really high-end one. Though I also know it's nothing I have a say in. Every so often my sisters and I will get shiny, new, lacquered ones for birthdays and Christmases, and sometimes for no reason at all. My younger sister gets a girl sitting on a prairie with an enormous, bulbous bonnet that looks more to be engulfing her face than protecting it from the sun. Paula and I get girl and boy twins in white nightgowns puckering up for a goodnight kiss. My grandmother says she made them just for us, thinking just of us. But I've seen her give others away, exact copies with only slight color variations. "You're the boy, Lina. Because you are like a boy and all. And Paula is the girl, look, see? How pretty. She inherited my skin."

But maybe I don't really understand the importance of slight variations and microscopic details. I've seen my grandmother staring at a mirror, at porcelain faces, at Paula's face. How symmetrical, how pale. And I think she has like X-ray vision or something. I think she sees Italy in it, Spain in it. All these places she's never been to, won't ever go to, but clings to. The places they told her that her blood came from, and she tells me my blood came from, too—but maybe Paula's more so than mine. And she doesn't say so—but it's obvious—how she doesn't like my younger sister, the dark-skinned one, and she likes me better but not best. So my mother sticks the porcelain heads back on and hides the visibly cracked ones when my grandmother visits, and I pull off their heads and limbs when no one's looking.

But I'm stuck now, even if no one is looking. He sort of imposed himself and I'm stuck. Fine, though, fine. I approach my sister while she's blow-drying her hair.

"So . . . Paula?" The whirring of hot, spinning, metal parts and the air getting crushed between them. I clear my throat. A little louder, "Paula?" Nothing. "Paula?" Louder, "Paula!" Until she finally turns around, a sharp-shooter's focus and the red glare of the laser scope set on my forehead. "How do you feel about . . . porcelain?"

So she doesn't answer, ok. That makes sense, sure. But then, that's not what I meant exactly, and not what *El Tenjano* meant either. And knowing that and not saying anything or doing anything feels a little wrong. Not wrong enough, of course, to do anything about it. But still.

I got back to school. It's pretty much unavoidable, isn't it? Nothing said, nothing done. I can always lie to him, I guess. Something meaningless, like, "She likes them when she likes them." Or else something catastrophic like, "She loves nothing better, and no one more. Go to her." But I probably won't. I'll likely just shrug, a painted, pastel expression on my face no one can really argue with. Though, I'm actually a little worried— if I tell the truth. Not really *worried* worried, just sort of aware. I'm a little aware that my sister's boyfriend might just kill *El Tenjano* if he finds out. Which I think he might if his girlfriend suddenly finds herself with, like, this really high-end, beautifully painted, gold-leafed porcelain doll about this tall. Matías is a *blue commando*, so you know what he's like. He wears the colors on his wrist, the metal-tipped boots. He has long hair, narrow fists. I heard he set a boy on fire once. And even if Matías doesn't get to him, someone else will. Cristian, Aron, Paredes, Carlos, Mario. Someone. Almost everyone in this halfway school ended up here because someone else didn't know where else to stick them. Expelled, suspended, flunked out, or just out of sync with the system—that's my sisters and me. Out of sync after two years in *Gringolandia*. My younger sister doesn't even speak Spanish, and I barely speak. Except, Paula seems really in sync here now. Like Colombia wiped her slate clean and welcomed her back with open arms.

The real problem is how little there is to do here, though. That's what really worries me—not really *worry* worry, just a sort of general uneasiness, or whatever. We are not expressly required to go to classes, and even when we do go, lectures are seen as an expression of a cultural obsession with 'structure' and 'standardization,' so they are generally strongly discouraged. "Children are naturally curious; 'structure' only gets in their way." So we don't go, and when we go, we only just sit and talk, and when we don't talk, we just stare at each other and peel the paint off of the half-rotten plywood tables. Sometimes we play chess.

One day I decided I was going to try to learn something. I got a calculator and filled the first five pages of a notebook with a list of cosines. I typed "1," pressed on the cosine button and wrote down the results up to six decimal points. Because that's how long I'd gone without learning anything. And I didn't even know what a cosine was, only that I thought it made me sound smart and it sounded to me a bit obscene. *Seno,* "Sine." *Coceno,* "Cosine." *Seno,* in Spanish: "breast." The first time I heard the word, I imagined that *Coceno* described either a corporation or a conspiracy of breasts. So that got old fast, and since we're not expressly required to be expressly awake in the classes we are not expressly required to attend either. So I gave that up and took to sleeping on the tumbling mats beside the Ping-Pong tables in a dog pile with everyone else. That's what I do now. Just lie here waiting for my turn to play or at least pretend to wait, as if I have something to wait for. And that's the part that worries me, you know? That there is really nothing to do with your turn, even when it comes. If it comes. Absolutely nothing to compete with the thrill of chasing a kid who's stepped too far out of his assigned place, and kicking him on the head, or pissing on him, or setting him on fire when he falls asleep on the blue mats by the Ping-Pong tables.

Nothing better to do than wait for *El Tenjano* either, though. I figure he'll show me the doll before he does anything anyway. Or at least ask me, "What did she say?" Because obviously I was supposed to relay more than just the bit about the doll. Something about how confident he seemed when he spoke, and how high-end the doll was, and what that meant about him, or her, or them, or whatever. Something about delicate things and knowing who you really are. I'm not really sure, and I don't think I really care. Though, of course, either way, I didn't tell her and wouldn't. But I still wait for *El Tenjano* to come back. I make tenuous plans to tell him about the kid who got set on fire, and that puts my conscience at ease. But he never comes back. Not to me, not to school. And maybe it would have been a big deal if it had been anyone who mattered, but it's *El Tenjano,* and I'm not sure anyone really notices until Clara stops coming, too.

Clara, she matters. She's better than me and much better than *El Tenjano,* though not better than my older sister. So people notice right away, start asking right away. She has light cinnamon skin, a wide, white smile, and I heard she gets around. She's pretty, anyway. From Tenjo, sure, but pretty enough for that not to matter so much—a little, but not too much. Enough to deserve a name, at the very least. So people ask for her by name, "Where is Clara? Where'd she go?" Boys, mostly. "Why isn't she here?"

At first it's just one of those questions that bounces aimlessly between us, but soon they take it up the ranks. They walk in a group into the wooden-beam cottage that serves as the administrative building, and right away the secretaries start crying. One, and then another, and then another. The pretty young secretary, and the girl with the coffee tray, and the older accountant lady, and they all have blood-shot eyes even before they start crying, and it's like walking into a wake. It's sort of embarrassing, but also sort of touching—in a weird way. How they all gather around another secretary—one whose job I've never quite been able to determine—and wrap themselves around her as if they are trying to incubate her, or suffocate her, or something. Then I realize who the secretary being smothered is: Clara's mom. Which I kind of already knew, because someone had explained it to me, how this was how Clara could afford the tuition here. But I just wasn't thinking about it right then. Not until the other women encircled her and started telling her it was going to be ok, and how you have to put your faith in God, and that stupid thing about the closing of doors and breaking of windows, or something like that. Whatever. Because all the time I'm thinking "*El Tenjano* is gone too, right? Am I not wrong, he's gone? Right?"

But I probably should be thinking about Clara, because she talked to me to talk to me and never mentioned my sister once. And that stuff matters more when it comes from someone who matters, you know? But it's not like *El Tenjano* ever mattered to anyone, so it was no use asking about him anyway. But Clara. That's different.

Once, I remember, she came right up to me one day, because they were organizing some sort of mini soccer tournament for girls, and she said, "Be on my team, we'll win." Which if I really think about it, wasn't particularly nice, because I was good. Or better than all the other girls at least—which may not be saying much, but that's all it takes. She said it in a nice way, anyway. Like, she really wasn't better than me, or she didn't believe she was, which she was. And this after my sister had launched a full-blown campaign against her. Some clever line about her face, or her butt, or both? I don't know. I think it rhymed.

But Clara's still gone; her mom's still crying. We are all still lying face up on tumbling mats staring at a concrete ceiling, wondering if anyone else is wondering, too. A boy swings his paddle and spikes a ball right at the corner of the Ping-Pong table. "Take that!" And for a moment I think about getting up to take the next turn but don't. It's not like I knew them, not really. Just these moments. Clara standing at the top of that hill, saying, "We'll call ourselves the jaguars!" Listing terrible possible names for a team of disinterested girls who ran like they were in tampon commercials. "No! I know—the panthers." And *El Tenjano* explaining what makes a porcelain "high-end," and me, not explaining to Clara that panthers are just different jaguars.

Time is brutal. It's like this one night when a cow tried to cross over into our school's field and got tangled up in the barbed wire, and I guess it must have slipped and strangled itself, because when we came to school the next morning, the groundskeeper was chainsawing it out in uneven chunks. So we sat there watching it happen. A dirty wheelbarrow stacked with slices of meat, hide still hanging from them like the wet hem of a prom dress. That's time. A pain to watch but you do it anyway when you have nothing else to do. And it all goes real smooth until you hit a bone, or whatever.

Just like this day, when Clara finally comes back. Suddenly and out of uniform.

She smiles and blinks in glittery shades of blue eye shadow. She says she's only there to visit her mom in the office, but she spends all her time outside with the boys. We all know she only says that so the administration will let her come visit. She's really not supposed to have contact with any of us. The boys don't care though, and they tell her so. "We don't care, fuck 'em. What are they gonna do to us, huh?" They surround her as if they're afraid she'll freeze to death, or maybe she's getting too much oxygen and they inhale it out of her. "But when are you coming back for good, eh?"

I'm not sure why they ask. If I know, then they know. Doesn't matter, they ask anyway. And when she doesn't answer and a few tears begin to gather, they close the few gaps around her and promise to skip class to come visit her in town. A cherry ChapStick smile and she takes turns hugging every single boy around her. Later I hear them say they'll take turns with her, and that it actually works out all right this way—"Better with a bed." But who's to say if they really mean it. Like I said that I'd sell that guy a picture, but then I saw the way his birthmark shook and stretched, and well. Or how I keep saying I'm going to leave this school, and I'm going to leave this school, and tomorrow, I'm going to leave this school— but I don't, and I probably won't. It's like that cow, you know? It's not a thing that happens quickly, a barbed wire strangling. A rusty-hacksaw metal line and a cow slowly tangling it tighter and tighter around its own neck while it tries to reach something on the other side. It takes effort to do a thing, and it takes effort to stop.

But I'll never see *El Tenjano* again, either way. He doesn't have anyone to visit here. And I can't say I'm not glad he doesn't show up in street clothes with a gift-wrapped porcelain doll. Especially after the administration got tired of the stories we were making up, so they sent someone to say something vague but official. It was hard to believe at first, but they didn't look like they were kidding, and doesn't it make it more believable, when something is so hard to believe? *He who least runs, flies.*

Even though I've lived my whole life here—save those two little years in the U.S.—I don't actually know anything about how these things work. So the image I have in my mind is probably wrong, but it doesn't matter. It's the only one I have. Clara and *El Tenjano* sit together in a room inside a cloud of cocaine dust. He brings in the bricks and builds a fort around her while she repackages and rewraps to later redistribute. I realize, of course, the scale of the operation is all wrong. Just as I realize that at least some of many unexpelled boys surrounding Clara when she visits had undoubtedly bought directly from her. But that's not the point. In the room in my head, *El Tenjano* sets down another brick on the wall, but he brings it down too hard and the tower explodes in tiny puffs of white air that fill the room and settle on Clara's sleek black hair. Everything momentarily suspended in porcelain-white particles of illicit wealth.

They wouldn't tell us anything more specific than that. Just, "The people who need to know already know." And the people who don't can easily guess. He was the mastermind, which makes him necessarily more important, while she—the broker—necessary less. And the rest with the cash and the habit, the clientele—further down the chain. And it all feels wrong. But Clara eventually stops coming, too, and no one ever asks where *El Tenjano* went, and they draw naked pictures of Clara on the half-rotten plywood tables, and I imagine they don't ask about me either when one day I say I'm never coming back and I actually don't. I pick up and go. I sleep in the next morning, and I'm enrolled in an all-girl Catholic school within two weeks. But, if I were to tell the truth, to really tell the truth, I'd admit I would go back, if *El Tenjano* went back.

Just to see how high-end that porcelain doll really is, you know?

LA LETRA CON SANGRE ENTRA

or

The letter with blood enters.

or

The ~~letter~~ [*lesson*] ~~with~~ [*written in*] blood ~~enters~~ [*is never forgotten*].

or

Spare the rod, beguile the child.

or

"A high price to pay for pink ink."

A Dry Tree

I want to tell you about Knute Cachan.

But first, I have to tell you about Diego, the angry goat. And Pepe, the Jack Russell Terrier, and Sandra's little brother, too.

Because it was thinking about Sandra's little brother, which reminded me of Pepe, which reminded me of Diego, which reminded me of seven-year-old Knute Cachan lying on the dirt, bleeding through a rip in the crotch of his pants.

Because we used to tie Diego to the rotten beams where the wasps made their nests, and they would hover above us like the clouds of ash that would descend on our small Cali school once a month, when the nearby dump burned its trash.

Because Pepe was a small dog who'd hump me in my sleep until he'd pant his throat raw and would wheeze for hours like so many of his toys, torn and squeaker-less.

And because Sandra's little brother stopped coming to school for weeks and weeks, and when he finally came back he walked around like an old toy cowboy. Legs wide apart, knees facing out. Waddling like they do in the movies, all night rides and day raids, and fused joints and raw thighs.

As if a dog had come right up to him, Sandra's eleven-year-old brother—no wagging, no barking, no growling—and dug right into him, teeth into testicles like a trowel into fresh dirt. One straight line running between the dog's teeth and the boy's balls. As if the boy had used his penis like a fishing rod and reeled in the dog. Tugging on a peninsula of skin, on nylon string, on a rusty hook, on the floppy cheek of the neighbor's dog. Turn the reel, wind the string, pull the dog closer in, closer still. Then a jack-in-the-box bear trap. Snap. Rip. Scream. And in my mind I see him try not to pull, try not to rip it any more than it's already been ripped.

Try to bounce on his heels and follow with his hips the jerking of the dog's head as it tries to separate the fruit from the branch.

Which is exactly what happened. Sandra told us while we watched her stiff-jointed cowboy little brother shuffle away slowly from a couple of sleeping dogs.

Which is what I was thinking about when my sister told me she wanted to buy Pepe prosthetic testicles after she had him neutered, "So he doesn't feel bad when he's around a dog with balls."

Though, really, I was thinking of Knute. A blond-brown boy who lived on the outskirts of Cali, in a tiny apartment with his mom. And he was too small for his uniform, too poor for that school, and had too strange a name to ever make more than one or two friends who'd talk to him for more than one or two minutes each. And I was one of them. And I used to say hi to him quietly in the playground, and never sit beside him on school trips.

Because Knute was always last for everything—last out for recess, last to get the joke, "Knute Cat Chow, give us your pen, give us your lunch. Cachan-cat-chow, Chow-Cat-Cachan. What you looking for, eh? What you looking at, man? Cat-Chow-Cachan, Cat-Chow-Cachan. How come your mom wear those dresses cleaning ladies wear? How come you got that weird name, Cachan? How come you say it in that weird way, Knute? How come you don't got a dad, Cat Chow? How come you are last to everything, every day, all the time?"

Last one to come goat wrestling with us. Last ever to wrestle, too.

Because when you first come up to Diego, the angry goat, you have to know that he hates you already. He may not know you, but he hates you all the same. More so. No one alive that Diego wouldn't hate on sight.

He eats the discarded martial arts belts we've tied him with, and he charges at the gardener who's four times our size. And you know, you just have to know, that if you don't grip his horns tight like the handlebar of a runway bicycle, and pull on them hard and fast, like you want to crash it and crumple its front wheels against a tree, Diego won't fall, won't topple, won't scramble on the dirt like he's trying to put out a fire. He'll hold his ground, because it's what he was born to do, what his father goat did before him, and his father goat before that. And then he'll charge.

Head down, horns up, jaw askew. A goat and an upward swing—and things will snag.

I didn't see it happen. Though I should have, because I was right there, at the edge. But everyone was talking about it for days. So it was almost like I'd been looking right at it, and not looking away.

In my mind Diego lifts his head effortlessly, a perfect arc. Dirt to sky, dust to blue. Two horns like open arms and Knute caught in their grasp, a second, maybe less. Something between impact and penetration, then

Knute follows. Up and into the air like a ballet dancer, as if he'd actually planned to pivot on his crotch, on the tip of a horn and swing his head and shoulders into the ground.

In my mind I hear the horn make contact, a cartoon thud and cloth tearing. Diego knocks it out like a ripe papaya, like scratching a pool table. Eight ball leaping off the green, clean and whole. Though sometimes it's more like a piñata, a hollow blow and a paper rip, followed by a crazed crowd of screaming kids. Because I did see that part. The kids running and Knute on the ground clutching with both hands the torn crotch of his pants.

Like when my older sister kicked me hard in the stomach and I fell over yelling, "You've castrated me!" Because I didn't know what it meant, but sort of knew what it meant. Not what it was but that it hurt enough to bring grown men to their knees. Because Knute always looked at me like he had something to say, like he was always about to say it, too. Because I read somewhere that a long time ago when certain Korean children were chosen to be eunuchs the elder eunuchs would smear feces on their genitals and allow dogs to chew off their testicles. Because there is some graffiti in Bogotá, right by the stadium, that reads, "Noemi Sanin has cojones. Noemi for president!" And that's not exactly it, or all of it. But it's a part of it at least, a small but big part. You know? Like how Knute would never say anything about where his dad was, or why we never ever saw him. Just that that was where his name had come from, and how his mom had taught him to spell it, and say it, and how it had nothing to do with cat food at all.

And I was the only one from school to go to Knute's eighth birthday party, and I probably wouldn't have, had I known it'd just be me and these two other scrawny kids that didn't even stay to the end. And his mother looked at me like she knew who I was, and she thanked me for coming even though it was obvious the wrapped box under my arm was a sixty-four-piece stationery store puzzle. And she was so earnest, it sort of made me sick, and there was so much cake and so few kids, it really did make me sick. Towering forkfuls from huge chocolate slices that I ate slowly and in silence while looking around for an explanation for his foreign sounding name, or why it was that he wasn't quite like us, or just not enough like us to be one of us. Or, more likely, just what it was that he always seemed to want to say and why he never said it.

And who knows why he had invited me, or if he would have invited me back, or even why there weren't any pictures of his dad in that apartment. Because really there weren't all that many pictures in there anyway. Except one of a white clown sitting on a bite-mark crescent moon and one of a pastel tree like those on which movie Indians would hang cowboys for their crimes. Because this was all before the goat. Before I learned the Indians in the movies were like the *indigenas* in Colombia. Before all the kids started chanting something about how Knute would only ever be an uncle and never, ever, ever a father. *"Lo dejaron tío, que no'lo dejaron tíoooo. Al gallinito pio-pio, tío-ío-ío!"* Which I didn't really get. Because Knute didn't have any brothers or sisters, so I didn't think he'd ever be that either.

Because I used to sit by the soccer field in high school, watching Sandra's little brother waddle around like he had fused joints and sunburned thighs, yelling at the girls across the field to come kiss it better. And I let Pepe hump my ankle, even after they cut off his balls. Even as my brother-in-law told me what a loss it all was. How his seed could have fetched him upwards of six hundred a pop, "Because his dad was a champion, you know?" Thinking, all the while, of the electric hum of a cloud of black wasps building paper nests above an angry goat.

About the day in social studies class when we learned about the Europeans, *y la colonia.* How we weren't what we'd thought we'd been, because we didn't come from where we thought we came from. How the teacher we called *La Bruja* told us how *they* had come, and what *they* had done. *Los Europeos, los Españoles.* And she explained what slavery was, what race was, and what rape was, too. And she took a piece of chalk and told us to remember these words, "*Indígena* with black makes '*Zambo.*'" As she wrote the words on the board, "While white with black makes '*Mulato.*'" And gave us quick mnemonic devices to study for the quiz, "Remember the word because it's like a mule." As she drew a lumpy silhouette next to the word '*Mulato.*' "Because it's the baby of a horse," a big outline with large hooves and a heavy mane, "and a donkey." A little, humpbacked sketch with toothpick legs and a bowling ball head. "So it's easy to remember. See?" And we nodded, thinking we knew more or less what she meant, and more or less who was meant to be whom between the horse and the donkey. "Pay attention, because this will be on the quiz." So we wrote it all down furiously as she continued to list mixes and remixes while brushing her thick black hair out of her face and wiping the sweat of her brow. "White with *indígena* makes '*Mestizo.*' White with '*Mestizo,*' '*Castizo.*' White with '*Mulato*' makes '*Morisco.*' '*Indígena*' with '*Mestizo,*' '*Cholo.*'" And white, she said, didn't stay white if it was born in the Americas. "White born here in *nuestra tierra,*" on our dirt, "makes '*Criollo.*'"

And when class ended, and everyone burst out of the classroom into the empty lots behind the school, I sat through recess running my finger over pale, printed faces on the page and tearing into the sun-made blisters on my chalk-white shoulders with my fingernails, while just outside black wasps lay translucent-white eggs and a fatherless blond-brown boy who'd never be a father himself lay on the dirt, bleeding red through a rip in his pants.

DE TRIPAS, CORAZON

or

Of tripe, heart.

or

[*Make*] ~~Of~~ [*from*] tripe, [*a*] heart.

or

When life gives you tripe, make heart stew.

or

"Get to it."

Caraba

Behind a sliding cage gate, there is a metal door. The cage was once
smooth and impermeable-white, but now it is all peeling paint scales,
and rust, and a high-pitched screeching that makes us grit our teeth as
the caretaker slides it open. "Come inside. Quick."

I rode in the back of someone's mom's minivan for over an hour to get
here. I rested my forehead against the window and watched the streets
grow dirtier and more abandoned with each passing block. I counted the
twisted, spindly weeds widening the cracks on the concrete and bearded
men pull food from trash bags the way bears swat at salmon swimming
upstream. And I pictured myself older than seventeen; pictured others
picturing me, thinking of me as really beyond my age and beyond their
grasp. I forced myself to stare unblinkingly into the street as I envisioned
them glancing over at me and wondering, "Why does she stare so pen-
sively? So quietly, so cryptically, so sullen." Because I fancy myself very
noble and very tortured and really, truly, very altruistic.

I rest my chin on my hand, try to ignore how very itchy my new
black turtleneck really is, and I'm in the process of imagining my shadow
stretching far and long behind me as I stand in the door frame of a vast
and spacious building when it occurs to me to ask what we are actually
expected to do once we arrive at the shelter.

"Cheer them up," someone's mother says flashing an instant coffee
smile. "It is, you know. So terrible, this thing they have." She shakes her
head and tightens her grip around the steering wheel. "So terrible and
sad. We have to cheer them up. It's only right."

Behind the cage, there is a metal door. Behind the metal door,
an underpaid woman soaked in rice steam and sweat, and behind her,
fifteen to twenty HIV-positive girls. Too poor or too alone, or too much or

not enough of something to go anywhere else but here. A public project turned private space, a hermetically sealed world populated entirely by girls ages four to sixteen and their underpaid caretakers. And what we are expected to do today is cheer them up.

The minivan door slides open and we get out. The cage door slides open and we go in. Yellow-white walls, a cold tile floor, and girls scattered all around while a song plays on loop. My turtleneck seems unusually tight. I scratch my neck under the collar and a strange order seems immediately apparent in the room. I have not yet crossed the threshold when I notice four or so specific stations scattered about the room like booths on registration day. Individual, simultaneous, independent-interdependent, the raindrops' *plicks* that make a storm thunder. The song ends and someone rewinds the cassette inside the tape deck, the garbled sound of magnetic voices in reverse.

Each station is more or less divided by age group, with the youngest girls sitting in a circle drawing pictures of the same five figures on the page, slight variations occurring as crayons are hoarded or shared. Beside them another small huddle, this one more tightly packed than any other. They kneel around something, bump their heads against one another when they try to get a closer look at whatever lays hidden behind the tightly packed circular fortress. The next age group appears in charge of the oversized radio cassette player, which they use to rewind and replay one single track on one single tape, repeating the words as it blasts from the speakers, rewinding and replaying and repeating as many times as necessary—though necessary for what, I cannot yet tell. I hear the rewind button suddenly pop up loudly as the cassette reel is brought back to the beginning. One of the girls presses play and the song begins a new loop. The next group stands only a foot away. Unlike the other groups, there is an obvious leader here, directing the whole scene. "No!" she yells and breaks from a line of girls attempting to achieve perfect synchronicity. "Shake it like this, and snap, snap, snap. And shake, shake." The other girls watch her feet and hips, and they nod, the less coordinated of the group nodding a little out of sync. "One more time." Next and last a much smaller group of older girls standing almost perfectly still. They huddle together, they stare, they whisper. My turtleneck itches and seems to begin to shrink slowly.

We walked in all together, but most of the volunteers paused only briefly at the door. A beat, a pause, and then they moved right in to pick up little girls and join in the dance, as if they'd all practiced beforehand. They sat girls on their laps, asked them about favorite colors and numbers and animals, told them how pretty they were—"So very, very pretty"— and the girls smiled and shrugged as if they had their publicists whispering in their ears. But I missed that beat, I should have followed, should

have shown up for practice, or should have at least known what to practice for. But I didn't. I stood still too long. Too long to move quickly again
without drawing too much attention, and then too long to move at all,
so I just kept still as if I were a leaf-shaped insect, as if I were staring out
a minivan window, as if this turtleneck were not entirely the wrong thing
to be wearing and tugging on while a group of girls my age, or almost my
age, stare and point and whisper.

I look around; there's nowhere to sit and all the windows are barred.
I reach behind me and feel the cold metal of the door, left, right—try to
look without moving your head, without appearing to be looking, try to
look. The kitchen. I move a foot slowly, sliding it over the tiles as if I'm
tightrope-walking across trigger wires and snare lines. So I step over and
around the huddled group of girls who have now lifted their eyes from
their glossy treasure and joined in the staring contest I've inadvertently
entered.

I feel immediate relief as the kitchen door swings behind me, dissipat-
ing, momentarily, the heavy steam that fills the room before it drifts back
and fills my nostrils and leaves a trail of dew on my forehead. I strain my
eyes and see, through veils and veils of rice and onion stew vapor the
only staff member on duty stirring the contents of an enormous aluminum pot. Then I walk quickly, trying to shake off paralysis, and a growing
feeling of sheer pointlessness, or, at least, the need to scratch my red-rash
neck raw. But I haven't thought this through either. I stutter, "Help?"
Reach for my neck and feel the sunburn sting of sandpapered skin.
"Do you want any?" She doesn't look up; she stirs while steam condenses
on her forehead. "With anything, I mean." I think of the minivan, the ride
back. The objective comparative value of telling a girl she is pretty and
helping to make her food. "I can help." She stops. Both hands around a
spoon like a carnival lever, like a sword in a stone, and as she rests her
whole weight on it, things begin to bubble. "Whatever, you . . ." I try to
finish, I try to start, but she just looks like she really needs a cigarette and I
don't say anything. I just want, very badly, to buy her a pack. But instead,
I watch her wipe her brow with the back of her hand and say, "What?"
Rice, steam, the muffled beat of song on loop. "What do you want?"

She doesn't need any help. Or else I can't really help with what she
really needs. So I walk back out of the kitchen, reluctantly but firmly.
Straight lines and feigned conviction. Or at least, an urgent need to get
out of her way. I push open the kitchen door and walk out so quickly I
crash into a little girl holding a well-worn supermarket-checkout magazine. She waves her arms back like some reverse flight mechanism. I try
to catch her but her arms are flailing and I cannot get a firm hold as her
spindly legs stumble back, trying desperately to get back under her. But
it's too late. She's going to fall, and there's nothing I can do. And though
there is something she can do, she doesn't do it. She holds on to the thin,

colorful pages like they are more fragile and precious than her own life and she falls hard on the stained tile floor. I try to say something like, "I'm so, so sorry," or, "Are you ok? Please let me help you up." But nothing so articulate comes out. Barely an "Oh," and "Ah," my hands frozen before me in a futile panicked-mannequin pose.

She doesn't seem hurt, though, and she doesn't seem all that bothered either. Instead she lifts her finger slowly and points up at me, while I suddenly realize the rest of her group is staring, again, directly at me. "Are you? Are . . . ?" She stammers as someone else helps the girl to her feet, though the help seems incidental to reaching for the magazine in her hands. "Are you?" She starts again and I realize the entire group is watching me carefully, polygraph stares, and this accident begins to seem less accidental. The girl who fell, who appears to have been designated by the group to approach me, hands the magazine over and closes the distance between us. "Are you . . ." she asks, "are you her?"

The girl now holding the magazine sets a finger down on the page, and the other girls crowd around. I take a step back but catch the faint scent of steamed potatoes and can step back no farther. The girls look at the magazine, up at me, the finger on the page, up at me like pigeons watching a tennis match. "She is," the girl who fell declares, looking right at me and brandishing a triumphant smirk. I try to smile back, but these things don't come naturally to me and I can feel my face like an untuned instrument, some strings too tight, others too loose, and not a single chance to play any recognizable tune. "I'm telling you," the girl who fell pulls the magazine out of the other's hands, "see here?" flashing me a glimpse of the page. "She is."

On a worn-out page, in a worn-out magazine, there is a picture of a beautiful woman laughing and posing and looking not a single bit like me. The staples are coming loose, and the intentional gloss has been replaced by the oily shine of fingertips and thumbprints. The woman is winking, she smiles, she faux leaps across a psychedelic *Goodnight Moon* set, and her curly hair follows like a cartoon cape. Red lipstick, tight pants, a shirt half-torn, half on, finger guns aimed at something just out of frame. "She has to be."

The group's eyes follow the magazine as it's passed around from hand to hand to hand. And they look at me askew, just off the corners of their eyes, like I'm an optical illusion, a 3D image printed lopsided and in the wrong colors. The girl who fell turns the page and points at another woman similarly dressed and posed, but with that girl-band uniqueness that ensures broad market appeal. "Look, see?" The group looks around the room at the other girls who arrived with me. The girl who fell turns the page again, "Right?" And they repeat the motion, one by one, in a strange process of elimination. They argue quietly, lifting their fingers and shaking their heads like Talmudic scholars, and I catch words like a dog snapping at crumbs tumbling off the table. Something about pale skin, curly hair and "What else? Who else?" And I struggle not to scratch under my collar, clear my throat, brush back the mess of disheveled curls around my face.

I push my shoulders forward, and then a bit farther still until I hear a click in my spine, as if I might be able to make myself concave, make myself drop beneath the layers of the visible world, sweep myself under the carpet, and—fingers crossed—no one will notice the lump. But then one little girl looks at another and nods. Another two look down at the page and nod as well. Another, more tentative half-nod, and another still even more tentatively abstains, but that's enough, and consensus has been reached. So they raise their eyes in unison, straight up and straight at me. "So . . ." the girl who fell starts, "you're her."

I'm not going to think about this moment for the next ten years. Not really. Then one day I'm going to find myself clicking through a continuous conveyer belt loop of YouTube videos, five standard members leaping and dancing and reacting to animated flying heads to be added in postproduction. The making of that video, and the interview filmed after the making of the video, and the variety shows filmed in between.

Click. Click. Unremarkable beats sprinkled with inexplicable stints into English rapping. The screen will flash, I will remember the shelter and rice steam. The band members will be transported to a Maasai village in a bizarrely conceived promotional tour. *Click.* The Maasai children will somehow hone in on three words they can pronounce, and they will chant them in a loud, monotone harmony. "Love is like an electric shock." *Maybe,* I will think, *it's not too late to learn to sing.* "Eh-eh-eh-eh-eh-Eehlectric." *And dance.* "Electric shock." Charisma, hugging, smiling naturally. How to hold someone's hand through a phone call, through the moments before the award is announced or the disease diagnosed.

But not yet.

"You are her, right?" There are minutes between us—full, plump, round minutes between discussions, assertions, and this question. Whole ones to find words or gestures or excuses for the unblinking group of girls before me. Minutes and moments for words and excuses that I do not find. I glance over at some of the other volunteers; they stand in a line knowingly or unknowingly playing their assigned parts, swiveling their hips to the beat of the looped song while small girls jump up and down around them, like corn kernels about to pop. "She's the mean one," one of the little girls whispers, "see?" And the girl who fell holds the magazine up like a stone tablet for the others to see. "Yes. The scowl."

It is the nature of girl bands to have stark distinguishing features for each member. A girl band is the promise of a world without redundancies.

And I guess I do scowl. I try to relax my face, try not to think, "Scowl Spice," try not to stand so still that I might never be able to move again. But it's no use, it's been decided.

I am, suddenly, transformed. I am an unclaimed territory, so they look down at their map, and up at me, down at their map, and up at me. They point from their peaks and ships and yell out, "It's just like Amsterdam, like York! Like South Wales, like Plymouth. Birmingham, Madrid, Moscow, Paris!" They cut the hole to fit the shape, "It's a star!" Don't seem to mind a rounded edge triangle and an oblong rectangle.

I shuffle in place as the whole scene slowly dawns on me, and I notice a few pale purple bruises on a few elbows, pale yellow stains on a few shirts, and more than a few pale blue circles under dark brown eyes still staring up at me, waiting for me to finally speak. I know they won't ask again too. I have to answer now. I have to say, "Yes, I am. I will." It's the only thing left to say, and I'm the only one left to say it.

A decade later I will close the YouTube windows and lean back on a broken chair. I won't have much to go on, an approximate date and scraps of lyrics I may still remember from a looped-tape song. I will type *All-Colombian girl band song boom boom*. Nothing. A few blogs and a slew of Shakira lookalikes. I will shake my head and try again, *Grupo femenino Colombiano boom boom*. And Google will correct me, "Did you mean, *Bum Bum?*"

"Popstar," was an unauthorized, low-budget Colombian American Idol, which lasted exactly one season and was outlived by its resulting pop group, *Escarcha*, or "Glitter," for a mere a few months. Popstar's true legacy being Glitter's only hit song, *"Bum Bum,"* pronounced, "Boom Boom,"—"Boom, boom goes my heart. Boom, boom. Each time I think of you, boom, boom." A three-and-a-half-minute song with a forty-five-second chorus that is repeated a grand total of three times before a saccharine end. A song which I will be able to hum on command over a decade after its release. "Caraba boom boom, you love me. Caraba boom boom, I love you. Caraba boom boom, my heart races for your love."

As the tape deck pops out and the song restarts an eighth or ninth time, I begin to slowly realize the vast discrepancy between what they have been promised and what has actually shown up on their doorstep. That a probably well-meaning someone must have said at some point— between commercials and pills—"Wouldn't it be nice if they came by? Then they could dance with you and maybe they'd hear you sing and wouldn't that be nice? I think that would be nice." Wishful thinking and miscommunication, "Do you think those beautiful women might ever come to the shelter to see us?" And what's the harm? Who's to say? "Anything is possible. If you are very-very good, go to bed early, take all your meds? I wouldn't be surprised if they came by tomorrow." Then, even more slowly, the realization that amidst promises and reality, these girls appear entirely willing settle.

All I have to do is say the word, one word, one single, "*Si.*" And not even that. A nod would do, a slight tilt of my heavy head to send them leaping, and singing, and dancing into choreographed riots of memorized lyrics, like all the other girls here are doing, around all the other girls who came with me.

September is one of the few bearable months in Iowa. February is antibody-white. July is hallucination-red. May is tornado-green. But September is tired of summer and unprepared for winter, and it curls dark yellow like the corners of a page left too close to the fire. You can sit on a step at night just wearing a sweater and watch the distant doorsteps light up with the brief red of end-of-the-day cigarettes. You can simply sink into the concave darkness as if you belonged there, and hardly anyone will notice. You can, in fact, feel almost like the sort of person who might go along with things, who might dance and sing and play the part, if asked. At least the sort to say something, say anything. The kind who would not simply look away from a group of small, hopeful girls not allowed to leave their cramped apartment for anything short of a medical emergency, and simply walk away. Try not to notice a few raw scabs and yellow bruises through their worn-torn shirts while the song starts up again and the other volunteers take their places—hands on hips, bright smiles. "Ready, on three."

NEMQUETEBA

He came from the east with the sun. Though from where, precisely, no one knows. Somewhere far away, they supposed, as they watched him ride in atop an animal no one had ever seen before so they had no words for it.

"What lies east of here, anyway?" they asked each other and themselves, standing close together, bare shoulder to bare shoulder, to fence in the warmth like a wild hare, or a lost curí, or a child born strange with wild eyes and a knotted tongue. "How far east can the east truly go?"

He carried a long staff and had long, white hair braided with gray moss and silver feathers. He sat crossed-legged atop that strange beast, he drank only when it rained and ate only when the wind carried seeds and grasshoppers, and the people could not help but stare at the soles of his scarred feet and the emerald-black of his eyes as they shone pale green when the sun was highest in the sky. And they all wanted to reach out and touch the beautifully woven blankets around his shoulders as he rode into Bacatá to teach the Muiscas how to live.

And maybe because it was such long journey, he was half asleep when he finally reached the valley, so he didn't say a word, didn't move a muscle. He sat quiet and still and high atop the beast with stilt legs and black conch-shell horns, until he heard in the distance an old woman coughing. Then Nemqueteba straightened his back like something that hears the screeching of its natural predator or the wailing of its offspring. He leapt down from atop the animal and landed as lightly as dandelion seeds—as dusk, as death. And he walked through the crowd like a stone skips over water, barely touching the surface and spinning constantly as he searched for the source of the sound. Around and around, until at last he found the old woman sleeping in a bed of mud and straw, and under a cloud of frenzied gnats. "Don't touch her," someone mumbled, trying—perhaps—to explain to the traveler that this woman was one of

those people made strange by the years and the cold and the mist that
sometimes rises from the savannah and builds gnarled nests inside people's lungs and between their ears. But Nemqueteba wouldn't listen.
He set down his staff, knelt beside her, and took her hands in his. "Hello,"
he said, and, "Did you sleep well?" And when she shook her head and
rubbed her bare arms to try to summon warmth, Nemqueteba took the
blanket from his own shoulders and, holding up a corner for her to see
the painted pattern, said, "This line," wrapping it around her shoulders,
"is where the universe begins, and this one," taking the opposite corner
and wiping the drool from her chin, "and this is where it ends."

Then he turned back to the people for whom he had journeyed so far.
He began walking across the plains, picking up bits of fur, and plants,
and berries, and the people followed him picking up bits of fur, and
plants, and berries, too. Following so closely sometimes they peeled the
skin off his heels with overeager steps, and he'd have to tell them to hold
back a minute while he walked carefully up to rabbit warrens and bird
nests and reverent, white-tailed rats, which sat perfectly still while he
lifted them gently and placed them inside his knitted *mochila*.
"Can you see?" they would ask each other. "Do you understand?"
As he sat on the ground surrounded by dozens of hollowed out gourd
bowls, mixing and mashing bitter berries and sweet leaves into brilliantly
wet colors they'd never seen before. "Look," he told them, holding a rabbit in his hand, "here and here." He pointed to the base of its skull and a
spot right beside it. "Like this and this," he said, holding it by its feet over
a bowl, breaking the neck and cutting the throat. "Blood makes the red."
"Look," how to weave blankets and *mochilas* and hats. "Look,"
to make pots, and plant corn, and drink *chicha* to keep warm. "Look,"
to rule through caciques and inherit through blood. "Just like this,"
to memorize the patterns of the universe, to weave them and carve them
and dye them and dream them. "And like this," to wash in the rivers
many times a day, and to stay away from stagnant water where lazy
things lay their eggs. "Here and here and here," where to cut, and how to
paint, and when to love and hate, and make and kill, and live and sleep,
and eat and die. "Just like that. See?" Because idleness is the greatest sin.
And when he slept, lying face down atop the strange animal's ribcage,
they kept watch. All of them sitting close in a circle around Nemqueteba,
resting their chins on each other's shoulders as they listened to the large-
winged beating of his heart and talked of the eastern most part of the east
they'd ever seen, and that was enough for them. Though only for a while,
because a sustained miracle is not miraculous. So slowly the men began to
sit closer and closer, and ask that the women sit farther and farther back,
"Because, look at us, are we not closer to divinity?" And then, slowly,
some began pulling the long silver feather from Nemqueteba's head to

trade for *chicha* or salt or red dye with which to paint serpentine patterns down their arms and legs.

"Look at this one," they said to one another, holding feathers covered in pale, luminous moss. And, "Look at mine," and, "Look at that one," and, "Look, just look!" When the sun began to set and the moss began to glow, when Nemqueteba would come back leaning on his staff, barefoot and tired and covered in red clay dust. And the people continued to follow him and copy him, and measure feathers to barter for an ounce more of salt and a drop more of *Chicha,* always coming an ounce and a drop short of having enough to season and enough to be drunk.

Having had enough of not having enough, however, one day someone got the idea to cut off one of the animal's long, lacquered horns and see how much salt and liquor and blankets and oblivion that could get them on the open market. So they gathered around the strange beast as it grazed in the field, and they stared up at it. The long black legs, the long black neck, and the long black horns growing into sharp spiraling points. "How do we get up there then?" one asked, while another turned the blanket Nemqueteba had made for him into a basket so he could gather stones. "Or do we get it to come down instead?" As yet another approached the animal slowly. "Gently now, tap it there, right there. Just like that." Measured steps and held breath. "Yes. That's it." They tapped the animal gently on the side as they had seen Nemqueteba do a hundred times before mounting it. "Now what?"

And the one who gathered stones suddenly let them fall back to the earth, while the animal slowly came down and laid its angular head on the ground like a gift at their feet.

It looked almost small stretched out like that, its face against the earth as if it wanted to hear the kicking of something growing beneath taut dirt, and it didn't even see it coming, how the man who'd gathered stones walked straight up to it holding an enormous rock over his head.

The others didn't move, didn't speak. Though later they would claim that they had—ardently, feverishly, desperately tried to stop the man from arching his back as if he were a bow and a great force were pulling back his string. "It'll never work, you'll miss," and, "What are you thinking? Are you thinking? Think this through!" Failing at last, but trying nonetheless, to keep the stone from falling, and chipping, and crushing the animal's eye sockets in a single strike.

"We tried," they'll say. "We told him." Though they did not and had not. Not when the animal had begun howling and screeching and wailing, half-blind and wholly desperate. Not when it had raised itself and bucked frantically, and not when it began swinging its head from side to side as streams of black blood spilled down its muzzle. Not when the animal kicked a child and broke its spine; not when it stumbled into a ravine and broke its own.

"What now?"

Now comes Nemqueteba from the field, covered in clay and gold dust. "Look," he'd said, carving the mold for a nose ring and one for a two headed turtled. "Look," pouring in the gold and throwing the clay mold into the fire. Then, "Where?" To the men panting and pointing back to the town where they'd just been. "What do you mean with a rock?" As he ran through the field and through the town, through the tall grass and toward his fallen steed. Then he knelt beside the still-warm body of the still-unnamed animal, as it lay crumpled at the bottom of a red ravine.

He reached out and ran his hand down the animal's long neck. Warm sweat and the palpable edge of broken bones trying to cut their way out. Nemqueteba stayed beside the animal all that night, and all the day after, and the day after that, and when Nemqueteba didn't rise on the third day, they began to worry.

They tried raising him themselves, but he was set in place as if with nails and divine appointment. They tried pleading and begging, setting down food before him as he had taught them to cook it, and a beautiful golden snake as he had taught them to carve it. And when that didn't work, some came down on him like hail, and pulled scraggly gray feathers out of his hair, ripping handfuls of white tresses and tufts of feather-beard, just to see if he was still breathing, still thinking—still Nemqueteba, still sitting still in a cloud of frenzied gnats. But he did not move. He sat motionless and expressionless, and he said nothing. And when the flies and birds and rain began to peel back the animal's flesh—skin and meat like faded patterns on old cloth, bones like sunken cities being raised—the people thought it would only be a matter of time before the white-haired man was nothing but white bones, too. And they started telling stories, of how he'd arrived from beyond the east on an animal no one knew what to call, and how he'd taught them how to mold clay, and dye thread, and weave blankets. How he'd taught them who should reign, and how only men should. And maybe because there were so many stories to tell about Nemqueteba, only a few noticed how the old woman, whom the mist had made mute and strange, walked through the crowd and knelt down beside him.

"Don't touch him," someone whispered, as she wrapped a blanket around his bare shoulders and patted him on the knee and spoke for the first time in years. "It's ok," she said. "S'ok." Smiling at Nemqueteba as if she had known him long ago in another life and land. As if she'd pulled him out of a lake as an infant, as if she'd carried him on her shoulder through a flood or an unlit universe. As if she were the mist weaving gnarled nests inside his lungs, and then the man who came with the sun finally rose. "S'ok," she said again, placing his staff back in his hands. "S'ok, s'fine." Patting him on the arm and pulling the blanket tight around his shoulder. "S'ok," she said, and Nemqueteba nodded. He held her hands and said that it couldn't be like it was before, that he'd had to change it and it couldn't be like it was before, and then he said that he'd be back, he promised, and she smiled at him as he walked out of Bacatá.

And because they all tried to follow Nemqueteba as he marched west-ward with the sun, no one saw the old woman paint the tall grass stale-blood brown as she dragged the carcass by the horns to the edge of the lake. No one saw her build an altar with the bones of the unnamed beast and whisper into it, "This is the beginning of the universe." And because none can keep up with the strides of a god, they followed as far as Soga-moso, where Nemqueteba slipped on some moss and left a footprint on a stone where rain still pools and mosquitoes lay their eggs. "And this, where it ends."

¿DESDE CUANDO LE TIRAN LOS PAJAROS A LAS ESCOPETAS?

or

Since when do they throw the birds at the shotguns?

or

Since When do they [did] throw the birds [start] at the shotguns [shooting back]?

or

A place for everything, and everyone in their place.

or

"But the center cannot hold us."

The Peach Orchard

A boy climbs a wall. He is alone, and he knows it as he reaches for peaches and plums. But they are too far from the wall, and this is the wrong wall to be climbing anyway, though he does not know this yet. He kicks his legs over and jumps down; bits of paint and brick follow, a wreath of broken brick and a boy in the middle. He rushes over to the nearest tree, the one loaded with small, yellow peaches. A foot on a stump where a branch was cut down and the front of his shirt turned inside out to make an improvised pouch. Green and yellow peaches on a cloth basket and translucent sap dripping from severed stems.

My father is not a particularly nostalgic or talkative man. He is not a man of expressed sorrows or sudden stories. He grew up in a small town in Colombia, and most of his tales revolve around the breaking of windows and stealing of horses. But then one day, from under the shadow of his favorite stolen horse story, he told me this one. About a boy who climbs a wall hoping for peaches and plums. And then he says, *Que pesar, pobrecito.* "What a shame, poor boy."

The sun sets slowly. A half-light through a sky made of milk skins and the sounds of footsteps approaching. Then yelling, a man between the trees that startles the boy and makes him rush for the wall while peaches fall from his shirt, like crumbs behind him. He is alone, and he knows it, and it's hard to climb one-handed. He holds his shirt against his stomach with his left hand and grips the edge of the wall with his right. He kicks at the wall the way a locked-in dog scratches at a door, until he manages to lay his body across the edge, one leg over, then another. A few more peaches sacrificed in the escape, a few others crushed between his body and the top of the wall. He clutches the sharp brick edge to keep himself from falling and accidentally cuts his hand. The light drains from the sky as he rights himself on the wall's edge, mumbles swear words, and licks blood mixed with dust from his palm. Then a sound like hollow thunder.

The guard stands beneath a tree holding a warm rifle while the wind gently slides over the leaves. Then one more sound. The painless thud of a boy hitting the ground. Warnings were uttered, loudly enough, the guard thinks, though clearly not loudly enough to be heard while kicking at a wall and panting for breath. The child is dead. A wreath of scattered peaches, a gathering crowd, and a body facedown on the dirt.

"I heard them talking, the town's people." My father recalls the event with the sober punctuation of unelaborated fact. I fill in the holes—the wind is mine, the cut, the sky, the warmth of steel. And he channels the crowd. How they kept saying what a pity it was and how the boy only had a little bit of fruit with him when they found him, "Over there, face-down. By the wall." And again, "*Solo unas cuantas pepas,*" and I begin to wonder if it might have been less of a pity if he'd been hauling greedy bounties in sacks and wheelbarrows. "The people, they just kept saying it—'what a pity' and 'only a little bit of fruit.'"

But maybe the facts are enough.

A boy climbed a wall. He stole fruit from a private orchard and was shot for it. The guard did not mean to kill the boy. It was a mistake. Something in the leaves and the light, and what are the odds that a single piece of metal would find a single vital organ in such a wide world filled with so many trees and walls and unripe peaches and bodies full of nonvital parts. There is a chance the bullet was only a nudge and the ground did to the boy's neck what stampedes do to eggs in fallen nests.

"Then they stopped talking about the boy, and they got angry. They said they ought to kill the guard who'd killed the boy."

I'm not sure why my father told me this story.

In high school I was once asked to do a report on the *Bogotázo* riots of 1948, the frenzied bouts of unrestrained brutality that burnt down more than half my city and that officially inaugurated the period of Colombian history knows only as *La Violencia*. The assignment required that I should find a "firsthand account," so I asked my father to drive me to his father's home in *La Esmeralda* so I could ask him what it was like to watch the world burn.

My grandfather is not a very social man, not an expressive man, not a talkative man. I always imagine his tongue like the circuitry of a bomb. Something not to be jostled or moved unless completely necessary, unless diffused, unless drenched in beer and whiskey and *guaro*. So I sat across from him with an opened notebook and pen and watched him take one amber sip after another while the light came into the room through dirt-yellow veils and then out again through the cracks in the walls, until he was ready to speak. "I don't know anything about that," he said, and I wrote it down just to have a reason to look away. "I was here, and that was there, and it's a big city." Again, while he poured more whiskey into his glass. "I wouldn't know anything anyway. How could I?" He drank it down as if to keep himself from drying up.

"Are you sure?" I watched him refill his glass. "Nothing at all?"

"Well," he said, "April 9th, 1948, there were riots." He recited an awkward assortment of commonplace facts: "Mariano Ospina Pérez was president, I think," and, "It was that boy who killed Gaitán—he started it all." And, "They were savages. They broke everything, and what was left they burnt. This is all written down; I don't have to say it."

A pause. The awkwardness between us and the light collecting between windowpane and veil. Another sip, a long one, and, "I had a friend in the army back then, though, he saw." He set down the glass and reached for his lighter. "They sent him to the rooftops," he said and motioned with his hands as if he were holding a rifle. "While the crowd was down there ripping up Bogotá," he aimed it at the veils, and then at me. "He told me later, about the orders that came through the radio that day."

In the 1940s Bogotá was not the sprawling, irrevocable empire of concrete and weeds it is today. It did not climb the mountainside with the improvised tin roofs of unofficial neighborhoods, nor did it tick with the deliberate violence of the eighties and nineties. It retained, for a moment, a certain sepia symmetry and temperate weather enthusiasm. Then came April 9th, 1948. Most photographs of the day capture one of two moments: the smoky horizon of rising flames, or the broken brick trail left in the riot's wake. Some, however, catch something between the two: people throwing themselves against the walls of buildings and houses, gutting the city with crowbars and hammers and bloody fingertips. As if there were forgiveness, gold, and a cure for madness buried under the concrete. As if the real city lay just beneath, and the shops and homes and liquor stores were only colorful paper, ribbon and tape meant for ripping and tearing.

The glimmer of an empty glass and a cigarette between my grandfather's lips. The faint flicker of that sharp glare that used to make so many tremble in his sight. "Kill the dogs," he said and lit his cigarette. "That's what they told him. On the roof, that day, through the radio."

My grandfather is ill now and, consequently, also sober. He vehemently denies ever saying anything of the sort, or knowing any such man. "I don't mix with the military element." And, "It was that boy who started it all, that's all I know. That boy—what's his name—he killed Gaitán."

The boy was Juan Roa Sierra. A man, technically, but maybe only technically. The last of fourteen brothers and sisters, born half a block from the birthplace of the man he would kill on a Friday afternoon in April.

Roa Sierra sits on the sidewalk on a Friday morning in April. Thinking of reincarnation, he lets his head hang between his knees. Or else he leans against the wall anxiously with a gun in his pocket, thinking of Jorge Eliecer Gaitán.

He is twenty-six and already eight of his thirteen brothers and sisters have died, while another rests his head in an asylum in Sibaté. And he usually feels it, all this death and madness, close to his chest and deep inside his skull. But not today. Today he wakes up with something to do and the look of a man certain to do it. His mother, Encarnación Sierra, makes him breakfast, pours him coffee and worries—as she always has, though perhaps a little more today. Because she can see that this boy, the last of her sons, who has so far managed to escape death and institutionalization, is slipping out of time and mind.

She has seen him mumble to himself while staring at the mirror. She has watched him sit before his own reflection for hours and hours, tracing the outline of his face with his finger as if he were connecting dots and waiting anxiously to see what image might emerge. She has heard him call out the names of Colombia's founding fathers as if he had just spotted them through the blur of a shuffling crowd. And then, she has heard him call back.

Bolívar? Her wide-eyed boy says to the mirror and then straightens his back and pulls back his hair in fistfuls. *Yes.* Then again, slouching and trembling and staring in disbelief. *Santander?* As if he were a deep well where every founding ghost lies trapped. *Yes, yes. It's me, I'm here.* And his mother has begun mumbling to herself, too. Rosary to her lips and whispered prayers.

But nothing comes—no answer, no cure. So she continues watching him watch himself, continues to miss what is to him so clear. Across the mirror national heroes stare back. He sees the irrefutable marks of reincarnation the way parents see themselves in the yet-undefined features of their newborns. He is Gonzalo Jiménez de Quesada; he is the general Francisco de Paula Santander. He is leading the charge for Bolívar against the Spanish Royalist forces come to take back their so-called colonies. He raises his fist in the reflection and sees himself in another's skin, yelling phrases straight from the general's mouth. "No man is unnecessary!" He tries to comb his hair to match the portraits. "Circumstance alone makes a man useless, or useful." But his hairline has not yet begun to recede, and he cannot replicate Santander's noble and expansive forehead.

On this morning Gaitán walks right past Roa Sierra. He hardly notices the young man looking into a little hand mirror the way lost sailors look into their compasses. Roa Sierra may be surprised at this. Shocked, even, that everyone in the street has not yet mobbed him, put him on their shoulders, and marched him right into the presidential palace. He feels the weight of reincarnation grow heavier with each passing hour, while his features fade into those of the dead general Santander. Regardless, Roa Sierra notices Gaitán. He has been, after all, waiting for him. And it's safe to assume that at this point Roa Sierra tightens his grip on the cheap gun in his pocket.

As Gaitán approaches the doors of his law office, he may remember he has an appointment with a Cuban student later, one Fidel Alejandro Castro Rus. He has his name jotted down on the schedule, three o'clock, but nothing on the particular business Castro hoped to discuss with the leader of the Colombian liberal party. Or perhaps Gaitán thinks of that young man, Roa something. The one who came not long ago to his law office to ask if Gaitán himself could not make the government find him a job somewhere. Because, he'd told Gaitán, he lived with his mother, and his siblings were dead, and there was a woman also, and a daughter with that woman, but no job anywhere. It is possible. Gaitán, a few feet away from Roa Sierra, wonders why he seems so familiar and remembers suddenly how he had turned the young man away, because he'd had a march to arrange, a speech to write, and what could he do anyway, unelected as he was?

Though, it is just as likely that the cool breeze of a gray Bogotá afternoon reminds Gaitán of nothing at all. This is not any particular day: it is a season of planning for a day when he might march into the presidential palace as the rightfully elected leader. So it is hard to tell one day from another. A spinning carousel of mornings and evenings and nothing but the notion that they are adding up to something more than themselves. So Gaitán has no reason to think of how his daughter likes to sit in the back of his Buick and point at birds out the window, puffing their chests and singing odd songs. No reason at all to think of family, friends, death, or irony at the precise moment the gun goes off.

Three distinct, short, sharp bursts of noise that echo through streets and ear canals, though Gaitán is unlikely to differentiate one spinning piece of metal from another. Then one burrows through the back of his neck and differentiation becomes irrelevant. The first sound has triggered an automatic reaction: Gaitán has begun turning toward the source of the sound before the last bit of metal burrows through his neck. And he is spinning now. Bullets like puffs of air on a pinwheel and a man turning as fast as he is dying. A witness in the street will later report seeing his arms go limp, his knees go limp, and the man who would be president collapse face up on the pavement.

Roa Sierra does not hesitate. This was the thing he had to do, and now he has done it. So he lurches forward, stepping around the fallen man toward the Avenida Jimenez, looking back only once to send out a final bullet into the air while a crowd gathers around a still-dying Gaitán.

A man across the street will later recall seeing one man run and one man fall. "I will remember it my entire life," he will tell reporters and writers, "standing there, not knowing if I should chase after the man with the gun, or go to the one that'd been shot." For a moment he does nothing. He simply watches one man disappear down the street like a skipping stone, while the other lies still on the pavement like something sunk at the bottom of a lake. And that is when he decides the man who ran could not be caught. So he crosses the street, leaps through traffic, and kneels beside the fallen man, while another witness cradles Gaitán's unconscious head in his lap, and sees for the first time the dying man's dark skin, broad forehead, and sleeked-back hair, and realizes he knows the man who is bleeding out before his eyes.

The man who reached the body first looks up at the man who has just arrived. He does not know this man, and his hands are stained with blood, but he looks at him as if he did, and he says, "I think they killed Gaitán."

In the absence of a specific noun to hold blame, Spanish resorts to the tacit *they*. *Mataron a Gaitán.* Before long the radio will repeat the pronouncement. "They," we don't know who, or we all know who, or does it matter who, "killed Gaitán."

Though the vagueness is not necessary. Roa Sierra leaps wildly through quiet streets with the revolver still in his hand. Two police officers apprehend him almost immediately. They take him by the shoulders and shove him against a wall. They take his gun and walk back toward the screams. *They* should be *he*. But that's not what it feels like to the crowd, so it's not what they say. *Mataron a Gaitán.* There is conspiracy in the sentence, the implication that Roa Sierra is more trigger than trigger-man. And there is plenty of reason to conspire, too. There are communists in the crowd; there are oligarchs in office; there is complicity in both and either of the established parties; and there is an official political police dispatching opposition members and leaders with singular impunity. But their rage is like a stone tied around their necks; it drags them down to the bottom where ears ring and reason drowns.

It will all be written down vaguely, and no one will clarify.

Gabriel García Márquez will write about this moment in his memoirs. He'll try to explain it, make sense of it. He'll backtrack two months before the murder, to Colombia's "March of Silence," and he will call it "a parade of mourning for the innumerable victims of the country's official violence."

February 7th, 1948. A silent crowd of more than a hundred thousand people moved through the streets like a mute tide. The sound of cloth resisting wind, footsteps, pigeons—nothing more. They didn't shout, didn't talk, they barely whispered. They filled the width of the streets, shoulder to shoulder, close enough to feel each other's breath on each other's necks and occasionally step on one another's heels. Then they reached the cobblestoned heart of the city, the Simón Bolívar Plaza of Santa Fe de Bogotá. And they stood quiet, still, organized, and fed up while they waved their flags and watched Gaitán carefully, as if his features hid traces of dead generals and liberators.

Red flags for the liberal party and black for a shared mourning. Because people in the cities kept losing their jobs over political affiliation, and out in the country they were cut down by waves of bullets and swinging machetes whenever they stood in the way of the party or corporation in power. The memory of *Las Bananeras* was still fresh in their minds, and by 1947, under conservative rule, over fourteen thousand had died in altercations and at the hands of the conservative police force. By late 1948, however, when Gaitán's death inaugurated the official violence, the number would surpass forty-three thousand and give birth to the first organized guerilla groups, sparking a fire that still burns today. And García Márquez will have to move from the destroyed city of Bogotá to Cartagena, where he will begin to write in earnest.

But not yet.

Now the mob moves through the city with purpose and practiced steps.

They still remember black February. The flags and the silence and Gaitán with his arms outstretched like Christ, saying, "Today, the capital of Colombia has witnessed a historically unprecedented event." People remember the air, warm with their breath and anticipation. "People here have come from every part of the country . . . to the Simón Bolívar Plaza, cradle of our liberties, to defend their rights." Gaitán spoke against the United Fruit Company, against massacres, against explicit and tacit cover-ups, and the image of a frozen moment of temporary immortality began to crystallize.

"Mr. President, you—a university man yourself—must comprehend what the discipline of a political party is capable of, when you witness how it can subdue the laws of collective psychology, to express emotion in perfect silence." Flags, and crowds, a stillness, and a dark-skinned man born in a neighborhood called "Fallen Aristocracy," speaking of peace and reform from a painted balcony. "There is no applause to be heard here: only the waving of black flags!"

The police officers round the corner with Roa Sierra in hand and they must see it already, the riots that will follow, as the crowd swells and men dip their handkerchiefs in Gaitán's blood.

The shoeshiners come first. They stand in the way of the officers, forming a wall, and then they try to rip Roa Sierra from the officers' grip like a piece of ripe fruit from a branch. Roa Sierra feels himself grow cold as night and pale as bone. He tries to hide behind one of the officers, but there are as many people in front as there are behind, all of them waiting for their turn to try to shake life off the branch. To hurt Roa Sierra as they feel hurt by him. So the officers pull their prisoner away and try to reason with the wall of shoeshiners, using words no one will care to write down. "Please step away, please let us pass. We have him, we'll see to it. It's done, he's caught, leave it to us now." But it does not matter. The wall is deaf, and the shoeshiners swing their fists and shoeshine kits at a trembling boy while the officers try to shield him with elbows and shoulders. A punch lands on the side of Roa Sierra's face; another graces his chin; another lands between shoulder blades, and still another on his chest. Then the tip of someone's boot strikes an ankle, and the boy feels shivers running up his shin and up his spine and he nearly falls. The officers stand on either side of Roa Sierra, gritting their teeth, holding the boy and trying desperately to circumvent the wall. They move to the left and then to the right, and a shoeshiner, seeing an opening between their shuffling, lifts his shoeshine kit high above his head and even higher above Roa Sierra's.

Most likely Roa Sierra has no idea where he has been hit or with what. It is also possible he does not know why he has been hit. But soon his vision will blur, he will feel heat emanating from his head and blood dripping down his shirt, and reasons and objects will become near irrelevant details.

The second swing is clearer and louder, and there is no confusion. A hard surface with a splintered edge to the side of his face, and he feels it in his teeth and the base of his skull and the pit of his stomach, though he does not understand that the mob feels it even deeper still.

They know they can do it now, so they begin to deal blows confidently. They kick him, punch him, spit on him, they lift their shoeshine kits and bring them down hard against him as if he is something that can be demolished and broken through. A man will report seeing a ten-centimeter gash leaking steadily across Roa Sierra's face mere moments after the officers had turned the corner into the street were Gaitán lay bleeding.

The officers struggle to find a place to hide Roa Sierra until the crowd settles down. They try a little Kodak shop, but it is either too small, too narrow, or packed too tightly with people wanting to beat the boy's life clean out of him. So they drag him through the sidewalks once more while the crowd shouts, "Stab him! Stab him! Stab him!" They drag him through a sliding metal door and into a pharmacy, where they find momentary respite. The crowd grows thick with rage. They shout at the police officers to let them have the boy, stab the boy, kill the boy. They yell as if they are hungry for him, as if they are sick with something that can only be cured by his spilt blood—like the officers are deliberately letting them die by keeping him from them.

What does Roa Sierra think about in this moment? Is there a mirror somewhere in the pharmacy, a shiny surface perhaps, where he might catch a glimpse of himself—the cheap grey suit, the gash on his cheek, how untidy his hair has become? Does he forget how firmly he is being held for a moment and try to put a finger inside the gash to see if there are *libertadores* and *generales* buried under reincarnated skin? Or, at least, to see how deep it goes?

Does he brush his hair forward like his former self, the general Francisco de Paula Santander and brace for the blow of the royalist force's muskets? Does he look at the glass on the counter and see himself in full uniform once more, a hand on his sword, a boot on the field, and Santander's words on his lips—his own lips, his own words, and his own voice, too? "Who is the emperor or king of this new empire?" Or does the illusion fade in? "A foreign prince, perhaps?" In the roaring of a crowd that pleads to be allowed to rip him to pieces, "Better cruel disillusion, than pernicious uncertainty." Or has he already accepted what must follow the murder of a man who promised them that they were more than themselves and deserved more than they were given?

In the meantime Gaitán continues to die. He bleeds while a man reaches to take his belt and another yells not to lay a hand on him. They try to hail taxis and cars but they all drive by, slowing down only momentarily to see the last moments of a dying man. He moves his lips as if speaking, or trying to speak, but he says nothing. His eyes remain open but glazed over, more a simulation of life than a sign of it.

Not too far away, prominent heads of state, secretaries, and generals from all over the continent, in their uniforms and suits, gather in the Ninth Pan-American Conference that would soon become the Organization of American States. In a neighboring city someone tucks away a copy of yesterday's paper, thinking nothing of the headline, "Gaitán is a leader in agony's trance." Though Juan Ortiz Marquez, Gaitán's close friend, may remember the stumbling moments after the March of Silence. A final murmuring and rumbling after the quiet, black and red flags were lowered and wrapped around poles while Ortiz placed his hand on Gaitán's shoulder. "Jorge Eliecer," he said as the crowd dispersed, "*they* are going to kill you." In Sibaté, Roa Sierra's brother sits in a room hearing trumpets no one else can hear, while boys in towns all across the nation steal unripe peaches from private orchards, and finally a car stops for the fallen Gaitán.

So they lift him into the vehicle and lay him across the back seat where he bleeds into the upholstery. Cars are small, and only a few can follow, and the crowd watches the taxi drive away toward the Clinica Central on Twelfth Street in utter silence. Then those who remain shuffle aimlessly around the room; nothing is certain in this moment and someone suggests the possibility of a political sleight of hand. "What if," he says, "what if they changed him between the run and the return and have brought us not the guilty man, but the one *they* want us to kill?" The idea will survive and become decades' worth of books, theories, and articles, but it will have no real life in that very moment. Gaitán's body is gone, the crowd is directionless and frenzied. With nothing to stare at and nothing to do, they dip their handkerchiefs in his blood, and they turn to the pharmacy.

The shouting rises and blends with the weeping and the failed speeches meant to sway the mob, and the crowd tries to pry open the sliding doors of the pharmacy with their bare fingers.

Inside the owners eye the officers and the man they've brought with them. Roa Sierra may stand trembling in the middle of the room looking into a little hand mirror or in a corner staring at the shiny metal edge of the counter like the space between the bars in a prison, while the officers watch the shoeshiners beat their kits into splinters against the sliding doors. One of the owners takes a step toward Roa Sierra, and outside a man yells to raid the hardware stores for crowbars and hacksaws. The most dangerous thing about the cowering man, the owner might think, is that dripping gash on his cheek, and there may even be a momentary impulse to wipe it clean.

Later people will point to this moment as evidence of Roa Sierra's guilt and a justification for what followed. The young man's almost-translucent skin, his incessant shaking, eyes opened so wide that it seemed like they could have slipped out of their sockets, and how he looked at a pharmacy employee who slowly approached him and asked, "Why?"

Maybe Roa Sierra wants to tell him something about the burdens of reincarnation and the trouble with linear time. Perhaps he thinks in his former words, "If I had taken another path, those who commit this calumny today would be commissioning my portrait." Likely, however, the blows he has already suffered make the whole scene fuzzy and incomprehensible.

Still, the employee must know, so he presses him again: "But why did you do this?" Why kill Gaitán? Why on a Friday? Why on the street? Why with a 34-caliber Smith & Wesson? Why three shots to the back? And why run, where to? Why? "Tell me who sent you to kill him, because right now, you are a lynched man."

And while the officer places a call to a station where no one will answer, Roa Sierra responds, "Oh sir." He stands in the corner of a stationery store, looking nothing like *El General* Santander. "There are powerful things that cannot be said."

Because the Ninth Pan-American Conference is taking place only a few blocks away, the city will be full of reporters to jot down these words later, which will sometimes be attributed to the officers and sometimes to the owner, and which will always end with Roa Sierra looking up to the ceiling and begging *la Virgen del Carmen* to stop the unstoppable.

None of this, of course, matters yet—only that metal can bend, and gates can give, and officers can fail to protect their charge. It only takes seconds, too: a few slip past the officers and grab Roa Sierra by the hair and the sleeves. He tries to kick and buck against them as if he thinks he might yet manage an escape, so they grab him by the collar and by the ankles, and start to drag him out of the pharmacy. But these men don't know that Roa Sierra is not alone in his skin; he has fallen patriots' blood in his veins, and he is not ready to fall again, not just yet, so he shakes and bites and kicks, and he thrusts his heel into one of the men's noses, and for a second he watches them retreat.

Roa Sierra stands up and steps back from the mob now shouting that they will pull him apart limb by limb. He looks for an escape, a weapon, a crack in the wall through which to slip. But there's nothing except the counter, and soon his moment has run out. The men are back on their feet and ready to strike again. Blood on this one's upper lip, and red spatters on that one's shirt, and all with something as ancient and desperate as hunger in their eyes.

So Roa Sierra takes a few quick steps toward the counter, places both hands on the glass, and begins to jump over it, noticing, likely, how the glass shakes under his weight and reflects back his image. One more glimpse of Francisco de Paula Santander before the mob catches him. "Between gallows and glorious death, there is no real choice to be made." One more time the sound of a faraway voice in his head and the sound of trumpets. "It was my duty . . . and if for this I am called enemy of the liberator, then so be it!" Halfway between a mob and a brick wall, between Roa and Santander, between this incarnation and the next, between everything and everyone and everywhere and nowhere, the glass suddenly gives, and Roa Sierra crashes through the counter and into the floor. One final yelp and a young man in the middle of a wreath of shattered glass.

He is not quite unconscious, but it does not matter anymore. Neither he nor Gaitán will ever rise again. The shoeshiners have already taken things off the wall and up from the floor. They hardly know what they are holding, only that these things are heavy and solid and edged, and Roa Sierra does not lift his arms or tuck in his head when they bring them down against him.

They strike his face, his chest, his side, and his head. They break the sockets like ice-cream cones, they crush his nose like an insect underfoot, and the body begins to pump fluid to suspend the damage and stall for repairs, as if it, too, thought it might yet manage an escape.

The bullet left the chamber at 1:05, and by 3:00 that afternoon Encarnación Sierra—the boy's mother—will have lost her tenth child. By then, too, the mob will have stripped Roa Sierra naked—except for his necktie, because you have to pull on something to drag a body. And they will shout in chaotic intervals, "To the palace! To the palace!" Once more marching through cobblestone blocks, just as they had two months prior, to stand in perfect silence listening to Gaitán's speech, "A Prayer for Peace."

The mob beats the boy dumb and blind. They beat him until his eyes are swollen shut, his mouth is swollen shut. Until he is swollen past reason and recognition. Until his teeth are gone and his ribs are splintered. Until every joint is disjointed and there is a soft sunken hole where the bridge of his nose used to be. Until his skull is soft, too, and it is like beating moss with a stick, little more than the sounds of a paddle striking the surface of the water and the occasional wet crack of something not broken all the way through finally giving way. Then they beat him some more.

Fidel Castro was there when the riots erupted. I've seen a picture of him in a jacket and tie looking both lost and at home in front of the scattered-brick outline of a former building. "There is no applause to be heard here: only the waving of black flags!"

The mob finally reaches the presidential palace, and they hold Roa Sierra up against the gates like a man trying to rub his dog's nose in its own feces. They believe the men behind the gates are also behind the murder, and they want to get their hands on them, too. Or maybe they only believe in the color red now, like a hungry dog believes only in meat. The red covering the sidewalk where Gaitán fell. The red on their knuckles and shoeshine kits. The red of the waving liberal party flags. The red pulp of their rage and that it must be emptied, must be unloaded and released, somewhere. And that this was the last place, the last direction of Gaitán's pointed finger, so why not here, after all?

But no one meets them at the gates. The president watches through the palace windows, surrounded by advisors and dignitaries, and he sends the army to shield him from his own country. Colonel Virgilio Barco will later admit to having given orders to his police force months prior to the riots, to blend into the crowds of silent marchers and Gaitán supporters and to incite them to violence and vandalism so as to justify more and more brutal reprisals from the government. And in so doing, he will also tacitly admit to having waited and longed and lusted for this moment of fire and looting. For the moment when the silent marchers would shout and wail and stampede through the city as if chased by every dark thing the abyss ever birthed. But now, when it finally comes, he hides. They hide. They pace around desks, look out windows, and lock their doors while their city burns.

There is no satisfaction to be had here. No verdict, no confession, no relief. And when this becomes clear, the mob digs its heels deeper into what's left of Roa Sierra. It is already more than one mob, though. There are three or four or five spreading quickly across the city and into nearby towns like the fires they've begun to set, and maybe someone from the military element does sit on a nearby rooftop cradling a rifle and a scope, waiting for orders to fizzle through the static of his radio. And then someone by the palace gates yells, "Crucify him!"

Do the words shock anyone? Does anyone reach for the gold cross that so many of them undoubtedly wear around their necks? Is there any sense of irony as the chant rises and fills the plaza? "Crucify him! Crucify him! Crucify him!"

Is the mob thinking of Gaitán at all in this moment? Of Jesus, Bolívar, Santander? On which side of the fence would *el General* or *el Libertador* have stood had either man lived to see what their country would become? "The time of your liberation has arrived!" Does the mob remember the silence of February as they descend on the palace's fence to rip it up and build a cross? Or is there only present time? The immediacy of fire and starvation.

Some one hundred and thirty buildings burn and five thousand people die during the day that would come to be known as *El Bogotázo*, then over two hundred thousand during the ten-year *Violencia* that follows, and almost two hundred and twenty thousand—most of them civilians—in the throes of the post-*Violencia* violence. Not to mention the over five million displaced, twenty-seven thousand kidnapped, twenty-five thousand disappeared, eleven thousand massacred, and the uncounted raped, maimed, and forcefully recruited.

And somewhere across the city, Encarnación Sierra weeps as she reaches into her closet for a black dress. She is a *Gaitánista*, a true believer and follower of the now-fallen leader of the liberal party. So she presses her rosary beads to her lips and makes plans to attend Gaitán's funeral. In the background the radio presenter's voice trembles as he repeats the news again and again, as if he could wear truth out of fact with sheer repetition: "*Mataron a Gaitán. Mataron a Gaitán.*" And while Encarnación is laying out the dress on her bed and weeping quietly into her handkerchief, she hears the radio presenter say her son's name, "Juan Roa Sierra," and inform the public that the killer was caught and killed, and justice "at least" was served in this small way.

Gaitán had been warned, by not only Ortiz but also nearly everyone he knew. Because it was clear to everyone: "*They* are going to kill you." But he refused bodyguards and security measures. "Not me," he said. "They won't kill me, because the people are my insurance. Because my murderer knows that he is killed the moment he kills me. That the oligarchs know the moment they kill me the waters of the country will overflow and it will be fifty years before they return to their course and anything to normal."

Though he is also the same man who a few months earlier said to his friends, "If they kill me, avenge me."

Knowing changes nothing. Gaitán knew they'd come, sooner or later. His killer, or killers, knew it would be a spark in a paper forest. The crowd, too, knows—somewhere in the labyrinthine crevices of their only-present time—that when they kick the boy, when they drag his naked body against the stone, when they step on his twisted fingers and limp limbs, he does not feel it. Stones into an abyss, into a lake that does not ripple. If he breathes still it is only an echo of life and not a sign of it. He will be dead on the street before Gaitán is on the gurney. And they must know, after all, that the purpose of the March of Silence had been to prove that they were above violence, beyond what had already been inflicted on them. And of course they also know no one will come to the gates of the presidential palace. No one will take responsibility; no one will acknowledge guilt, or blame, or even the absurd coincidence that Gaitán would be killed at the height of his political threat and popularity by a dazed schizophrenic boy. *These things happen, what are we supposed to do about it? They killed Gaitán!*

Gaitán refused bodyguards, Roa Sierra pulled the trigger, Colonel Barco told the police to incite riots, the corporation opened fire on civilians, the men in power watched the city burn, the radio said to kill the dogs, the boy reached for the fruit, and the mob stood outside the palace gates all the same.

Because *they* also know the city is even less guilty—the walls, the pavement, the glass panes, and the painted windowsill feel even less than the boy the mob drags by his necktie like a dead pet on a leash. They know the people who run the coffee shops and drugstores and restaurants, and they know their children and the sound of their voices when they beg them to please, please stop. But they do not stop. They gut the city. They pry her open, they hear her scream, they do not care, they pull her apart piece by piece. And while the city writhes and twists under the mob's sharp heels and mob-set fires, in the tumult someone yells, "We did not come here to steal, but to destroy."

Knowing does not stop them. It does not cure them or calm them, and they pose for photographs beside Roa Sierra's unrecognizable body.

The image is not hard to find. It is in every article and every high schooler's book report. Roa Sierra is stuffed into a plywood coffin too small for his swollen body, holding what appears to be a white wool blanket. And it occurs to me, sifting through dozens of reprinted articles on my desk and screen, that amid the chaos someone must have walked back through broken streets and shattered doors, back into an unburnt home, out of the noise, away from the destruction, and he or she must have reached into a closet or atop a bed for this one white blanket around Roa Sierra's body. A woman, man, human being amid the chaos must have.

Stepped through the rubble and between the cluster of post-riot police to cover the nakedness of a dead man.

In the photograph, men and women cover their mouths and noses with one hand while holding purses and hats with the other. They surround the slightly opened coffin and peer directly into the camera with pained faces. It reminds me of something I once read: that as President Ospina Pérez watched the mob through the palace windows, he worried—most of all—about what the cold-war-obsessed U.S. would think of Colombia. What the world would think of him—the nephew and son of former presidents, a "university man" who'd seen Paris, and London, and Louisiana. "What will," he asked, "they make of us now?" When this is what we make of ourselves.

And at first it seems trivial. But I worry, too.

"Mr. President," Gaitán said to the tide of black and red waving flags in February 1948, "at this time we do not ask you for vast economic or political treaties. Only that our country will not walk down a path that will shame us in our own eyes or the eyes of strangers."

I look at the trail of bruises and blows on Roa Sierra's skin and wonder if the blanket was brought out for him or for *them*. For one of ours dead in a box, or for those people walking past him, turning their heads and covering their mouths with white handkerchiefs. Was it one last act to cover Roa Sierra's final offense of public nudity? Or the less forgivable offense of still existing after so much was done to wipe him out? Still, the possibility remains that it was done not for *them* but for him and for Incarnación. I hold on to this. One final act of final kindness for a man out of time and mind.

The bullet left the chamber at 1:05 PM. Gaitán is declared dead by 1:55. Less than an hour between Roa Sierra's gun and the doctors' scalpels. By 3:05 the hospital is surrounded by soldiers hungry for Gaitán's body, just as the mob had been starved for Roa Sierra's. But the men around him cannot make up their minds. They debate, argue, retrace their steps, and tug on their ties. "Should we bury him in La Via Real?" one asks. "No," the others answer, "it's been destroyed." Shaking their heads in unison. "Then beside Bolívar's monument," another proposes, but again the answer is, "No. Too close to the palace. They will destroy it again." And they light their cigarettes and pace and let their heads hang with all the weight of a day that may never end. "An anonymous grave then," another suggests before knowing how many anonymous dead will be poured into ditches throughout the next fifty years. "No," the others respond. "It will make him a martyr." And while they all nod and take long drags from their cigarettes, another adds, "Not just a martyr, but not our martyr, *their* martyr, and then what will that make us?" And while they continue to argue, a much greater, subtler, and almost inconceivable fear begins to form. That all this was done by a wholly unknown boy from a poor neighborhood of Bogotá. That a great man possessed by ideology and animated by the will of the people, could be—would be—killed by anything less than a great conspiracy.

The men will find some relief in the stubbornness of Gaitán's widow. They will stand in her living room as she grips the sides of his coffin. While soldiers gather outside, dust settles on the stacks of papers in Gaitán's office, the mobs burn down the city, and they will hear her say, "He doesn't leave this house until the current government is toppled."

His daughter will write about it all in a book she will title, "Bolívar had a white horse, and my Dad had a Buick." She will write about her mother's trembling hands and the smell of ash and death on a damp night. And about the men who came into her home and dug through her living room floor to bury her father beneath concrete. Because the government will not be toppled, power will not be shared, and the crowds cannot be trusted to leave the body in the ground.

But not yet. Now she watches her mother sit beside her father. She listens as soldiers open drawers, take papers and notes and whatever else they like, and maybe she sees a brown bird out the window puffing his chest and chirping in the dark.

After the guard shoots the boy on the wall, my father stands outside the small house in Zipaquira that served as the town's precinct and jail, listening to the men inside.

The officers rest their hands on the cold walls and sigh. They knock on the doors, hear the flimsy rumble of cheap metal, and they try not to look at the bent hinges.

The tops of peach trees are visible over the orchard walls. Inside, an orchard security guard sits on a bench in a small cell. He rests his elbows on his knees, lets his hands hang limply, and stares through the bars at an empty spot on the floor on the other side. It is a small room, and he can see the officers testing the door and pushing on the walls, and he knows the mob will come for him this night. He takes short, steady breaths while the men guarding him kick the walls as if they are the flat tires of a broken-down truck. What are the officers thinking about right now? Do they remember a past life? Pressing their hands against sliding gates, feeling shoeshine boxes break and chip against metal and concrete. Or further back: to the heat of the battlefield beside El General Francisco de Paula Santander. There is a chance they've been here before. Endless reiterations of themselves endlessly attempting the same endlessly futile task. That the two guards in the jail are the same two in the pharmacy, and the same two standing beside *El General* Santander as he looks across the colonial square that would soon become the Simón Bolívar Plaza, at thirty-eight unarmed Spanish prisoners. And then, they hear *El General* sentence them to death. They may notice, these two soldiers, how their general hesitates for an instant before giving the order. They may wonder, as the men who carry out executions, what it takes to be the man who orders them. And they may even begin to see the signs of a rift between Santander and Bolívar, the first seeds of descent that will lead Santander to plot against the *Libertador's* life. Or else, surely, they can tell that their general knows that the mob can just as easily lynch the Spaniards as it can lynch him.

More likely the soldiers know that Santander is thinking about the prisoners the Spaniards hold that very second, and how probable it is that they have all already been executed. Maybe that's when the soldiers waver. When they shift their weight from one foot to the other, take off their boots and lay down their muskets so they can sit cross-legged on the dirt wondering what it means to become extensions and abstractions of a national body that is forever dismembered, until Santander shouts for them to stand up. To be men, and shoot the other, lesser men in the plaza, and in the church, and the cells, and to shoot the survivors too, and shoot them again if that doesn't do, and use their sabers if they cannot make themselves take aim. "The laws of war authorize us to destroy the destroyers," wrote Bolívar. "It is just to do with them what is customary for them to do with us," wrote Santander.

More likely than anything else, however, is that the officers in the Zipaquira jail know the boy who was shot on the wall. His mother, possibly, his brother, probably. And as my father tells the story, I have to wonder if, instead of all this, they would rather tear the orchard guard apart themselves.

If the argument they are having, really, is not more about whether they should leave the door closed to spare the man, or leave it ajar to spare the building. Because the walls were too thin anyway, the doors too weak, the mob too angry, and maybe my father was too tired too, because he never finished the story. He looked away as if through time and former selves, and I did not press him, like I do not press my grandfather in his living room, and do not expect a different ending every time I read the chronicles of *El 9 de Abril*.

I've been here before.

Gaitán's body remained beneath concrete and floorboards for forty years before being moved to the Cementerio Central in the heart of Bogotá and to the front of the Colombian thousand-peso bill. Roa Sierra's naked body remained two days on the steps of the presidential palace while the army marched in circles, locked front doors, and aimed their rifles at anyone setting so much as a foot in the direction of the palace. Roa Sierra was identified by his mother, lover, and three remaining siblings before being tossed into a deep pit of anonymous bodies while President Ospina Pérez denounced the riots on the radio and declared that Bogotá could not have and would never have done this to herself. "Foreign," he said through the speakers. "Yes, foreign were the criminal hands lifted against us that day. Not the Colombian people . . . to set fire to our buildings, stores, schools, temples, homes, and modest workshops. It was a foreign spirit . . . we stand now before a communist movement."

I'm a nostalgic sort of person, though not a particularly sentimental one, and I've only ever seen one lynch mob in my life. A breaking news rerun shown in the evening news for audience convenience. The television announcer raced through the bullet points while people joined the mob in the street and on the screen. This man had killed his wife, she told us, and killed his baby, too. The neighbors began pouring out of their houses and filling the street shoulder to shoulder to SWAT-team shield like they were trying to fence in a wild hare. They yelled at the police and pushed the cameraman farther and farther back while the officers tried to hold their ground. "No man is unnecessary." People in red shirts and dresses pressed themselves against a wall of black SWAT uniforms, as the officers tried to hold each other up and push the crowd back without pushing it down. "We are authorized to destroy the destroyers." And I watched the mob spilling over shields, helmets, and nightsticks, as for a moment they became one single, uncoordinated blur of force, and it was hard to tell who was pushing and who was resisting. "There is no applause to be heard here: only the waving of black flags."

On the second floor of the house, a man could be seen through dirty veils. He paced and peered and ran from one end of the room to the other as if he could already feel the mob digging its heels into his back and fingers into his eyes, and I watched him grow more and more frantic as the crowd grew more and more desperate to shove the officers out of the way and march into the man's home. "There are powerful things that cannot be said." Eventually the announcer would praise the police force for sneaking the man out dressed in SWAT gear. But before that, while the neighbors descended on the man's house like lead rain and literally pulled the bricks out of the walls, the announcer said that the man had had his way with his own baby girl before suffocating her with a blanket, so I cheered on the mob and whispered, "Go on. Kill him."

PELEA DE TIGRE CON BURRO AMARRADO

or

Fight of tiger with donkey tied.

or

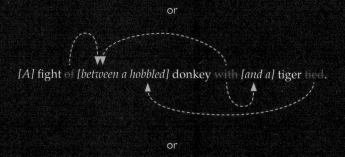

[A] fight ~~of~~ [between a hobbled] donkey ~~with~~ [and a] tiger ~~tied~~.

or

Easy as donkey cake at a tiger tea party.

or

"Shouldn't take long."

Practice

Like our first day back in Bogotá after a two-year stint in the U.S. Like this man we see by the *Autopista* under the 129th Avenue Bridge. A white shirt and a thin belt, gripping a boy by the arm with one hand and a splintered stick in the other. I am twelve, jetlagged and dazed, and so it takes me a minute to see him. First, my older sister's face. An expression rippling out from her eyes. Narrow and unfocused, then wide and sharp. Teeth gritted, fist clenched, and a quiet gasp. Then she turns away as if the wind were carrying sand. Then I turn, too. I see it, too. The man raising the stick and swinging it hard against the boy's hip. Against the boy's knee. Against the boy's thigh. And the brown-haired boy, who may or may not be the man's son, twists under the man's grip and screams only once when he doesn't seem to be expecting it. A muffled sound from his throat like something wild, mute and yet unnamed hearing the trap snap before feeling metal teeth cut the tendon, crush the bone. Then silence. The boy rubs his hip like he's trying to warm himself, clutches his knee like he's trying to keep the joint from falling out, and not a noise, not a whimper. He shudders and turns solid with tension and practice. A stick like a baton, a beat, a metronome. *Up,* hold your knee, *down,* hold your breath. *Up,* hold your hip, *down,* hold it in. *Up,* suck it up, *down,* drink it down. One second before the next strike, and then again before the next, before the next. Like dancing, or swimming—all about breathing and tempo.

And the boy hardly flinches and we hardly look. Because not looking takes practice, too, so we practice, too. The man striking the boy wants to catch a bus, so he stays. We, back at last after two years in *Los Estados Unidos*, want to eat familiar food, so we walk away.

EL PEZ MUERE POR LA BOCA

or

The fish die by the mouth.

or

~~The~~ [A] fish[*'s death comes through its*] ~~die by~~ mouth.

or

Loose lips sink ships. Mouth agape, watch the fish escape.

or

"Best to say nothing."

Drowning Lessons

The rule was this: each life raft could hold every person in our group without sinking, regardless of weight or size, all but one. Because metaphorical rafts are not bound by physics but by the arbitrary rules of mad storytellers. The game was this: Each person on the raft would then have to make a case for themselves in order to be allowed to remain onboard, to stay and survive together or else to be expelled and drown alone. "The final decision," the counselor explained, "will be made by the group. Who stays, who goes." Catholic school necrodemocracy. "We will assume there is a storm and whoever leaves, no matter how good a swimmer, will drown."

This was all explained in the shadow of an adobe convent on the second day of a school-mandated spiritual retreat. Because confinement and isolation breed contempt, and these are the loadbearing pillars of all-girl Catholic schools. So most of the time we were fine in our plaid skirts, itchy knee-high socks, and assigned classroom. But most of the time we were lying about being fine and would tell extraordinary lies about ourselves, about each other, and about what and who we were and would become. Hoping, secretly, that talking was like coughing into a petri dish, and soon our lies would bloom into this one's weight gain, that one's pubic lice, and our own unequivocal triumph over the rest. So we drifted into smaller and smaller clusters, tried to break bones with words, and when all else failed we threw metal sharpeners at sleeping classmates and stole each other's overweight boyfriends. That was when the school had to resort to calling on stained-jeaned, rolled-sleeved, bearded counselors to convince us we didn't really hate each other and ourselves.

Meaning, roughly, once a year.

So we were herded on to a bus and sent away to bucolic scenes and quiet convents for two days of marathon bonding, self-reflection, metaphoric rafts, and gore-filled Christian allegories.

"Hurry in, come on. Sit now." These things were carefully calculated. "We don't have all day, hurry in, come on."

A room full of fifteen-year-old girls at the end of a long bus ride, smelling faintly of sardines and knockoff Chanel, and a counselor in torn jeans and a ponytail telling everyone to sit down on the floor, because that is how the indigenous people used to do it. And then it began. "Listen," he said, and no one listened. The whispered rumble of pebbles rolling down an unpaved road. Again, "Listen." And again, fifty or so girls zipping and unzipping their backpacks while some of the other counselors tried to manage the volume like desperate traffic cops at a three-car pileup. "There is a dead dog."

Silence. The counselor nodded. "Dead." And the girl who always cried when we watched educational films let out a gasp.

"The dog is lying on the ground, just like that, on a wet street." He pointed at an empty spot in the room and yelled, "Look! There!" Nothing to see. Cracked tiles, dust. But he yelled again, "Look! Just look!" Some strange the-emperor-is-fully-clothed trick of repetition. "Right there." He gesticulated madly, covered his mouth with his hands as if he might vomit, and pointed again at the empty spot, this time his finger followed a trail toward his feet as if the floor were slanted and the blood raced toward him. "Oh God, there's so much blood!" I watched him shake his head and look up at the opposite corner of the room as if he had caught someone's eye. He quickly began to wave his arms dramatically as if flagging someone down for a rescue. Then he slipped out of place and character and ran to that corner to pick up the play from there. "What?" He said in a high-pitched voice. "What is that you found? Dead, you say? Show me!" And he would take a step to the right or a step to the left and change his voice, and change his posture, and say "What?!" Again, and nod again. A man playing checkers beside a wall, another drinking and humming, a child with a ball, or a hysterical woman who had to be dragged like an acrophobe to a ledge, to a cliff, to the spot where the invisible dog lay scattered like a deck of cards.

Some characters would sprint, some resist, but in the end they all plunged into the sight—a heart like a red hood and ribs like lonely trees. "Oh God, you are right. You're right, look at the legs, and is that bone?" Then he'd repeat the process, slipping in and out of personae until he had built a mob of rubbernecking ghosts around the invisible body.

Walking to the equally invisible raft the next morning, I made a list in my head of all the reasons I should live and others die. "Up ahead," a blond counselor instructed us as we approached a second group of girls sitting in a circle on the grass. "Keep going, just up ahead." Seven or nine girls maybe our age, maybe a bit younger, some definitely younger, and some maybe slightly older. "Don't stop there, we're up ahead, keep going." And as we walked on, I heard them speak of Jesus and Mary Magdalene, and about how this or that reminded them of how life had been before the convent. "Right, over there by the logs." And it was how they rounded their vowels and emphasized their consonants that gave it away. The visible invisible class lines, the ghost maps of education and ancestry.

Something like the unseen outline of a dead dog in a one-man play. The night before, despite the lack of scenery, props, and plot, the play had only gotten bigger and bigger with each repetition, and the play was all repetition. The counselor said, "Oh my God! Oh my God!" over and over, and over again. He said, "Come look!" And, "Are you looking now?" And, "Do you see it there?" And, "Careful now!" And, when one of us uncrossed our pins-and-needles-riddled legs, "Don't step on the tail? Watch your shoes!" A loud, spindly man with a greasy ponytail, leaping on the tiles and gesturing as if he were playing a demented game of hopscotch-charades. The girl who always cried, cried steadily between the gasping interruptions of breathless sobs. "Look at it, do it. Look at it now." He told us the crowd kept growing around the dead animal, larger and larger. Because no one cares about a stray dog, but everyone likes a spectacle. "Just look at those eyes, look!" he pleaded, and I did look, as if there were something there to see. Dirt-brown eyes, neither in nor out, barely eyes anymore, squashed grapes and broken saucers. "Look at the tongue, too. God, oh, God!" He drew a trail with his index finger, as if it were following the path of a flailing-fish tongue flapping away from a broken muzzle. The counselor motioned as if he might vomit, and a girl sitting at his feet ducked, because he seemed sort of lost in his play and we weren't sure how much of it was just pretend anymore.

A pause, almost-silence.

The girl who cried muttered that she was not crying for the dog but because it had reminded her of something else entirely, while outside the rhythmic creak of the insects and amphibians of the Andean moors ushered in the night. "And then!" The counselor interrupted himself, "right then, this man out of nowhere." Later, inside the convent, we'd be lead through long and quiet hallways of empty rooms offered to us for the night. Most of my classmates would choose to stay in a few adjacent rooms so they could spend the night in huddled sleepless unison. I know, because I would hear about it for weeks after, flashlights and bottles and cell phones and joints and sleepy boys back in Bogotá mumbling confused hellos through the static of bad reception. I, however, would choose a room at the end of the hallway by the staircase, realize I can count all the nuns in the convent with just my finger, and wonder, as I count, how nun recruitment works, and if they sleep in adjacent rooms too, or scattered throughout the building.

"So this man, he shows up late and out of nowhere, and then he leans in—I mean really leans in and really looks at the dead animal."

The counselor walked to the corner to illustrate. He stuck his head close, almost into the make-believe body opened like a popup book. "Really, really look." Then he straightened up, furrowed his brow, looked around the room as if noticing us for the first time, and asked, "And do you know what that man said?"

From my assigned raft I stared across the field at the circle of girls sitting on the grass around a nun. They spoke while pulling fistful of grass from the lawn. They wore oversized, secondhand sweatpants and sweaters with cartoon mice in polka dot skirts, and I imagined one of the many empty rooms inside the cold convent was filled to the brim with stuffed garbage bags of donated hand-me-downs and plump moths. "Lina, stop." Someone had tugged on my sleeve as we had walked past them. But then one of the girls in the circle had turned to the nun and said something about understanding the story perfectly, because, for example, she felt she was just like the woman in it and she was about to say something else so I didn't turn away, not right away, and the girl who had been walking beside me had to tug again on my sleeve and whisper in my ear, "*Prostitutas.*"

The counselor did one last nauseated pirouette and declared, "The man who really looked said, 'Man,' and 'Oh man, but did you see . . . those . . . teeth . . . man? Did you, man? Look at them, look how white they are, and look at those fangs, just look at them!'" He motioned to the other invisible characters in his pretend throngs, to come look, too. He ran back and forth, as if he were filling a pool with a bucket, character after character, nodding and whispering and nodding again. "I see. I do. Look, look! How white, how true! Shit man, are you looking?" There was unanimity, how magnificent and white the mangled animal's teeth, and the legion nodded.

When I looked around my own randomly selected circle of peers, I felt almost confident. I played soccer, I carried a lighter, I wasn't a picky eater. I grew up playing "little apocalypse" and had been the only one chosen to hold the cow eyeballs on dissection day in biology. I felt certain I had a chance, and it is likely my confidence showed because the counselor asked me to go first and give the reasons I should be allowed to stay and live. So, I took a deep breath and leaned forward to try to explain my list of aptitudes as clearly as I could. Background, experience, skills, and the potential long-term benefits for the group, given my survival, but before I'd even really started the girl beside me began to cry in the same panting sobs of the night before.

"Silvia, what is it? Why are you crying?"

"Because," she said drawing breath, "I," interrupting herself with shallow gasps, "don't," like she'd been hit suddenly with a torrent of freezing water, "ha-a-a-ve," all her muscles contracting at once and shrinking the alcoves of her lungs into tiny crawl spaces, "a reason." I stared confused for a moment, still holding in my mind the next point in my list, while another girl changed seats so she could console the crying girl. She rubbed the girl's back with one hand and wiped away her own tears with the other. "It should be me," she said. "I don't have a reason. It should be me who goes."

It didn't take more than a minute before the entire circle was crying as well. Before I realized the error of my strategy, and I was voted off unanimously for being the only one not to volunteer for drowning. A matter made only easier for the group when I pointed out that I was the only one with a pocketknife to which they responded that I was also the only one who had failed to console the crying girl.

It is a persistent character flaw. I take things too literally. I'm told the dog is dead and his teeth are white. I think the dog must have had an owner, because I've never seen a stray without rows of yellow fangs. I think someone should check for tags; the owner should be notified. I'm told I'm going to drown. I wonder if there was a plane crash, how we got there, where it is that we were going, and what our packed carry-ons hold. I wonder if I'm drowning in the ocean or in a lake or in the panicked snake thrashings of an angry river. If we can vote the counselors off the raft, or if I can refuse to leave, because I think I can take most of the girls. Especially the crying one. Or, maybe, if we could just tie the rafts together like circled wagons so my body won't float away, and they will have something to give to my parents if they ever get rescued. It's not the point. The dog's teeth are white. "Do you know who that man was? Do you? The man who saw the teeth, the man who really looked?"

This is the point. "Every dead dog has his white-teeth lining." Or the benevolent man always sticks his face close enough to stain red the tip of his nose. There is redemption in the staring, he says. The raft is a metaphor, he says. So I'm asked to go stand a few feet away so the rest of the teary-eyed group can finish the game while I drown out of earshot. "That man. That was Jesus."

I didn't really resist. I stood between little imaginary rafts pretend drowning in an ocean of grass and class and chance. I looked across the field at others who had also been chosen to drown, and beyond them to the other girls' raft. "*Prostitutas*." The nuns explained it all later, while they made me an *agua aromática* and my classmates slept in a pile in the stillness of a white *paramo* dawn. A very old nun ran her hand down the back of a very large white cat, wispering "S'okay, S'okay," and then said that these were girls looking to leave their old lives behind. The cat lifted its head to meet her hand while she explained that they held classes and seminars every other Saturday on the green by the convent, to explain the life of contemplation and sacrifice, and to give them a second chance.

I briefly thought the life raft exercise had something to do with the man who noticed the dead dog's teeth, but I couldn't quite piece it together, and drowning took so long and the day got so hot, I eventually just stopped trying to make sense of it. I paced for a minute and waved at the others who had also been chosen to die. Though only one waved back reluctantly, while the others did not seem to see me through their tears. Across the field the other girls talked about poorly lit motel rooms and street corners and long, quiet hallways and convents. Johns, Jesus, sweaters and habits, and the counselor with the ponytail looked to be delivering some intense and important speech to his raft.

I tried walking back to mine but was told to stay dead for a bit longer while they finished the exercise. The girl who had sat beside me and cried now trembled only a little while the others appeared to be taking turns telling her all the reasons she should live. I tried sitting down but the grass was wet. Then I tried yelling, *I'm dead! I've died, can I go home now?* But no one seemed amused except one of the other girls in a dirty wool sweater on the other side of the field.

I looked across to them again. The nun nodded as her girls told their stories; the counselors nodded as their girls cried; and most of the drowning ones were allowed back into the rafts eventually while I stood in the middle of a bright green field, imagining limp bodies being hauled out of the water, groups pulling together in coordinated efforts that would have made any counselors proud—"Ready, on three! One, two . . ." Fistfuls of wet shirts and hair and soaked rag-doll bodies at the bottom of sinking rafts. On the opposite side of the field I saw the others; there weren't that many girls in the nun's raft, but they all looked like strong swimmers.

or

Himself put in the mouth of the wolf.

or

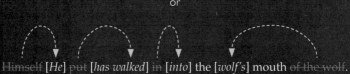

Himself [*He*] put [*has walked*] in [*into*] the [*wolf's*] mouth of the wolf.

or

From the pan and into the wolf's belly.

or

"Hope you brought a flashlight."

Lamia

"When you die, there will be slime," my grandmother knows; she died
once. She told me. "But I came back. And I saw it, the other place." Slime.
"You'll look down and your hands will be covered," whenever I'd sleep
over, or my parents left the room for an hour or a minute, "and you'll look
around and the walls will be covered." She'd fix the crucifix or her dead
husband's picture on the wall, and she'd lean in and say, "And you will be
covered, too, because everything will be." Where you go, when you die.

I imagine walls like open wounds, a tide of sludge rising up to your
knees. A steep incline and fingers into the thick of it, to steady yourself—
something between muscle and moss that gets under your fingernails and
in your hair and mouth and eyes. Like being swallowed, like a throat constricting, tightening as you go, and you do go, because it is too slippery to
climb back up, too narrow to turn, and down below something like a light
flickers.

When you run away from home in Bogotá there will be sewage.
Because the sidewalks aren't safe—the streets, the corners, the bridges,
the churches, and the flyer-littered alleys between alleys and lanes.
So you pull out the manhole covers and jump in when you hear the Social
Cleansing—*Limpieza Social*—vans pulling up. Climb down, crawl across,
get your shoes and socks soaked through. Because they have acid and
they have guns and they have gasoline and matches and PowerPoint clip
art. And they hand out their flyers outside schools and around street corners in broad daylight.
    And they can spell *Eradicate*, and *It's your turn*, and *Malparidos gono-
rreas hijueputas,* and *We know who you are, kidnappers, pushers, junkies.* And
even when they can't spell, they don't let it stop them: *AIDSied whoares,
lazie, thiefer, potehead fukers.* A little clip-art man sits in fetal position on

the top right corner. A revolver for a head, like a little Anubis, a little mal-formed dog—a small, blind animal fighting gravity and encephalitis with a weak neck. *Good little boys go to bed early, bad ones stay up late. You've been warned.*

When you go to clean up the streets of Bogotá, take acid. Take matches, take little cans—be careful not to spill because the carpet will smell of gasoline forever—and take extra change to make more flyers if you run out. While you are at it, take the Virgin with you, too. Like the *sicarios* on their hits, back in the days of the Medellin Cartel, the Cali Cartel—Rodriguez Orejuela, Pablo Escobar. *Virgen María, dame puntería.* "Holy Virgin, give me aim." But go otherwise empty-handed, with only the change in your pockets, the gas can, the gun. Because no one is paying you to clean things up; no one is telling you to go, or go out, or put them out like damp finger tips around a burning wick.

No one and nothing, except your own conviction. Except that you know someone who knows someone, or you know someone, or you yourself know firsthand what it is to be sitting in your living room on a quiet weekday night and hear the thump of unfamiliar footsteps down your hallway. To register the mask but not quite its meaning, the indus-trial glimmer of something being waved around, the urgency in the fog of words drowning out the radio, or the television, or your own stupid heart racing to catch up with the sudden change in pace—the metal edge of that waved-about thing against your chest, your cheek. Then you are caught, and caught up, instantaneously. When you feel the heat of some-one's rage burning through their wool knit sweater, out the muzzle of their gun—through metal, gritted teeth, and chapped lips. Luminously clear and succinct, if not repetitive, the list spouted out, the many things they'll do to you and the people you had almost forgotten were standing by the kitchen sink, lying in their beds, and sitting right beside you on the couch—if you don't do as they say. "*Malparidos gonorreas hijueputas.*" Words soaked in oil and stuffed down your throat like they can choke you with them, light you up like a Molotov cocktail, like they won't just come back up undigested and burning—like it's their right to make you burn.

"Like it's their right." Remind yourself of it and take your time writ-ing this, dragging the little gun-headed Anubis to the corner of the page. Click and shrink the image, one size smaller to fit every extra paragraph you write, because it all has to fit in one page and because you have a lot to say. "Like it's . . . their right!" Because it isn't, you know. It's gone too far and must be made to stop, enough is enough, so you write a manifesto, an open letter, with the vague impression it may never reach the exact people you want to reach. It's a big city but it's ok, letters must be sent, must go somewhere, read by someone, others will do, others are guilty, too. So take the gun, the can, the flyer, the rosary beads, and the others who know what it's like to feel something sharp and foreign against their ribs and between their legs. Because everyone knows someone who knows someone, and many know firsthand, too.

I imagine walls like open wounds, wet socks, white vans—a handsome man I used to know, or know about, walking down the street, sitting in the gutter. A man who used to run away, and run away again every time he was brought back full of smoke and PBC and acid and kerosene. His father used to kneel by the sidewalk once a month, used to put his hands in the gutter to get that legitimate grime under his fingernails. He kept a second set of clothes in a plastic bag just for those days when he had to go down dark streets and into dangerous neighborhoods looking for his son. He would put on the dirty jacket, the torn pants, the thin, rag shirt and matching shoes, and then he'd reach into the gutter and draw streaks down his face, arms, and chest with the three-week-old black sludge. So he could slip by unnoticed into neighborhoods littered with broken bottles and heels, wet mattresses and flyers, to pay for a room so his son might have a place to sleep when the drugs wore off.
Because who else was going to pay, someone always has to.

When you go walking in Bogotá—that is, when I used to go walking after the rain, past a man dragging his black clay pot back onto the sidewalk, to sell hot cinnamon liquor in plastic cups, I tried to be careful. Because he was likely to burn my hands when he ladled the *canelazo* into the cup and said, "God-bless-you-love," all in one breath. Because the plastic was thin, and the heat made it soft, melted it in parts and I had to pull my sleeves over my hands like oven mitts and pay attention to the world roaring past me—even if it spilled over, burned my skin, and soaked my sweater. Because I'd been mugged there a few weeks before, over by the pink-neon club with a strange name—*The Footrest? The Stool? The Ottoman?* And I knew, like everyone knew, to take my chances with the traffic because no one crossed the bridge after eight. To walk with purpose, and look over my shoulder every so often. To carry small bills in different places, to sit on the seat near the aisle and never the window, because sometimes they come sit beside you, press themselves against you and you against the metal, the glass, the dust of dead insects crushed to powder on the windowsill. And maybe their breath burns your cheek and you don't even notice if it's a knife or a sharp stick pocking you through the cloth of their pocket. And feel yourself, sometimes, wishing you had a gun, or a hammer, or a holy fire to breathe down the neck of the men who press sharp things into rib cages and throats.
And if you think that guy doesn't seem to know where he's going, or he walks with both hands in his pockets in too straight a line behind you, walk over to the kid resting on the curb with his feet in the gutter,

and sit right down next to him—offer him your *canelazo* if he seems surprised. Because your hands are warm now, and this is why you get it a cup every other night anyway, and it's about to start raining again, and the man who writes poems for a fee begins to cover his stand with a green plastic tarp again. And the news say the flyer-threats have not materialized anyway.

But you're not sure, because how can you be, and because why not. Who and how are they to really know. And mostly because one day an indigent man yells at you in the street. He sees something in the way you walk or leap over the gutter. The way you paused a street away to look at the improvised Liquid Paper whiteout graffiti on a light post, the flaky outline of a man and a woman having sex. How you traced a finger over the single white line smile of the crudely drawn man's face while he plunged into the whiteout woman bending over just for him. Or, more likely, how you met the indigent man's eyes and forgot to look away quickly enough, so he yelled, "You with them?" He paced and stared. "The *Limpieza Social* people." Like he's seen your face before, traced on a light post, sketched on a flyer. "Come to set fire to me too?"

So sit beside the boy with the PBC cigar, or sprint through traffic if the man who follows, lingers—if he never takes his hands out of his pockets and doesn't seem to mind the pouring rain. Or just stay on the curb a bit longer, he won't touch you while you sit beside the smoking child, as if you were sitting under a cloud of frenzied gnats and surrounded by moats of black slime. "Poems, sonnets, letters, acrostics! For your lovers, for your friends!" See the man with the stand hand out sample poems written in colored marker for people he's never met, watch the people stuff them in their pockets, drop them on the ground and in the gutter. Hear someone curse in the distance, someone yell to keep the music going, the echo of a horse's hooves hitting the pavement. See the waning glow of gold, green, and blue lights reflected off of a wet street. And see if you can help it, being a bit in love with this city, even after all this, even now. Even knowing that inside her there are children being digested in the sewers. Lighting up and wrapping up, wet cigarettes and blankets.

"When you die," my grandmother told me, "there will be slime and a tunnel." She straightened the portrait of her dead husband hanging on the wall, the crucifix, the rosary—the altar of the Virgin splitting the serpent's head in two with her heel. And she told me, "I know, I saw it. When I died once." I sat on the edge of her bed, six years old, wide-eyed and restless under a framed pencil sketch of a curly-haired homeless child. "But I came back, so I know what's on the other side." She never told me how she died, how she came back, or why. I always assumed an asthma attack, in her sleep maybe. A slip into deeper sleep, dreams wandering down a constricting throat, into the purple mazes of swollen lungs. But I don't know. She didn't tell me that part, only the thing about the tunnel, while I sat on her bed cradling my favorite Ninja Turtle, and staring out through the tattered eyeholes of a worn-out Batman mask she bought me for my birthday and I refused to take off for months. "You will see a light flickering in the distance, and there is nothing you can do, because it is too steep to climb back, too narrow to turn, and too full of slime to go anywhere but down."

When you run away take candles. Not to temper the darkness of Bogotá's tunnels of sewage, but because there's a tide, and it carries rats, and they'll bite down on anything that fits in their mouths—noses and ears and fingers and genitals. And when you go walking, walk with purpose, wear good shoes, and carry a bag of bread. Sprint through traffic if you don't want to meet the man walking toward you, try to give out the bread to the children sitting on the curb puffing away on *bazuco* cigars, and try, try not to be offended when they toss it in the gutter. Because *Limpieza Social* already tried that, and some kids died and some just got really sick, and now they don't take bread from strangers.

CRIA CUERVOS Y TE SACARAN LOS OJOS

or

Raise crows and to you they will pull out the eyes.

or

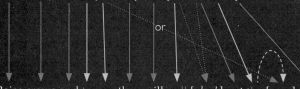

Raise crows and to you they will pull [pluck] out the [your] eyes.

or

If you lie down with crows, you get up blind.

or

"Can't help it."

Epigraphist

This is where the bus hit. And this, this is Paula, my older sister. And this is Bogotá in the summer. As if there were summers at the equator and not just one uninterrupted season of rain and sun and rain again. A single blur of continuous days that crash one into the other, leaving parts and marks and scraps in one another's backs and faces. Blurred and bright and bruised. And this is the license plate number imbedded like braille on my sister's hip.

This is Paula, after the bus hit, in a neck brace on the couch when I come home from school one day. And that's me laughing, because she looks a bit like a flipped-over armadillo, and when I chuckle she chuckles, too. So I think there can't be any real harm under neck brace and bruises, so I keep right on laughing.

But that's Paula, earlier that day, flat on her back in the middle of an intersection. Breathless and cold while a driver considers the human dent she may have left on his front fender. So that's me, later, beside her on the couch, not quite laughing anymore. Looking at bruises and scrapes and partial license plate indentations on muscle and skin. And me, again, listening to explanations of intersections and bus drivers circumventing unconscious bodies. Screeches and thuds and metal and meat.

This is the moment when bus meets sister and sister flies and driver drives.

That's me, staring at the yellow-purple etching of a fresh bruise that slowly appears like a 3D painting you have to stare at cross-eyed to finally see. Me, wanting to run my finger on the swollen grooves of what could be a 5 or an S. Trying to think in concrete numbers, like the ones pressed into her hip. How far did we run that time when she sprinted angry and barefoot through a rain-wet street in Bogotá, for how long had I trailed after thinking I could keep her from falling into puddles and running into traffic? How many years between us? How many rooms shared while growing up? How many schools? How many days spent in games of simulated destruction?

"Let's play slavery, Lina."

"Let's play Apocalypse, Paula."

She tells me to stand perfectly still, and because it's my turn to be the slave, I do. I put my hands behind my back, perfectly aware we are too old for this game, her sixteen to my thirteen, her razor to my eyebrow.

I tell her the world is ending and even though she's nine and I'm six it is still my turn to pick the game, so she agrees. We turn bunk beds into bunker, and she peeks out through a pillowcase curtain as I command her to narrate the burning of the world while I count supplies and survivors.

How many times will I let her shave off eyebrows and cut off eyelashes? How many nights arguing whether the door should remain open in case the devil climbed through the window, or closed, in case the men with guns should rush up the stairs? How many hours practicing extinction and belonging? How many times will she let me burn the world? And how many hands and fingers around my sister's purse and inside her pockets while a bus turns the corner and she lies on the ground—flat, motionless, and flammable?

That's me walking through Bogotá, day and night in torn jeans and burnt tennis shoes with the bleakness and incandesce of adolescence dripping from my skin. So many times, I've lost track. Those are the strangers I'll never know, pulling my sister's unconscious body on to the sidewalk by the strap of her purse. And that's me one tired night in Bogotá, sitting on a curb with my head between my knees while ten-year-old homeless *gamin* boys smoke *bazuco* in the alley.

That rushing, blunt, tingling sensation—that must be the feeling of so many fingers hiking over my sister's body; pins and needles and spider legs checking for change, and wallet, and rings. And that must be what it feels like, finally, to wake up to a heart still beating under an Andean sun in the middle of a city that plays and kills and smiles with the same set of fangs and claws.

That's a two-hundred-peso coin I'm rubbing between my fingers, sitting on the curb while the homeless boys smoke. I feel the little ingrained *indígena* pattern with my fingertips and watch the cars drive through red lights and stop signs. That's what I give the boy smoking *bazuco* beside me. Two hundred pesos, barely enough to buy two cigarettes from the newspaper stand in the corner. A piece of metal etched with a symmetrical pre-Columbian symbol and the words *Republica de Colombia* around the edges. The emblems of meaning and ownership that make currency current only in one place and only in one time, and worthless anywhere and any-when else. A coin in a doped boy's hand like the ones they hope to find in Paula's jeans when she wakes up suddenly in the middle of pulsing traffic with strangers' hands in her pockets.

That, over there, is the street where it happened. Over by the *Plaza De Bolívar* where so much has already happened. And those are the black stars cops paint on the road over the spots where meat has met metal and metal has won. "Black stars are warnings where not to cross, because that's where people've died. Don't you know anything?" Like they've seeped into the city, all her dead and dying. Struck back where they were struck. Like a dent on a fender, or a fender on a hip, or a spine against the edge of the sidewalk, or a dog pissing on a fence.

Try to avoid crossing where there are constellations and clusters and the paint is still wet.

Like imprints on a hip, patterns on a coin. Scabs and scars and black stars.

That's me, by the way, hopscotching between speeding cars on painted road stars. Kicking up dust and hanging from buses, trying to chase Bogotá down wet streets as if she might run into her own traffic and fall into a red ravine.

And that's Paula, flying and falling and absorbing the shape of metal numbers and letters with her hip. And her, again, falling asleep in a neck brace while we watch TV. Me, too, falling asleep—on a bench in Bogotá, in a bus Iowa City, behind the wheel in Provo, in so many planes and so many waiting rooms, as if Bogotá keeps chasing me into other people's traffic. As if moving is end without means. As if I'm hardly paying attention while I turn the corner, which I never have, and never will. Like Paula, when we are kids, standing on the sidewalk, gripping my wrist and pulling me back so hard I feel it in my shoulder and neck as I whip back around to the sidewalk, torn between her grip and the wind-tunnel wake of a car speeding past me. A second late on that tug and the car would have clipped me at best, ripped me apart at worst, written its name in my ribs and skull.

or

Where one least thinks jumps the hare.

or

Def. **1.** a fast-running, long-eared mammal resembling a large rabbit, **with very long hind legs.** • Lepus europaeus (brown hare) and **2. Hare-brained adj.** rash; ill-judged.

Rabbit

Hare

3. to run or go very quickly, usually in an uncontrolled way.

"**I saw** her **haring** off down the **road** like her feet were on fire."

Where one least ~~thinks~~ [*expects it*], jumps the **hare**

Def. f. **1.** Mamífero del orden de los Lagomorfos, que mide unos 7 dm desde la cabeza hasta la cola, y 20 a 24 cm de altura. Tiene el pelaje suave y espeso de color negro rojizo en cabeza y lomo, leonado en cuello y patas, y blanco en pecho y vientre, la cabeza proporcionalmente pequeña, con hocico estrecho y orejas muy largas, de color gris con las puntas negras, el cuerpo estrecho, **las extremidades posteriores más largas que las anteriores**, y la cola corta, negra por encima y blanca por debajo. **Es un animal muy tímido, solitario,** de veloz carrera, que abunda en España. Vive preferentemente en las llanuras, sin hacer madrigueras, y **descansa en camas que muda con frecuencia.** Su carne es comestible apreciado y su piel más estimada que la del conejo.

3. f. coloq. Hombre **tímido y cobarde.**
4. f. *El Salv.* Persona **lista y astuta.**

or

Out of nowhere come the blue hares.

or

"Ready?"

Burn

Gustavo's grandfather's fingers were like melted candles. Smooth, waxy stumps burnt nearly all the way down to the knuckle.

Our parents talked, at and around us, while Gustavo's grandfather reclined and huffed. The day flashed by, the rain came down, the mosquitos laid their eggs, the pupas squirmed in the dirt beneath our feet, and we stared at melted fingers until finally he let us touch them. "But you have to pay attention," he'd say, "Pay attention." Because they meant something; they were made of consequence and fire, and he said he'd tell us what a smooth stump meant if only we promised to sit still for a minute and "Pay attention." A difficult task on any normal day and an almost impossible one on the days Gustavo's wheezing grandfather would let us take turns touching the shiny tips of his wickless fingers as if they were lucky pennies, as if they could be convinced to grow back, fingers burnt so short and strange and smooth. "Are you listening?" Not really.

Christmas came and we watched our own fathers and grandfathers set up fireworks in front of our houses and in the middle of the street. Then we'd forget all about Gustavo's grandfather's fingers and what they meant. Something about pink and green fire against a black sky. "This is what happens when," memory fragments, "This is why you never," burnt short and smooth, too. "Never ever . . . Are you paying attention?" Not really.

Time to gather in the *salón comunal*, the public building with the green, metal-door reserved for birthday and graduation parties. And on Christmas, the epicenter of our shared *Novena*. Tambourines, maracas, and tin cans full of stones—because there are never enough maracas and tambourines, and who'd settle for just singing and clapping after wielding the cacophonic power of a colorfully painted, seed filled, dried gourd shell.

"Come, come, come. Come unto our souls Jesus, come, come, come." Between verses of prayer and scripture and fire, there was pudding and fried *buñuelos* and fermented *masato* with a dash of cinnamon. "Come unto our souls Jesus, come, come, come." As loud as lungs allow, "Come unto or soooooooooo-uuuuuuuls." Until a stone flew out from a crack in the can and hit someone in the eye, or some premature fireworks set the sky ablaze. "Don't take so long, don't take so long, Jesus come, come."

In December—after *La Novena*, after Christmas, after presents and dinners, *arroz con leche, aguardiente y café*—came the cleansing fire. Before midnight of the New Year, when all of Colombia smelled of gunpowder and pork and burnt skin, we would gather around dozens of *Año Viejos*, the papier-mâché dummies lying in gutters and on sidewalks. Painted smiles, lazy eyes, lumpy torsos, and limp limbs. Old, worn clothes stuffed with newspaper, oil soaked rags, fireworks, and every bad memory, wrong turn, and bit of terrible luck from the previous year. Every *Año Viejo* must burn before every *Año Nuevo* can start. Then, finally, some sugar-high kid running in mad, Catherine-wheel circles would finally push something over, or trip over a pile of matches, or an unlit fuse and off they'd go. Domino chains and cycling flames. One body would catch fire, and then another, and then another. Lighters, matches, cigarettes, and shouts. "The old year is dead! *¡Que viva el Año Nuevo!*" And we watched the *Año Viejo* dummies convulse with light, shooting green and red and yellow sparks from fingers and eyes and bowels.

Then we shot out, too. From houses and community centers, through the streets that a month before we'd filled with handmade lanterns to light the Virgin's path on her way to Bethlehem. We ran like mad, writing our names in the air with sparklers, playing Roman-candle tag, burning holes in our shirts and shoes until we ran out of sparklers and Roman candles and fireworks and time, and then we rolled up newspaper and kept running with paper torches as if we wanted to burn the whole world down.

HUITACA

Before the moon was made, back when the earth rested atop four guaia-cum trees, Huitaca used to sit on the cold hills of the Bacatá savannah surrounded by fog and smoke and men, while she drank *chicha* from a hollowed-out gourd and spoke slowly in long drags, as if there were noth-ing on earth worth the quickening of her pace. Skin like wet clay, gray-green eyes and a smile as sharp as the edge of the world, and her listeners would have to hold each other back so as not to close the circle too tightly around her.

Another sip from the gourd and another story. She would talk of the world, tell them that it was very wide and life very brief, and what a shame to spend it all sowing and plowing and weaving and toiling so feverishly under the fevered notion of a long and narrow life. So she drank and she gambled. She traced a hypnotic finger across the cloth and confused the patterns that Nemqueteba, the civilizing god, had taught them to weave and paint into their blankets. "Let the patterns go," she whispered. "Take this, leave that, come with me. No rush, no hurry." Say-ing it like she meant it entirely, but only really very casually in the sort of way that made the Muiscas want to mean it for her. To make up the dif-ference and talk to her as equals, sitting there beside her, speaking in long drags and drinking *chicha* from hollowed-out gourds.

Which, of course, was not what the greater god, Nemqueteba, had taught them. Not what they were meant to do at all, and they knew it. And Chibchacum, god of the harvest and the river, faithful servant of the civilizing god, knew they knew it, too. But neither knowing changed either doing. The Muiscas continued listening to Huitaca; Huitaca con-tinued to speak; and Chibchacum continued to watch them sleep all day on beds of blue-green moss, let their fields go fallow and their cotton rot. And it drove him mad to watch them watching Huitaca as if the sight of her were the air in their lungs, her words the water in their blood, and every movement of her shoulders the earth beneath their feet. "How wide the world," she would say. "How wide the day, and wider still the night," and when she laughed it was like stirring coals in a fire. The crowd growing larger around her, and Chibchacum's rage more twisted and barbed inside him, until one day it grew so thick and gnarled, he could barely breathe through it. Barely make himself whisper to the seedling to sprout and the branch to reach. Barely look at dust-covered shrines without shaking furiously, as if beneath his skin millions of wasp eggs were beginning to hatch. So he gritted his teeth and clenched his fists, leapt down from his mountain, and landed with his heels on the spine of a hill, on the head of a snake, and he made the whole savannah shiver.

Then, the bare-shouldered god of fertile earth and green stalks walked the length of the plateau and the height of the knolls looking for water. Past creeks and lakes, brooks and rills, swollen black clouds and swollen-bellied frogs until finally he found two thick rivers nipping like hungry hatchlings in a nest. He bent down, wrapped his hands around their necks, and, arching his back, he pulled them out of their banks, and snapped them together like the tangled antlers of two angry stags.

And the god of the harvest watched as the rivers bucked and jerked, coiled and spilled, and wiped out the world.

Nearly everything died and nearly everyone drowned, too. And the people who remained clung to the side of the mountain, to floating trees, and to dead bloated animals, and they cried out to Nemqueteba, the civilizing god, pleading and begging and praying for his mercy and his wrath. "Mercy! Mercy!" they cried. "Wrath, great god! Thy wrath!" Tempting Nemqueteba to punish Chibchacum for punishing, and Huitaca for tempting, and to spare the tempted and the punished who held on to the sides of the cliffs, and the cracks in the rock, and the small bodies of their children even long after they had stopped shivering and gasping for breath.

So Nemqueteba marched down from the highest peak, cut his feet on shards of stone and bone, trudged through flood and mud while wet birds and mice climbed atop his shoulders and white-feather beard. And he raised his staff above his head and struck the mountain as if it were made of eggshell and arteries. A cliff made waterfall, made drain, made spout.

Then the civilizing god walked the length of Bacatá and the depth of her flooded plains, leaving bloody footprints in the mud until he found Chibchacum, water up to his chest, mud between his toes, and the weeping nephews of the ruling Zaque on his shoulders, heirs to the drowned confederation of Muisca tribes. Then, "Chibchacum," Nemqueteba called out. "Chibchacum, what did you do?"

And Nemqueteba's words struck the god of seeds and seasons the way the mountain had been struck. As the water slowly descended—from his chest, to his waist, to his knees, to his ankles—the drowned world resurfaced, and Chibchacum's whimpering could be heard under the thrashing of fish suddenly dropped into patches of grass and mud and wet, unfinished blankets. "Chibchacum," Nemqueteba started once more, "bow down." And Chibchacum set the two boys down, tried to put words to thoughts, or thoughts to words, but neither yielded, and he simply closed his eyes and bowed his head.

Because there was no one he loved more than Nemqueteba, but there was no one Nemqueteba loved more than the Muiscas. Then Chibchacum understood. What he had done, what it had meant, and how long gods live and how much longer Nemqueteba would remember this betrayal. And all this knowing already weighed so heavily on him, he barely felt the earth being lifted from guaiacum treetops and lowered unto his shoulders.

On the other side of the savannah, Huitaca sat on a hillside, surrounded by the remains of her drowned followers. That's where Nemqueteba found her, drinking from her gourd and running her hand down the neck of a broken-boned stag still gasping for breath. "Huitaca," Nemqueteba called out, but she did not turn, did not raise her eyes. She only continued patting the animal gently as it tried to raise itself on splintered legs and mangled hooves. She ran her hand down its neck and up to the edge of a branch sticking out as if it were sprouting from between the animal's ribs.

"Huitaca," Nemqueteba called out again.

But again, she did not turn. So he walked toward her, on mud mixed with feathers and blood, while the stag huffed and shook and tried to raise its head from under the weight of its own splintered antlers.

"What did you do?"

Huitaca did not turn.

She kept her eyes on the branch lodged solidly between meat and bone while she clutched what appeared to be a piece of the animal's shattered antlers. One hand to hold the shard and another to console.

Nemqueteba took a deep breath—the air so thick and damp, he almost had to swallow—and he walked up to Huitaca and sat beside her.

"How wide the waters too, then," he said, staring into the panicked eyes of a dying deer, and Huitaca finally turned.

Eyes like emerald dust mixed with ash and sand. Something almost like a smile, almost like defeat, but not quite like it, nothing like it. She took a drink, licked her lips, held up the gourd and shook it to show that there was still *chicha* left inside. "Wide and deep," she said, and handing the gourd to the god sitting beside her, she stood up.

"Huitaca," he said again, and again. Nothing back. She walked around god and beast to stand right in front of the animal's head, gripping the sharp piece of antler in her left hand as if it were the only fixed point in the universe and she were expecting a second flood to wash her away any second. "Huitaca." She raised the bone shard above her head, one hand around the other. "Wait." Without making a sound, she brought down all her weight on that shard. Both hands, fast, hard, bone into bone, one single motion, right between the deer's eyes.

A flock of birds took off. Frogs croaked. God and Huitaca stood still while the animal twitched. And it felt so quiet that for a moment, Huitaca thought she could hear the loosening of internal strings, life unspooling inside the animal and inside her like a map back to the beginning. A deer's forehead like a spout, blood spattered across Huitaca's face like a red-starred sky, and silence across the muddied plains.

"Huitaca," Nemqueteba said one last time as he gently placed his hand on her bare ankle. "Huitaca." And for a few seconds she felt something like black wings outstretched inside her chest, a condor warming itself in the sun and life winding itself back into her—air in her lungs and water in her blood—when suddenly the animal's legs began to kick wildly. It began to kick desperately. Groaning, and shaking, and tossing, and howling, and beating its head against the ground like all the fish left alive were beating themselves to death against mud and stone all across the savannah, and then it began making the loneliest noise Huitaca had ever heard. Like whistling, like roaring, like the world was ending, or it should have ended. And then Nemqueteba lunged forward, landing on the bone shard and driving it the rest of the way in.

The silence of the dead and the quiet of survival.

Water draining out of the savanna, birds gathering twigs, red streaks on the white of Nemqueteba's beard.

Huitaca began to step back but one more time she felt a hand on her ankle. And the temptress looked down at the civilizing god who seemed to be crying while he held on to her as if she were the only fixed point in the universe and he were expecting a second flood. And then in one single motion and without making a sound, he stood up and swept her off her feet. Off the ground, and off the mountain. He tightented his grip around her ankle and swung her around—spun her around, and around, and around, so hard and so fast that all her joints came loose inside her, and the deer blood leapt off her face, and her own blood leapt from her skin, her fingertips, her toes, her legs, her arms, her heart, her lungs. He swung her and spun her. So fast and so hard, she turned translucent white—milk water and quartz, white smoke, bleached feathers and dandelion seeds— and then he let her go.

And Nemqueteba gave Chibchacum the width of the earth, and Huitaca the breadth of the night, and the Muiscas the light of a new moon and the shaking of the ground beneath their feet.

TANTO VA EL CÁNTARO AL AGUA
HASTA QUE POR FIN SE ROMPE

or

So much goes the pitcher to water until that at last itself
breaks.

or

[The pitcher can only] so much goes [be filled so many times]
the pitcher to water until [before] that at last itself [it] breaks.

or

It's only a matter of water.

or

"Some cracks are hard to see."

The First Jaime

Jaime sneaked into the train while no one was looking. The reasons are unclear. Though, even more than fifty years later, his brother still suspects it was all to visit him in the rundown, downtown office where he used to work. "Because," he says, "sometimes I'd give him something to do, or a little money to buy a soda and an *arepa* in the corner store," or even, "sometimes, enough to buy a coat," so he wouldn't shiver walking back the long way home.

But Jaime did not wait in line, did not pay the fare, did not sit by a window. He sneaked in, climbed up the side, and waited between cars. We don't know why. Maybe he didn't have enough for the ride, or maybe he'd seen someone do it before, or maybe there was no reason at all, "Because," his brother tells me, "Jaime was simple like that." Didn't think things through, couldn't think things through. Even at nineteen he struggled. Secret cliffs and hidden ravines between the points in his mind, and straight lines would sometimes get lost, fall off, and disappear before they could connect point to point to point. "Like that," his brother says. A dark flyover map of single flickering lights and no highways between them. So Jaime sneaked into the train, who knows why, and he hid until he saw from a distance the building where his brother worked. Then maybe he thought, "So close, why wait?" So he jumped off the train and hit the ground so hard bones popped, ligaments snapped, and his liver came loose inside him.

"I'm sure that was it. He saw the building and then jumped." More than fifty years later I sit across from the first Jaime's brother in a dimly lit living room beside newspaper-covered tables. "He must have thought, 'Why wait?'" He shifts in his chair and occasionally holds his fingers as if he were holding a cigarette between them, as if he still smoked, and needed still to flick off the ash before it fell to the floor. "Because Jaime was simple like that." *Como simple, eso de pensar, pues, no mucho. Pero*

Bueno, "But good," and maybe he can tell I don't quite understand what he means, because he clarifies: *No en ningún área en particular, no-no.* "Not good *at anything.* Just," he pauses, "good." He's not an expressive man, not a talkative man, but he says it in the gentlest way I've ever heard him say anything in my entire life.

A leap and a miscalculation. A train going too fast, a slick edge, and a gap hidden by tall grass. Then a knee like a guitar tossed from a window. Hollow wood meets wet cement. A burst of splinters and the sound of strings snapping, twisting, tangling, and dangling. Jaime on the ground, on his back, looking up. A brief blue moment of Bogotá sky. Width and depth and the clanking of metal wheels on metal tracks.

Then voices. People gathering to see if there is anything to see. Jaime on the ground. "Are you ok? Are you alright?" But none of the people standing over him are his brother. Not one familiar face, not one voice, not a one, not at all. So Jaime doesn't know what to say, even if he didn't have trouble talking, and he does—have trouble talking, trouble getting up, trouble walking. "What are you doing? Wait. Don't put weight on that!" And he must have screamed, he thinks he may have screamed, because there are so many people, and so many faces, so many voices pushing themselves up against him like ants around a sugar cube or a dying grub. And they seem to understand, seem to know what to do and where to go as they carry him off, so he doesn't have to talk that much, at least until they reach the hospital, the doctors, the nurses, the questions and questionnaires. "Call my brother, my mother, my father." Call someone, anyone.

"We had a cousin who was like that too, like Jaime," Jaime's brother tells me, as if it explained everything. *These strange things happen to people like Jaime who happen to be a little bit strange.* "But not exactly like Jaime. He could make just about anything out of wood. You know, how sometimes people like Jaime have these skills, born like that, too, I guess." And it's strange to see the first Jaime's brother sitting next to the second Jaime. My grandfather next to my father, his second-born son, the one he named after the brother who leapt from the train before it was time. "Not Jaime, though." Seems to want to flick invisible ash from his invisible cigarette, "He couldn't do anything like that. Not *good at anything.* But *good.*" Then he looks away from me. "But who knows why, really." And though it's a shaper turn, I follow. Because it's one of those always-true things; no one ever really knows why anyone else ever really jumps.

A hospital room and a ticking clock. Jaime on a stretcher, then a bed. A nurse, a nurse, a nurse. Then a doctor, at long last, a doctor. One who studied far away and explains just how far in words Jaime can't pronounce: "De Unitet Staits off Ahmerika?" And he looks at Jaime, or at his leg, at least. Makes him stretch his ankle, "That's right, just like that." And raise his leg off the bed, "Your foot flat on the bed, like that." Sets his left hand on Jaime's ankle as if keeping it in place, wraps his right arm around the calf, and seems to lean back as if about to pull it like the band on a slingshot. "Ok now, I'm just going to . . ." And Jaime hears screams, or he thinks he hears a scream behind bright colors and behind black glass. "Ok then," the doctor steps back and produces a pen and prescription pad from the breast pocket of his white coat. *No es nada,* he said. "Nothing we can't fix with a few screws."

"Top-notch stuff," my grandfather tells me. *Una cantidad de cosas complicadísimas.* Complicated words for complicated procedures, for important men with important jobs, with no time to explain that it'll be no time at all before skin grow over screws, and Jaime's back off his back, back on his feet, and right back at home, where he belongs. *Que con el bisturí y que con unos tornillos. Bueno, ahí.* Blood, scalpels, swelling, screws, and skin that begins to turn the color of mustard.

"'Just a few weeks.' That's what the doctor said, 'He'll be fine.'" But, of course, Jaime wasn't and wouldn't be. His leg healed, but he kept having to lean over to spit blood into a bedpan, to feel the force of a body kicking itself, inside itself, against itself, as strips and chucks and pieces of itself filled a bedpan that had already been emptied twice. And a nurse helped Jaime lean back so he didn't fall off the bed, as if he were leaping from it, as he'd leapt from the train when he thought he could sprint to his brother's office building, walk through the door, and surprise him with a handful of fresh grass and a knotted ball of white feathers. And though Jaime's brother doesn't quite remember Jaime's mother being there, she must have been, she had to have been. Because Jaime was her favorite son and she said so to Jaime's brother every day.

Perhaps it was she who held the bedpan and pushed her simple son back against the propped up pillows so she could catch a glimpse of him, and he his breath. So she could wipe the blood off his chin and tell him it would be all right, *mi niño,* just a moment, it'll pass, *ya verás,* "Tomorrow, you'll be fine," she may have said, she could have said. At least she would have, I think, if she could have, I think, stood the sight of her favorite son's body breaking down and spilling out in violent, burning, choking bursts. Her simple boy, pale yellow skin, wet red lips, looking off into the corner where his older brother sat, holding his hat and crumpling the brim.

My grandfather sitting next to my father in the yellow light of an unchanging room. My grandfather next to his second son, the second Jaime. Because the Ferreiras do that, dead cousins and sisters and brothers and babies. A living cousin after a stillborn aunt. A daughter after a little girl in the back seat of an uncle's car who flickered out of life on impact. Names like rooms in a hotel—vacancies, quotas, and checkouts. As if someone had already paid for the week and left early, as if we can't bear the thought of wasting a good name. So there are these endless loops of name repetition—Maria Alejandra, Maria Alejandra, Hernando, Hernando, Daniel, Daniel, Margarita, Margarita—and it turns out my father is one, too. And I could ask my grandfather. I imagine asking, "Why the name again? Always again. Did he remind you of something? Were you hoping for someone?" But my grandfather flicks invisible ash into the carpet and I know I can't actually ask. Because he barely talks to the second Jaime, barely talks at all, barely knows my unrepeated name, barely knows what to call me beyond *niña. Qui'hubo niña.* "Hello, girl."

"Hello, Grandfather." Stutter, repeat. *Hola Abuelo.* Partly because I don't know what to say and partly because I like the word. Because I never get much of a chance to use it. So I say it clumsily and as if it quenches something, *Abuelo, hola.* I told him over the phone that I was in the country. *Just for a couple of weeks, I'm on my way to Quito, my aunt Lucero, you see? She paid for a ticket.* And I don't know why I call him, why I visit. He's not an expressive man, not a talkative man, not a man I really know, and most of what I know is not particularly laudable. But I still do, to say hello, maybe, to say *Abuelo,* likely. An inexplicable dark-flyover-map impulse. *Hola, Abuelo. Would it be ok if we came by?*

The television is on upstairs. I could hear it the moment I walked in, a car chase and my younger cousin saying something between the screeches of B-movie sound effects. For a moment I stood at the bottom of the staircase. I could have walked upstairs, said hello, sat on the edge of the bed and watched cars drive off bridges and into walls. I could have—simple straight lines and forward leaps.

But I don't walk up. I don't think I can, or should. Last time I saw my younger cousin was at her sister's funeral, the second Margarita to die young and suddenly. I was fourteen and she was eleven; she had her older sister in a box, and I had my own in a dark flower-print dress beside me. A funeral-home basement full of women in black veils and girls holding trays of coffee and tea so hot it melted the edges of the plastic cup and burned my lips. Rosary beads rattling through fingers in unison like the rhythmic clatter of trains on time, on tracks, on route. Margarita in a loop, in a secondhand name, in a wooden box.

Jaime's brother is only twenty years old when his brother is dragged away from the train tracks and into a yellow-white hospital room. He only owns two suits: one gray, one blue. The gray is his favorite one. He pays for his family's bills and groceries. His brother's clothes, his sister's dresses, tuition, books, shoes and hospitals bills. He is not his mother's favorite son and is reminded frequently, which he sometimes takes out on the girls he dates.

He's not a very tall man, but he's not short either. Wide around the shoulders, meticulous, good with numbers, and strangely strong for a man his size. One day in the future he will walk alongside his secondborn son down a street in Bogotá, and a man will fall on his wristwatch like a bird on a crumb, then Jaime's brother will simply straighten out his arm and send the man flying into a cement lamppost.

But not yet. Not now.

Now he sits in the corner of the hospital room in a rare moment of almost silence. He listens to his brother's shallow wheezing, and he wishes he had a beer in his hand. He's come straight from work in his gray suit. And even though the fabric is too thin for Bogotá weather, he's come to love it: "Not good for the weather, but *good*." He doesn't have much, and he loves even less. So that's the one he's wearing while he sits in the corner just as he did the day before, and the day before that, and the day before that, and every day since Jaime was admitted.

Then Jaime wakes up; he wretches on the floor. Feels crushed from the inside out and has trouble straightening up on the bed, so his brother helps him. Puts his hands around Jaime's bony shoulder and feels him shaking, sees him looking up at him the way he used to when he would walk through his office door hoping for something to do, though he wasn't very good at anything, and knew enough—at least—to know that much was true. But Jaime is exhausted, and it's hard to tell what he can and cannot understand anymore. Maybe sometimes he concentrates on the feeling of screws holding his knee together and tries to feel anchored to something, someone, somewhere. Maybe he pictures himself like one of the suspension bridges his brother studies in the University; maybe he hates the doctor who studied in *Los Estados Unidos* for forgetting to check for internal damage. Maybe he dreams of trains. Maybe he didn't slip at all. Maybe Jaime cries when he sees his brother sitting in the corner in his best gray suit while a nurse goes to empty the metal pan, and maybe there is nothing to think through anymore; Jaime is a simple boy and this is a simple thing, and he knows he's going to die.

"So," I say partly to fill the silence of my grandfather's long pauses. "Did my grandfather love Jaime very much?" Because I can't use *tú* when I talk to Jaime's brother. *Tú*, informal *you*—¿*Tú como estas? ¿Tú dónde has estado? ¿Y tú a dónde vas?* In fact, I can barely use the formal you, *usted*—¿*Usted como esta? ¿Usted donde ha estado? ¿Usted a donde va?*— though it feels slightly easier, it still takes effort. So I end up awkwardly addressing the man sitting across from me in the third person, as if I'm talking to an invisible interpreter who'll make all my words familiar and intelligible to him. I say, *¿Mi abuelo lo vio todo?* "My grandfather saw everything?" And, *¿Mi abuelo quería a Jaime mucho?* Did my grandfather love Jaime very much?"

And I watch him straighten his back, and I realize how stupid my questions must sound. He's not an expressive man. "Well, not so much," he says. "Anytime there was a little money for the movies or anything like that, they sent him with our sister."

The Ferreiras do this, too—children like songs and seasons and suits. Favorites and least favorites and those in between. My older sister was both my grandmothers' favorite, my father was his mother's favorite, and my grandfather was his father's favorite. "But," my father tells me, "there is no use in being the favorite of the parent who is never home." And paternal favoritism almost always means maternal exclusionism. So when my grandfather says that they sent Jaime with his sister to the movies, he means, "Not me," he means, "Never me," he means, "Maybe enough people loved Jaime already."

But then he also says, "See, Jaime was very beautiful." As if this answers not the question I asked, but the one I meant to, or should have asked. "Very handsome, really. And I was apparently very serious." Because what's the use in asking why his mother preferred Jaime over the son who assumed the financial responsibilities of his absent father? Why both my grandmothers preferred my older sister, this one that one, that one this one, trains? Planes, Huitaca, Nemqueteba, the gray suit or the blue? So instead I ask him what Jaime looked like. *Can my grandfather describe him?*

"Hm," I watch him scratch his chin. "No."

Not at all? Dark hair? Eye color?

"Hm," again. I picture him in a hospital room for hours and days watching this boy spit out wet chunks of his own organs. "No."

"Imagine," he says, deciding that there are better things to discuss. "This holy eminent doctor from one of those famous U.S. hospitals, something like Maya, or Maju. Just imagine."

Does my grandfather mean The Mayo Clinic?

"What do I know? One of those over there." He motions with his hand as if he were waving flies away, *far-far, away-away, Gringolandia, fairytale land.*

"He looked at the leg and didn't even think to check the organs." *Idiot.* "And back then was not like now; we kept a proper mourning." Because he thinks that wearing black anywhere but a funeral is just one more of the many ways my generation is ruining the country. Another disappointing side effect of a disaffected youth, like casual Fridays and Taco Tuesdays. *About how long then?* "Well, long, but different for each one. Six years, for example, if your mother died—six years, all black. Now, there are brides in beige and mourners in navy blue." He shakes his head,

"Just, disrespectful. And Carlina," he calls his mother by her first name as Ferreiras tend to, "she did have a few black things, but us? Not a one."

So what did my grandfather do? "Well, since I had nothing black, some beast of a man told me that I should get that nice grey suit that I liked so much into a tint shop. And I liked that suit a lot. It wasn't too thick, like nicer ones, but it was still good." *So my grandfather dyed it black?* "Huy!" He scoffs, "I took it into the shop, sure. But when I got it back it was one single wrinkle, the whole thing, just one long wrinkle." He never speaks of the funeral or of Jaime's death, though he must have been present at both. And what he does speak of, he changes. He gets Jaime's age wrong. He makes himself much older, and Jaime much younger, and he stretches out the time it takes Jaime to die. A miniature boy hanging out the window of a train. Pale, narrow-shouldered, wide-eyed, and fourteen as he jumps out of a moving train, kicking his legs and swinging his arms wildly as if he half expects to never hit the ground. Barely out of childhood, though not really ever out of childhood, spitting out chunks of liver the way magicians pull scarves from trick sleeves. My grandfather in the corner of a hospital room so small he has to pull in his knees to fit, wrap his arms around them, and try to hold his breath so he doesn't suck all the air out of his brother's lungs. And he tells me he doesn't remember how long he wore his one-wrinkle, once-gray, once-favorite black suit, but he brushes his hand over his sleeve when he says it, as if just talking about it wrinkles his shirt.

My grandfather doesn't get choked up about these things. Doesn't get choked up, period. He's a civil engineer from a very long line of civil engineers who see the bridge for what it is and not what it might represent. The screw, the steel, the cables above, the water below, and the man walking across. A screw is a screw, a cable a cable, water, water, men, men. *Un puente es un puente es un puente es un puente.* A wrinkled, black suit is proper mourning garb even when it used to be gray and adored. And then in one single, un-mourning tone, he tells me about the first Maria Alejandra, the daughter he lost when she was only three months old.

I can hear Hollywood bullets being shot in whatever Saturday afternoon movie my cousin is watching upstairs. My name was going to be Margarita, too, which would have made me the third and longest living one. *Why Margarita? Because of something? Because of someone?* "I just liked the name." *No meaning?* "Not really?" *Why not?* "I saw your face. Not a Margarita." Though not a Lina either. Not an *anyone* for a month when my mother couldn't decide what to name me. "*Hola, niña.*" And I was just *girl*, just there, untethered, mid-leap.

But Jaime fell and fell apart against the ground. And then Jaime's mother fell apart, too. He was so beautiful and so good, though not good at anything in particular, "Just good." And he was Carlina's favorite. Because he smiled, he beamed—electric sun grin, electric sun son—and he was such a happy child, a forever child of lightness and light. So any time she had any money, of course, she would give it to him. Because their father was never there, and the eldest son never smiled, never laughed, always seemed to think too much and know too much, and who could ever like that? Who'd want to give such a son anything, when you could give it to Jaime and see the gleam of his gratitude and the simple wildness of his happy confusions? But Jaime leapt from a moving train. So there was nothing left to give him, and no one left to give things to. So she folded his clothes neatly, and she dressed him for the funeral. Then she dressed herself in black for longer than was required, and she put the boy in the ground and his clothes in a drawer, and then she grew old.

Memories flickered on and off like so many cigarettes in the dark, ankles swelled, spines bent, and her mind faltered. Until a beggar came to the door on Christmas day. He said, "I'm cold," because Bogotá evenings can chill the blood. He said, "Won't you please give me something, *Doña?* To warm me, *Doña?*" And he was dirty and hard to describe, but somehow good, and somehow beautiful, and somehow familiar. So she looked him over once and then again, and again. Back at the kitchen, back at the man. A dark flyover map of single flickering lights and only a few highways between them. And she could barely believe it at first, and maybe she wouldn't have, were it not right there in front of her, Jaime at the door asking if she wouldn't give him something to keep warm. So of course she ran back into the house to fetch the clothes she'd kept for all those years, washed and folded and tied with string. "Of course, of course. They are yours, of course. So of course, you can have them, they are yours." And it was odd to see him, and odd to see him dressed like that, but so good to see him at all. She put the clothes in Jaime's arms and took him by the hand, car grease, and dirt, and broken fingernails wrapped in Carlina's wrinkled fingers. "You are my favorite," she tells him, "you know that, right? Always, forever, you know." And because Jaime was simple, he didn't say anything back, didn't nod or clasp her hands. A sweet boy smiling with a bundle of old clothes under his arms as he walked away, a woman watching from her doorstep until he is out of sight, not quite remembering why she was standing, there so she goes back inside.

Then highways lit up, points connected, lines appeared on the darkened map. The world grew sharp again, edged again, and Carlina rushed to the door as fast as swollen ankles and knees allowed. Out into the night stumbling and yelling for the man to come back, "Please! Please! Come back, come back!" To the corner of this street, and the corner of that one, running through the fog and remembering how she dressed Jaime one last time before placing him in the coffin and pulling down the lid. So she yelled again, as loud as she could, again, for the man to please come back, please bring back the last things left of her favorite son, the first Jaime.

"But it was alright," my grandfather says, and my father agrees. The Ferreiras are practical men, and this was a practical thing. Clothes and names are for those alive enough to mind the cold and need something by which to be called. "Better someone use them, not just keep them in a drawer. And we convinced her of it later, so it was all right." *But,* I hear myself interrupt him, *it was the last thing left of him. No?* And for a moment it seems like my grandfather is considering the question, thinking of what to say next, or how to say it. He shifts forward and looks straight at the brown curtains behind me as if he were a man lying on his back and looking up at a brief blue sky. But then I realize he has decided to answer not the question I asked, but the one I probably meant to, or at least the one I should have.

"When it was time to move him from the coffin to the ossuary," he says looking down at the newspaper-covered table, "it was me who had to go." Stern and precise, he feels no need to meet my gaze or even speak in my direction. "They pulled him out, opened the lid, and everything, everything, was gone. Only bones left." His hand clears the air in front of him as if he has begun to see clouds of invisible smoke rising from empty ash trays. "Nothing, except . . . the cast." I imagine a plaster shell and a body made of hermit crabs skittering away, while I stare at Jaime's brother's steel-cut expression. "So the men, they broke it with their fists and with a hammer to get at the bones beneath." It reveals nothing of what it was like to see plaster dust and human dust mixing and rising from his dead brother's box, to hear the dry crack and pulverizing crunch of hammers and fists against plaster and bone. To see a brother in a hospital room tilting his head like an overflowing pitcher and fill bedpan after bedpan with his own blood. To be the loathed child of a present parent, the favorite of the absent one. To grow up to do and be the very same. To be elsewhere, to be drunk, to swing large fists at small heads, to slam doors, and to yell. Though not at the first Jaime—never at him. I watch him pause, clear his throat, flick ash, and stare at the coffee table. Newspapers and filled-out crosswords, one stacked over another, over another, over another. He shakes his head, I hear trains coming. "It was the hardest thing I've ever had to do," Jaime's brother in a once-gray suit, in a cemetery shed, in a loop, watching men stuff his brother's bones into a metal box the length of a femur, the width of two skulls.

PATADAS DE AHOGADO

or

Kicks of drowned.

or

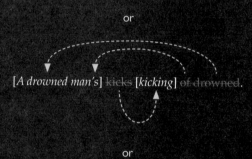

[*A drowned man's*] ~~kicks~~ [*kicking*] ~~of drowned~~.

or

Drowning men grasp at straws.

or

"Give it a second, it'll stop."

Thinking It Was Something You Could Hunt and Kill

This is the way it goes. Lina hears a pop. She wonders what it is. Not a pop though; there is meat in that sound, around it. Then a scream. It's Lina screaming, but she doesn't realize that right away. Then an instant without thought or sound.

Kai is standing over her when she opens her eyes. Lina's on her back and she is stupid, but Kai will help her up. Though he will, however, still tell her she is an idiot when she puts weight on her leg.

"Stop standing on it, you idiot," and she smiles and maybe laughs a little. Children run to her sort of excited because something different is happening, "What happened? What's wrong? Are you ok?"

And of course, Lina says, "Of course!" But she's wrong. Kai knows it already, but Lina is stupid when it comes to these things.

When she drives herself home in a blizzard, and warm things begin to get cold, she'll feel something rattle inside her leg. That's when she'll start to get it. "Please, please," she'll say, "Please God. Don't let it be as bad as it feels." She may cry a little and clutch her knee as the snow falls on the road, but she will still remember to return that movie she never watched to the video store.

Needless to say Lina doesn't go to a hospital as perhaps she should. She is a cliché and the knowledge that this is what she is does not save her from it. But that is not exactly why she does not go to the hospital; even clichés have occasional lapses into common sense, and there is nothing like raw, torn things to snap you into them. But she has terrible insurance and even though she does not yet know it'll take her a full year of dodged, past-due calls to pay off the whole thing, she does know it'll be worse if she goes to the ER. So, instead, she drives herself home—though first to the video store.

She's a little distracted, and the tires slide on layers of black ice and dirty snow, so she ends up parking about two feet from the rusted, dumpster-like Hollywood Video drop-off box, which is about two feet too far for her to reach. But she tries anyway; she's like that, knowing how something's going to end and doing it anyway. She lowers the window and tries to lean out by pivoting on her ribcage, by stretching her arm out, long and taut like a tug-a-war rope. She is almost there, she tells herself, "Almost." Though she is not, and for an instant she is hanging halfway out of the car window with a DVD case between her fingers before the pain in her knee slurps her back in like a loose strand of spaghetti. So she falls back inside, she clutches her knee with one hand and turns the steering wheel with the other, moving slowly toward an empty parking space across the street while the driver behind her plays telegrapher on the car horn.

As she steps out of the car to return a pretentious foreign film, she briefly hopes she is exaggerating and the pain is really mostly in her head, but then immediately she self corrects and hopes it's actually worse than it feels. "Wouldn't it be nice," she thinks, "to be brave."

The road is Teflon and loose gravel. Ice covered oil spill, and she has to stretch out both arms like a tightrope walker to simply stay upright. She tries to walk across the parking lot, tries to imitate her normal gait, but it is like walking through a nursery of sleeping infants with a game-show buzzer strapped to the bottom of her shoe. Weight on her heel, *Buzz!* Weight on the outside of her foot, *Buzz!* Tiptoe-toes and a half limp forward. *Buzz-buzz!* She is attempting to place all her weight on the inside of her foot when she hears tires spinning, and suddenly she is standing in a blinding stream of an SUV's headlights. The car slides very, very slowly toward her. She stares into the light and feels winter chewing on her toes through her cloth sneakers and tries to pivot on a torn knee. The driver slams his fist into the horn. Lina feels she is being run down by a flock of impatient geese, and she shuffles forward, dragging her feet across the ice like she is trying to clean a spill with paper-towel slippers. But the road is at an incline, and she has not made it far before she begins to slide back on black ice. "You are an idiot!" A man yells from the driver's side. She shuffles forward again and slides right back again. Forward, back, again, again. "Move, idiot!" Lina on ice and on a loop, a honking horn and more impromptu abuse out a rolled-down window. So Lina looks up, a moment through a windshield, a driver waving his hands like he's trying to land a plane, and she takes firm hold of the car's grill, puts all her weight on her injured left leg and pushes forward with her right. A foot like a skate-board and the inside of her knee like the grinding gears of a shattered clock, as she rides a torn leg to the edge of a metal drop-off container, and she crashes into it. Now she knows for sure that this is not an injury that'll go away on its own, and she begins whispering tragically predictable pro-testations into a frozen Hollywood Video storage box.

The pain she is feeling is not special, it is not unique. It's not inside her leg. It is on the ground and on the ice, in trying not to slip, to keep legs and self together, in the tension and anticipation of an imminent icy blow. But her knee has been turned into a tiny but powerful amp, she can hear every bump and every crack. The sound of an acoustic pebble travels through an electric limb and fills her like an avalanche in a concert hall. "Idiot!" She watches the SUV drive away and understands perfectly that every bit of this is self-inflicted.

She hangs onto the metal side as if it were the only fixed point in the universe, and she is expecting a flood. She tries to remember that thing about reality being the thing that continues to exists after belief is dispelled, or whatever—a saying she doesn't particularly like, but which makes her think, momentarily, that maybe it can work in reverse, and if she can only believe enough, she will be able to wind herself back in time to the moment right before she heard that scream, and pop, and Kai saying, "Stop putting weight on it, you idiot." Or, at the very least, believe herself into a warmer place where people will agree in big exaggerated motions that this is objectively disastrous, and catastrophic, and nothing can compare, though even Lina knows better. It's all the same, however, because she won't actually remember the saying until weeks later when it'll matter even less.

So instead, she clutches the box with one hand, slips the video in with the other, and as snow melts on the back of her neck, she reaches down, rubs her knee, and whispers, "I'm sorry."

When Lina gets home there is about an inch of snow on the ground and her leg has begun to swell. She stands at the bottom of the staircase counting steps and patches of ice. She stares for a while, then counts again. It does not occur to her to call anyone. Though she does make a mental note to call work and let them know she might be late the next morning. She tastes the salt of drying sweat on her lip and worries it might be hard to take a shower standing on her only working leg, imagines a doctor scrunching his nose as he inspects her the next morning, and she decides that no matter what she will shower, and the patches of sweat on her shirt begin to freeze. It's not rare, though perhaps worth noting, that she has not slept in a couple of nights and perhaps she shouldn't have been driving in the first place. Not perhaps, but probably definitely. She does not think to ask someone, anyone—her roommate who is awake upstairs—for a ride, however. This is not who she is or ever has been.

Finally she puts her right foot down on a step and pulls herself up by gripping the rail. She wants desperately to be alone in a familiar space, to lie down on her stomach, with her face on the carpet so the knotted, gnarled, and twisted branches of all her private heartbreaks and disasters won't sprout out suddenly and rip through her abdomen—ribs, leaves, and red-green trees. Fantastic and foreign, and sometimes hard to explain to friends and family back home.

Lina curses. She's loud—but it's ok, she tells herself, because everyone is asleep. She may mumble something like a prayer, nothing specific, just, "God, oh God." She is aware of the length of little ligaments and tendons, the woven hinges of shoulder and elbows and knees. She's dislocated shoulders and ribs, torn ankles and wrists, broken noses and thumbs. And she realizes, also, that this injury is a speck, and what is means to her is not what it really means at all. She sets down a foot on a frozen step, salt grains amplified through swollen speakers. The prophetic pain of a lingering future limp. She reaches a bit farther up the rail, but does not pull right away. She simply lays her forehead against the cold metal and feels the sleep that has evaded her for nights and nights descend on her with the snow. "I'm an idiot." She tries to think things like *work tomorrow morning, Kai and Sab on Saturday,* and *Korea in six months.* Of course she realizes these things aren't real anymore, if they ever were. And even when and if they were, they were only ever pieces of the cardboard corpse of a person she might have liked to be, had she stayed in just one place long enough to be known for something other than being the person who came from somewhere else. And that's when she hears the voice. "Help? Help?"

It's a strange thing, she thinks, to find in the snow. A boy of ten, maybe eleven. Dirty and alone at night in a college town. "Do you want help?" She hears him but doesn't turn around. She grips the rail a bit tighter and feels a sudden sense of urgency to overcome the staircase. "I said," he starts again, "do you want help?" But still, she won't respond because she's a little stuck. Like one of those jelly-thick, post-insomnia dreams, when she wakes inside a dream exhausted and sleepless. She is always aware she is asleep. She tells herself so: "You are sleeping. You can't be tired. This is not real." But the realization does nothing to the weight in her arms and the feeling that her blood has turned toxic and dense. She lies down at the edge of a cliff in her dreams and tries to fall asleep anyway. She has insomnia, and she dreams she has insomnia, and all the websites she consults say that as long as she is still dreaming there is nothing to worry about, but she hangs her head off the edge of the cliff—red and raw, as if the gravel had sanded her down to muscle and bone—and she worries anyway. And when she hears a boy behind her, in the middle of a snowstorm, she doesn't respond.

The boy stares up from an inch or two of snow and asks a third time, "Do you want help?" And finally Lina looks over her shoulder. "No." She looks just for a moment, just a blurry snap, and turns around again as if she's being chased. Maybe it's the knowledge that someone is watching that amplifies this little show she's putting on for herself. Maybe it's something else. "No," she says again, "I'm fine." Again, "Fine." She let's go of the rail with one hand and picks up the pace. Then a thought, which will later seem strange and inexcusable, but right now it feels like the only logical thought in her mind. She makes a fist, turns the heel that can still turn and thinks she can still pivot on her good leg and land a punch hard on the bridge of this boy's nose—if she has to.

One hand after the other, one foot, one step, one after the other, after the other. She pulls once more and then again, clenching her fist between each pull, waiting for a tug or a small hand on her back, to let her know when to turn around in a full swing and plunge a fist into a small boy's head. Seeming suddenly intent on breaking something in someone else's body. So she pulls on the railing, she knows it's nearly time, she begins to turn and sees it in her mind. Her fist on the bridge of a ten year old's nose, like a man under a bridge with a stick, a man in a van with a gas can, her grandfather with a bottle in his hand. She's ready to pivot, ready to fall upon him as if she were his natural predator and he were hers. A body like a sled, a spine like its stanchion, the sharp edge of a frozen staircase like the ridged back of a rocky cliff, but the tug never comes, and by the time she reaches the top, he's gone.

Lina limps the rest of the way, doesn't give the boy a second thought. She takes a hot shower, which is an incredibly stupid thing to do, and she really should know better. The water strikes the surface of her knee and widens the blood vessels inside it, ushering in a flood of blood and liquid, and makes it swell like the small, distended bellies of the parasite-infested children. And only then does she begin to think about the boy at the bottom of the staircase.

She does not go back to the staircase, but the scene comes back to her. How dark that little boy's skin, how strangely and lightly he was dressed in the middle of a Utah snowstorm. How perfectly alone, how terribly late. How much he looked like so many Bogotá homeless *gamin* boys, shelter kids and displaced children at intersections, holding rain soaked signs and outreached hands. Sitting on sidewalks and in gutters, lighting up cocaine-paste cigars, limping through the rain while yelling at something conjured and imagined in a mist of glue and cheap *bazuco*—one too many hits, one too many blows to the head. And it strikes Lina, suddenly, how she knows all her barely-in-their-twenties neighbors and how none of them have children, and when she thinks about it she can't be sure he was wearing any shoes. Lina doesn't sleep that night either, not more than an hour or two pinpricked in a wide-awake blank of a night. She's stuck on a loop, hearing a pop and a scream, telling a barefoot child who leaves no prints in the snow to go away, to leave her alone. "I'm fine, I'm fine." And as she dreams of trying to put a five-hundred-peso coin in a homeless kid's hand while he swats away invisible spiders, she lies on the couch holding her knee like a bible, like a dream, like a gun, like the side of a cliff and the door of a train, or the rail of a frozen staircase in a snowstorm.

DEL AHOGADO, EL SOMBRERO

or

Of the drowned man, the hat.

or

 [*From*] the drowned man, [*take*] the hat.

or

Every drowned man wears a silver-lining cap.

or

"We call it the bright side."

Empire of Toes

"Why don't you ever write something I can read, Lina? Why not write something in Spanish, or at least translate something you've already written? Your parents, they tell me all the time, and everyone's read something. Everyone but me. It's all only ever in English. And we spend so much time in waiting rooms, I could really use something to read. I would like to. If you would only translate for me."

A PATA LIMPIA

or

At clean leg (*Snout v. Mouth.* "Leg," animal, object.)

or

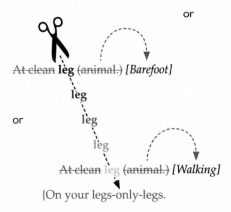

~~At clean~~ **lèg** ~~(animal.)~~ [*Barefoot*]

lèg

or   lèg

lèg

~~At clean~~ leg ~~(animal.)~~ [*Walking*]

{On your legs-only-legs.

Not driving, not riding, not rolling, not running.}

or

Walking.

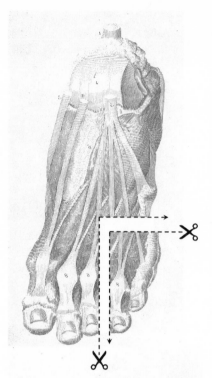

The toes have turned black, the two at the end. *Circulation, lupus, cancer, cortisone, chemo, radiotherapy.* All of the above, none, some. It does not matter. The toes, they'll have to go.

The foot is unevenly swollen. Bulging, sporadic, yellow-white blisters travel down from above the ankle to the tip of my aunt Chiqui's big toe. The words and proportions are all off, too big and hungry for the confinement of mere *blisters* and *scabs.* It is not one whole, but a mismatched union of painful shapes trying to split one from the other. An angry amalgamation faintly reminiscent of a foot. It is a postcolonial map in a child's coloring book. A featherless tropical bird; a bloated chameleon shedding burnt skin. It is a country at war with itself.

The yellow peels off in thick slices, the pink glistens raw, the brown sinks into crevices, the white stands on end, the black flakes off. The toes are both symptom and cause, consuming and consumed, stuck on a loop. They are the living dead. They cannot return to pink circulation, they will not fall off of their own accord, and if they are to go it will be neither quietly nor alone. So they scream necrosis up my aunt's leg, beckoning all flesh to join their purple-black empire, and I get an

email that starts with, "Things are complicated," and ends with, "They want to cut both legs off."

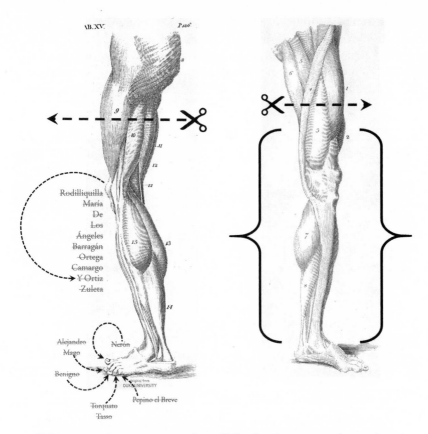

Rodilliquilla
María
De
Los
Ángeles
Barragán
Ortega
Camargo
→ Y Ortiz
Zuleta

Alejandro   Nerón
Mago

Benigno

Torquato   Pepino el Breve
Tasso

"These toes, they are tremendous." That's what my mother writes
from a corner of my aunt's hospital room while nurses unwrap, wrap,
and rewrap—swollen ankles, blackened flesh. She said the same thing
about Alexander the Great. He was short and bent on invasion, too. Rep-
lication, repetition, reiteration—to name cities and states and rivers after
himself, to fill the whole world with Alexander so that none could cut out
any piece of him without hitting a major artery. That's what they want,
these two toes. To leave no doubt of themselves. To spread, to reiterate,
to name and rename. So I more or less hate them, but am a little in awe,
too. Anything with such conviction deserves a name, at least. So my
mother christens them, Pepin the Short and Torquato Tasso. While I look
for the torn scrap of paper where I wrote the name my mother gave my
knee when I tore it up, too—Rodilliquilla María de los Ángeles Barragán
Ortega Camargo y Ortíz Zuleta. It is the current cat's sometimes-surname.
The previous cat's on-and-off nickname. The previous-previous cat's
more-often-than-not name, and she's named my aunt's toes after her own,
too. Her tiny toenail-less nubs, constantly curled, and constantly clawing
the carpet. Like a man hanging from the ceiling by the weeds growing
through the cracks, by the nose hairs, by the scalp. As if expecting at any

minute for the world to be turned upside down, for the sky to stretch out a long, plucking claw, or a surgeon's pliers and saw.

And all my sisters and nearly all my cousins and I have the same middle name. And I am determined to name my first daughter after my first niece and count her toes and name her knees and draw maps of Alexandria on the soles of her feet.

So these doctors, they're fixing to cut off my aunt's legs, but they don't know her. My aunt, she's tremendous. "Over my dead body," she tells them. *You can have my legs when you pry them from my cold dead hip joints.* And she means it. She means to die if they mean to cut, and above all she means to live, so she does—that's who she is. Though it is too late for Pepin and Torquato, and the doctors saw them off. Or maybe they pluck them off, like black strawberries to be burnt with all the other orphaned limbs.

So the foot is folded into itself, like an empanada—to save on stitches and leave smaller scars. As if one might not notice a three-toed foot on an eight-toed aunt. And though it's no longer very good for walking, it is beautiful and brief and hard to describe, just like the woman who wiggles the remaining three they have let her keep. The woman who lets me takes pictures with my phone as she reclines and takes another shot of morphine. Who turns the handle of the "As Seen on TV" foldable TravelScoot scooter I've hauled back from the States for her, until the engine whirs like a swarm of bumble bees in a tin cup. Who cuts off a taxi and makes the children drop their ice creams, while I run like mad beside her, trying to keep up.

So she rides Heavy Bastard— because that's what we have named it—as fast as she can through the bright grey world of Bogotá's cracked streets, just to see if it's much changed since her tour of emergency rooms and intensive

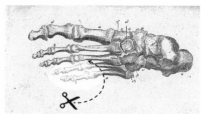

care units. So I carried that heavy bastard through the wide and narrow hallways of airports and airplanes until it left a purple groove on my shoulder—because a thing with wheels meant to carry people, was not designed with wheels for those who carry it—just so she might see that she is not so changed to see the world she's sure no longer wishes to see her, a few pounds more, a few toes less, nothing more.

She doesn't lie about the pain; that's not who she is. And she doesn't go out to the park ever again after that, either. It's not who she can make herself be anymore. She stays in, flips through catalogues and magazines, points at deals and sales, and explains to me how to get to this store, and that store, and how this chair right here—"Do you see it, the reclining one?"—will finally fix her back, and it won't hurt anymore, "You'll see. You'll see." Four months inside. Stacks of newspapers and empty pill packets. The time it takes to get a medical assistant certification online; the time it takes for fetuses to grow toes inside the womb. The time between Alexander's coronation and the burning of Persepolis down to black splinters, white ash, and forty lonely columns left where a great palace once stood.

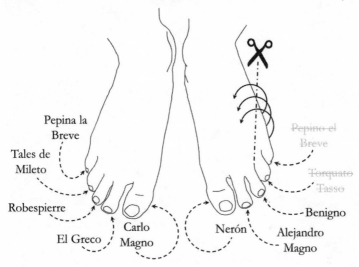

But not yet. Now, I sit at the foot of her bed, beside a reiterated foot, and I stare at the spot where her new chair is going to go. She points to the page of an opened catalogue and laughs as if it doesn't hurt, "Lina, look." A sale of mugs emblazoned with the Virgin of Chiquinquirá's face which turn blood red when filled with hot liquid. "You can write about this right? All the crazy things that happen here. And then be famous and rich." And I laugh, too, and promise to write, promise to translate, promise to come back. And then my mother walks in and raises her hand, three fingers extended, "Hail!" she says, "to the chicken foot." My aunt's new nickname. "I say hail!"

NADIE SABE LA SED CON QUÉ BEBE EL OTRO

or

No one knows the thirst with what drinks the other.

or

No one knows the thirst with ~~what~~ *[which another]* drinks ~~the other~~.

or

Nobody knows the thirsts that I've known.

or

"But let's pretend."

The Death and Burial of Concepción Dolores

"Yaneth."
"Yes, Lina." *Dime.* "Tell me."
"No." *Dígame usted,* "You tell me."
Y que quieres que te cuente, "And what would you like me to tell you?"
"A story. Something good, something that really happened."

My grandmother's nurse wears faded scrubs adorned with dancing syringes and twirling Band-Aids. She has freckles like dirty footprints running down her face and arms, and the milk-molasses brown skin and dark eyes of the mixed races that trace the roads from the comparably pale capital to the darker coasts.

¿A ver, que te cuento? "Well, let's see. What should I tell you?"
My grandmother stares blankly at a detective on the screen as he kneels down to talk to his dog partner. Lips out of sync while the Rin Tin Tin lookalike drools.

Above anything else worth noting, however, Yaneth is patient. She can sit for a very long time and say the same thing over and over again as if she's rehearsing for a play, "Yes, Doña Josefina," "No, Doña Josefina," "Of course, Doña Josefina," "Right away," "No," "Yes," "Yes, no." As if she's cracking a safe, every sentence a turn of the dial.

"Tell me about Concepción Dolores."

Yaneth is from a small, hot city near the coast. Sometimes she will close her eyes and smile, and talk of sweet fried fish, hammocks, mosquitos, and warm, shallow rivers. She has many brothers and sisters and aunts and uncles, more than she actually should. Because some of those uncles and brothers are actually first and second cousins taken in at this or that time for this or that reason to be raised as sons and to be called not "uncle," but "brother." It's not very hard to get her to talk about

Chiriguaná, especially on a rainy Bogotá day, like so many Bogotá days tend to be.

Though she's been here a long time now, and she says she's used to it now. She sits beside my grandmother and crosses herself a hundred times, then a hundred times more. On the screen a dog jumps through a windowpane of fake glass. "I've been here a long time. Ever since I came to work as a maid. I'm used to the rain now, but . . ."

This is a familiar story, at the end of the day you can always go to Bogotá, be a maid. God willing you have some luck, a godmother to arrange things for you, so you end up with people who actually pay you, who don't make you work on Sundays, with a father who travels and whose eyes don't wander. You can actually make it—that's what Yaneth says, anyway. "But my mother she worried about me—all alone in this big city. All that work in the day, all that study at night. It's a lot, you know?"

"Of course."

"She worried. I'm the last of five, and a girl, so she worried a lot."

"So, what did she do?"

"She came from Chiriguaná, moved right in with me."

"Why?"

"To take care of me, cook, clean, make sure I ate, slept."

"Then?"

"She got sick."

This part is familiar, too. Should be anyway. A cancer like a bleached sun drying her up, a skull like a husk, limbs like brittle snakes, peeling scales, and razor bones.

"She had it a long time, the cancer. But then it got much worse, much faster."

I imagine Yaneth's mother a bit shorter than Yaneth herself—same freckles, same smile—lying on a hospital in Bogotá under sterilized hands and iodine lights. Then a doctor walks in; maybe he's polite, maybe he's not, maybe it doesn't matter. He explains—politely, vaguely, technically—the situation. *It's too advanced, all that can be done has been done, odds are against you, your insurance cannot cover it, your body is not responding, there is a chance, there is no chance. You are going to die.*

"And?"

"And what?"

"And then what happened?"

"Then she turns to me, she says . . . have I told you before what she says to me then?"

"Yes. But tell me again."

"She turns to me, she says, 'Yaneth, don't let me die here.'"

And Yaneth wipes drool from my grandmother's chin, reminds her how important it is to close our mouths when we are eating and to swallow. *Traga mami, traga,* "Go on, swallow, love, swallow." She takes a big pretend gulp herself and slides her hand down her throat to illustrate, as if she's revealing a magic trick, as if she's swallowed a rabbit whole.

"She says to me not to let her die there, and not so far away, and so alone. You know?"

"I imagine."

"It wasn't easy. Leaving my dad up in the coast where he was, to come take care of me." A smile like a broken back and the rapid-fire sound of commercial breaks. "And Bogotá is so far, and they loved each other so much, so long—all their lives, five kids you know?" She has a way of saying things that makes you believe them. Make me believe. Even things like, "They loved each other all their lives." Which, I imagine, has something to do with how relentlessly she believes them herself. Her parents met in a town dance at the red brick heart of Chiriguaná. Her mother in a white skirt under a white moon, freckles down her face and arms like barefoot prints in the sand, and her father barefoot too, as he walked toward Concepción Dolores to ask her to dance. Then, the rest of their lives, four children, five? Brothers, cousins, hammocks and rivers. "Never seen two people love each other so much, so it was real, real hard, you know? To come take care of me."

My grandmother mumbles something, maybe a prayer, I can't tell. I can hear my mother across the hall trying to cheer up my aunt Chiqui, telling her the colostomy bag is only temporary, the cancer, too. *It'll pass, you'll see, hang on.*

"She picked him up and took him home. When my dad died, my mom did. Right after that surgery to pull all the tumors out of him and all." I imagine someone lifting the skin from his rib cage like a tent from its poles, a tangled orchard beneath, and doctors plucking tumors like black plums. "No matter. She just got on a bus, and all the way to Cartagena to get him." Six hundred kilometers on bad roads in a hot tin bus, to pick up his body and take it back home to Chiriguaná.

"And she must have known already, what was coming her way, you know? She must have." Across the hallway, in the second bedroom of this two-bedroom apartment, my mother tells my aunt that the next time will be better. Counting down surgeries like days until Christmas break. *They'll close the fistula right up and that'll be that, and back to normal sooner than you think, and you'll see, you'll see, I've seen you much worse, and I'll see you much better, too, you'll see, you'll see.*

"Why?"

"Hm?"

"Why must she have known?"

"Because," Yaneth is patient, "of what my brother heard her say."

"What'd she say to your brother?"

"Not to my brother. To my father. My brother only overheard."

Yaneth's mother travelled all six hundred kilometers between Chiriguaná and Cartagena to the unrelenting heat of the Caribbean coast just to stand beside her husband's body, to squeeze his hand, and for a confused second expect him to squeeze back.

"He was right there when my mother leaned in and whispered in my father's ear. 'I'm right behind you.'"

My aunt won't be cheered, and Yaneth's mother won't survive, and maybe they both know better than to believe the people who tell them it'll be fine. But Concepción Dolores—*Conception Pains*, because she was born on the eighth of December, right about the time the Holy Virgin would have begun to feel immaculate contractions—won't let herself die in Bogotá either, no matter what the doctors say.

I imagine warm breath on a cold ear. *Esperame que ya me vengo contigo.* "Wait for me a minute, I'm right behind you." Maybe they really did love each other all their lives, maybe it's true how some cannot live without others. *Espérame, que ya me vengo.* Yaneth is convinced, at least, and she has so many brothers and sisters, "I'm the last of five, see? Those two really loved each other." Or maybe Concepción Dolores simply felt it, beneath her skin, the blossoming of a cancerous spring while she still stood in the drowning heat of the Cartagena coast.

My grandmother stares at a K9 Division German shepherd as he listens intently to the demands of black-leather-jacketed terrorists on the screen. For a moment, at an angle, it's easy to imagine that my grandmother can still recognize me, and I want to ask her, "Do you remember, Mamo? Do you remember your husband, the Colonel? Do you remember the jungle? Do you remember the coast where you are from? Do you remember home?" But even if she were still wholly there, if she remembered me and remembered it, she wouldn't tell me about Barranquilla where she was born and raised. She spent her entire life trying to forget and to make others forget alongside her, to pave over her coastal accent with the Bogotá flatness, and to remind us every so often about the nice plot she bought in a nice Bogotá cemetery. "Bury me here, where I'm from."

Yaneth straightens her Band-Aid-decorated scrubs and says that when her mother got back from burying her father, it was ok for a little bit but then way, way worse than it'd ever been before. Concepción Dolores had gone from healthy to sick, to healthy to sicker, to just ok and then to nothing left but pray. From Chiriguaná to Bogotá, to Cartagena to Chiriguaná, back to Bogotá again, to a hospital again, again. Renewed diagnoses, black plum tumors, and bleached white hospitals rooms. Back, again, to beg Yaneth to take her home one last time. "'Don't let me die here,' that's what she said to me. And what was I going to do?"

Math. If your mother asks you take her home so she can die, you do math. At least you would, if you were Yaneth. You'd calculate kilometers, hours, dirt roads, ticket prices, and discomfort, and—if you were Yaneth—you'd come to the conclusion that a car is the best option, and then you'd find one.

"Like a taxi?"

"No, no. A friend's friend with a Renault who said he'd drive."

"Like a favor?"

"No, no, no. For a fee."

"And then?"

Paperwork. "So much paperwork," she laughs as if it's a joke, and repeats it as if it's a particularly funny one, "*Un papeleo tremendo.*" Stacks and stacks of it, initials and dotted lines. "Had me sign everything, everything" and everything twice. Because hospital administration and legal services take these things very seriously. They made her sign over and over that she knew, that she knew, that she knew what she was accountable for, what they weren't, what was happening next, and what certainly, certainly wouldn't. *Can't sue, will die, signature here, and here, and initial here, and here, and here.*

"What was I going to do?" Sign and sign and sign and initial and sign. Show that she knew and knew and knew to the satisfaction of lawyers and administrators, and then check her mother out.

Chiriguaná is one of those tropical-heat cities in Colombia, forgettable for their proximity to more important cities, and surrounded on all sides by swamps, sugar cane fields, and coffee. An outward spiral of old villas and cool adobe houses that become apartment complexes and barred-window constructions the farther you walk from the still vaguely colonial town square. The town becomes fainter and fainter, too, the farther you go from the cathedral's stone steps—turns into farms, into grass, disappears into Venezuela, Santa Marta, and the Cesar River. This is where Concepción Dolores was born, where she once lived and would have lived all her life had her dandelion children not scattered themselves across the country. Had her youngest not gone off to that big city in the mountains, to work and study and go for days without sleeping between bleach, dishes, and textbooks.

So Yaneth took her mother by the arm, "Mamá, take it slow," and walked slowly-slowly at her mother's pace, "Almost there, almost," reassuring her with each step that "it's ok, there's no rush, Mamá, no rush." Though the entire endeavor is threaded with rush. Home before midnight, back before too late, in bed just in time—final rites and last goodbyes. So Yaneth held her mother's arm and leaned forward to meet her at old age's height and help her into a grey Renault 12. I almost see it, Yaneth telling her to watch her head and watch her step. "That might be hot, that might not lock. No rush, Mamá, no rush," and Concepción Dolores trying to rush all the same, having somewhere to go for herself and no one else for the first time in a long, long time. Maybe she brushes her own hair back with a plastic comb, does up her coat, and misses a button. I imagine trembling fingers and a smile like tinsel loosely strung over thin branches. As if someone on TV had just pulled her name out of a hat: "Concepción Dolores! It's Concepción Dolores!" As if everything might just turn out all right.

So, very slowly, Yaneth's mother crawled in and curled herself against a rattling door. She heard the sound of the engine, the groan of the suspension, and the cacophonous palaver of furious traffic. A moment, quiet. Driver, Yaneth, and Concepción Dolores, on the road for Chiriguaná— fried fish, accordions, and mosquitos. Yaneth sat in the back seat next to her mother. She held the Gatorade bottle to her mother's lips when she asked her for a drink. She screwed the lid back on and asked if her mother was too cold, or too hot, too something or other within her grasp to fix. But Concepción Dolores shook her head, saying that no, she was fine, comfortable, warm, though a bit tired perhaps, and that she was going to close her eyes for just a minute, rest her head on the door, for just a minute, because it had been the longest day to wait for the brevity of night.

"It's like falling asleep," she says. "Just like it."

Yaneth looks out the window and back at my grandmother. The tear ducts in my grandmother's left eye have somehow become clogged, and the left side of her face swells with puss and gunk and yellow-green bacteria that Yaneth has to drain daily by poking a hole into the swollen skin and squeezing the angry pustule. "I saw her rest her head on the door, and then breathe in, and breathe out, and it was like this." She makes a tight fist and holds it up for me to see. "Like this," loosening her grip slowly until a fist becomes a limp collection of fingers, "see?" Like a motion capture video of a blooming rose. "See?"

"Yes, I think so."

"Like falling asleep," she says. "Just like it."

A few blocks from the hospital, papers signed, coats buttoned, bags packed, Yaneth's mother loosened her grip around life and left her daughter alone in a grey Renault 12 to consider the legal repercussions of the unsanctioned transportation of human remains across Colombian highways. So, still within the boundaries of Bogotá, in the growing heat of the back seat, Yaneth does math. She counts and considers: the number of military checkpoints between Bogotá and Chiriguaná, the ever-creative schemes of the major drug trafficking cartels to slip past those checkpoints, the number of wrongly imprisoned men and women in the many *guandocas* across the country, the very unreliable nature of our legal system, and just what the underpaid friend-of-a-friend driver might do if he were to discover that the sleeping woman in the backseat sleeps more soundly than he can imagine.

"So, what then? What did you do, Yaneth?"

"Nothing to do."

"Nothing?"

"Keep going."

"Like nothing had happened?"

"Like nothing."

"Pretend?"

Pretend. If you were Yaneth, at least, that's what you would do. Pretend it never happened. Turn to your mother's body and talk to it as if it could also pretend. Say, "Good idea, Mamá," and "I'm tired, too," and, "Yes it is getting a bit warm, want me to help you with your sweater?" Pull out arms very gently from sleeves like there may be rogue, telegrapher nerve endings sending signals to towers beyond the grave. Rest your head on her shoulder or pull her head onto yours. Lean in, say, "Yes, yes, Mamá," or, "No, not there yet, Mamá." Try to balance her limpness with your own, mimicking the carelessness of death with feigned sleep, and tell your mother's corpse, "Yes, you are right. It'll be good to be home."

"How long?"

"Long enough."

"For what?"

"For there to be no point in turning back."

"How far is that?"

"As far as Bucaramanga. More than half way there."

"And then?"

"Then I told him."

"The driver."

"Yes."

"And?"

"He wasn't happy."

"But he kept going?"

"Yes."

"Why?"

Because it's hard to stop things with momentum. Pendulums, stampedes, avalanches, and lies. More than halfway to Chiriguaná, they'd passed more than half a dozen checkpoints, and no one had bothered to wake the cancer patient. Halfway anywhere, turning back is the same as going forward, so he kept driving because it made sense, and Yaneth kept pretending, even though it didn't.

She made the call from a little restaurant on the side of the road, talked to a brother, or a sister, said, *Nuestra mamá se nos murió*, "Our mother's gone and died on us. Have the priest ready. Be there soon." And then she climbed back into the grey Renault, leaned in and whispered into a dead ear, "Are you getting too hot, Mamá?" and "Almost there, hold on." Past Bucaramanga, past the checkpoints, and past any point in pretending.

Just like falling asleep, or falling. Things with their own unstoppable forward force.

I can hear my mother across the hall begin the long process of leaving this apartment. *It's time to go,* she'll say, and, *We have to catch a bus, it'll be dark soon, it won't be so safe.* And my aunt will reply with distraction. She'll change the channel to something my mother has been wanting to watch for ages, pull out a brand-new shiny something that needs to be seen to be believed, or a brand-new shiny problem that desperately needs solving. *I'll come look at it tomorrow, this is beautiful, but we really must go.*

I look at the screen, a new episode of the detective and his dog comes on. I wrap my arms around my knees and rest my chin on my forearm.

After the burial of Concepción Dolores, reality forced its way inside, and Yaneth started to drink and sing, lying all night on the tile floor of her one bedroom apartment. "Stacks and stacks of cassette tapes with *rancheras,* you know the type?" Mexican odes to maternal love on worn-out magnetic strips played on loop while Yaneth sang along, drank along—along and alone with her face pressed to the cold tile until she fell asleep every night. "If I wasn't working, then that's what I was doing. My mother, she loved me a lot."

I watch the dog on the screen tackle a drug dealer and ask, "So what finally did it, Yaneth?"

"What did what?"

"What broke the depression?"

Yaneth takes a deep breath and yawns. My grandmother notices the smallest changes in Yaneth's demeanor, and they seem to intermittently reassure and upset her in a way nothing else seems to reach her anymore. She looks out the window at a clear night sky and mumbles, "It's going to rain."

"My friend at the hospital, she did me some therapy for free. I was working in the hospital back then, so 'round lunchtime I go by, and she sat me down and said to me, 'Yaneth, you are depressed.'"

"So, therapy."

"She told me, 'You need to throw away the *rancheras* and quit with the drinking and crying. Got to move on.'"

"And it worked?"

"Oh no, not at all. I just kept on weeping and singing and drinking, I just didn't tell her."

Though I cannot hear it, I know that in the next room my aunt is saying that's it's too much hassle to leave, too much trouble and too dangerous. *Might as well stay, no?* It is what always happens. Though it is unclear how this might be arranged in a cramped, two-bedroom apartment.

"So . . . nothing then. It just wore off eventually?"

My mother appears in the door frame and walks straight to my grand-mother. She gives her a kiss on the cheek and tells me, "*Deberíamos empe-zar a coger camino,*" We ought to get going soon. "*Despídete y nos vamos.*"

"My mother, she appeared to me."

"What do you mean?"

"In dreams, she came to me. That's what did it—*she* told me to stop."

I stand up and walk over to say goodbye to my grandmother. I can hear my aunt's last-resort distractions across the hallway, and it strikes me, how she has lived this long in perpetual proximity. My grandfather died when his three daughters were only children, and my Aunt Chiqui wasn't yet twelve, and yet she took up his mantle. For her entire life she has lived no farther than a hallway away, within constant yelling distance of my grandmother.

Where I sat a few seconds ago, on the edge of the bed, that's where Chiqui must have sat a few years ago, before my grandmother's senility set in, before the surgeons parted my aunt's body like a biblical sea and walked across it with scalpels and clamps. When pretending wore its feet into stumps and my beautiful aunt finally had to tell my grandmother, "*Mamá,* I have cancer."

It's a small room; there are only so many places to sit. I kiss my grandmother on the cheek and half expect things to click back to a more familiar routine. At this point in the evening, before her mind left her and I left Colombia, she would have told me, "God bless you and keep you," and then, "I'll probably be dead the next time you come." She looks very frail and soft and helpless, like muscle and memory have all but dissolved away. When I press my cheek against hers, it's like a Ziploc bag of may-onnaise, and she drools on me. She's smaller than she was, but this is not saying much; she was short to begin with, as I am now. Then I straighten my back, and towering over her, I try to picture it.

My aunt sitting on the edge of my grandmother's bed after months of hiding her diagnosis. "Mamá," she says, staring into my grand-mother's honey-colored, still perfectly lucid eyes, "I have cancer." What does my grandmother think in this moment? Does she think at all? Does she see a vision of herself as a child again on a hot Barraquilla evening, walking on a dirt road with her younger sister tugging on her left hand and the enormous weight of an empty basket pulling on her right? Does she remember that basket, which her parents would hand her before sending her to beg for the priests' dinner scraps at the rectory? A litera-ture teacher's salary lost in drink and cards and women. Or is she really thinking about her eldest daughter? Can she really see her sitting there before her, her dark eyes watering, her dark skin growing pale though never pale enough to pretend she has better blood running in her veins than the "lower class" Barranquilleros my grandmother tried all her life to distance herself from?

Why does she say what she says next? Why does she say anything all?

"Serves you right." My aunt turns, her mother is unmoved. "It's what you deserve."

My grandmother pulls back after I kiss her, merges with her recliner, beige on beige, with a confined stare as if all objects in sight have exactly the same value. Nothing painful or special or memorable in sight. A television, a chair, a person, a portrait of a man in uniform, and dog detective on the screen. Only Yaneth and imagined rain clouds adrift on a clear sky. Then, unexpectedly, she speaks. "When are you coming back?" An unfamiliar voice rising from my grandmother's husk, as if her throat is made of chalk and sandpaper. "When are you coming back?" I stutter, I haven't heard her voice in ages, and I'm actually not sure. She turns to Yaneth, as if she might know, or might have the power to make me answer. "Is she coming back? Will she come back?"

Across the hallways I can hear my aunt asking my mother to come back into her bedroom, *Solo un minutico,* for just a minute more. *Déjeme mostrarle esto rapidito un momentico y ya se van.* "Just one last thing before you go, I swear." And I can hear it, the thinly veiled plead for company. A voice like something almost drowned, a mouse I pulled out of a swimming pool once—taut belly, shallow breathing. My aunt on the phone when I'm in the States and I call her in the hospital, hear her get tangled in the IV lines coming out of her wrists, her arms, her neck. *¡Linita! Llamaste.* "You really called," like she never really expects me to, and never really wants to hang up. "Are you coming back, Linita? When are you coming back? Will you be here for Christmas? How many years now?" And, every so often, when the diagnosis is particularly bad, she tells me, "Sometimes, I think, you really shouldn't come back." Because, she says, "What is here left for you? Just to watch us die."

Yaneth looks down at her lap and sets an index finger in the middle of her right thigh. "Like this," she tells me, and I understand that her finger is the needle. "I'm the only nurse in my family, see? Only one who could do it."

"Do what?"

Yaneth doesn't pause. She doesn't look out any window, to any ceiling or floor. She lifts her index finger and sets it right back down on her thigh. "The formaldehyde. It had to be me."

I have to imagine a priest, but it's hard to place him. Yaneth stands over her mother's body lying flat over a knitted blanket on a small bed. A brother or cousin or uncle must have carried her there, this seems clear,

Yaneth has another job to do. There may have been some need for prying limbs loose, if the long trip made the body mold itself to the backseat, or perhaps it's still in the grasp of the sleeping fantasy and falls limply into the cousin's, or brother's, or uncle's arms as soon as he opens the door. The room is small and cool, the muffled prayers and sobs blending together and seeping through the slit beneath the door while everyone waits outside for Yaneth. A priest is likely somewhere in the room, but it's hard to place him—this is Yaneth's moment. So she stands one last time over what is left of this woman who loved her so much. Then she hikes up her mother's skirt and lifts her sweater, wrinkled skin and the odd bruises of cancer and age. And then she drives the syringe into her thighs and abdomen, and pushes down on the plunger top, all the way down and through the painless resistance of a body quiet with death. Formaldehyde soaks through, a holy flood filling veins and valleys, tunnels and capillaries, and the inner vaults of what once was Concepción Dolores. It submerges cells and tissue, suspends decomposition and the natural stiffness of death; it is the substance of pretense.

Yaneth shrugs but my grandmother does not relent, she seems quickened by inquisition, and staring up at me she asks again, "Will you? When will you?" In the room across the hall I hear my aunt tell my mother of all the things she should have done, would have done had she left, not come back, and I don't know what to say. I just stand there, stupidly, blankly, as if I've forgotten where and whom I am, but Yaneth has been doing this a long time. A bent wire-hanger smile and she doesn't miss a beat.

"Of course she's coming back, *Doña* Josefina, of course."

LO QUE POR AGUA VIENE, POR AGUA SE VA

or

That what by water come, by water itself go.

or

That ~~what by~~ [*which comes through*] water ~~come~~, [*leaves, also,*]
~~by~~ [*through*] water ~~itself~~.

or

Water bringeth, and water taketh away.

or

"Don't get too attached."

Pain Pays the Income of Each Precious Thing

Like this. They drop this girl off at school after a visit to the dentist. Midway through the day, when all we do is throw stones at the rain. Her gums are numb, so incredibly numb; she opens her mouth wide and digs her fingernails into them, swearing all the while that she does not feel a thing.

Or like this. I hold the cat that has never liked to be held against my shoulder while you try to clip its claws. I press it down against my body like a baby full of helium and needles. It tries to wriggle out of my grasp, digs its claws deep into my shoulder and right above my ribs, climbing shoes on a mountain side, spigots on a maple tree—little itchy dots and pinpricks of red sap.

Or better yet, Jesús—who looks after the garden behind my elementary school classrooms in Cali.

Jesús, Jesus. But only the teachers ever call him that. A notch below their social class, and two below ours, he lets us yell, run, chant. Lets us call him, "*Chuchito! Chuchito!*" A round man in a blue overall jumpsuit, chest hair caught in his zipper, machete hanging from an unused belt loop. "*Chuchito tiene caña, tiene caña?*" Whom we'd surround and harass like so many featherless, wide-mouthed birds in a nest. *A ring, a ring o'* spinning and chanting and begging and pleading, "*¿Tiene caña, tiene caña, tiene caña?*" Until he'd take the machete from his hip like a holy staff, a brass serpent, a jaguar's tail. "*Porfis, Chucho, porfis,*" Pleasies, please, please, please. And hurriedly cut sugar cane down for us. Swift, sweet— soft, sugar-soaked pulp still sheathed in splintered stalk. Grant us, Jesus, our daily cane. One swing to pluck, another to split. And we ran swinging green stalks like swords above our heads.

Like this girl, back in school after a visit to the dentist, telling us her gums were numb, so incredibly numb; she opened her mouth wide and dug her fingernails into them. "Thee? Notheen." But it's hard to believe, and we tell her she's faking. We know that everything that hurts always hurts, and hurts right away, and sometimes for a long time after. So she reaches for a pencil. "Am noth lying," She drools, she protests. She pecks a tiny path of graphite holes across her gums with the pencil, colorblind stars on a pink sky. "Cannoth feelth ith. Noth ath'all." But we shake our heads. We say no. And no, no. "Faker." Because maybe we don't believe her, or maybe we want to see what else she cannot feel. So she reaches for a stapler.

Like this. My mother sitting in a cemetery coffee shop. Atop the metal table a wooden box full of her older sister's ashes. She lifts the lid and presses down on the ash-filled plastic bag, surprised by how little is left; how thorough the ovens, the fire. Ten years of cancer, hospitals, referrals, intubations, ambulances, electric beeps, and iodine-colored hospital hallways. Ten years awake and asleep, waiting rooms and induced comas. A thousand needle-mosquitos on a handful of veins, a hundred blood tubes clinking, a lifetime sedated and punctured. And it all fits in a box. A little wooden box. So she presses down and feels something sharp in the ashes. "Do you want to feel?" she asks me, because, "Not everything's burnt all the way through." Fingertips down on sharp bits of charred bone.

Like Chucho quietly going back into his garden, machete swinging from his hip, while we chewed through math class until the edges of the stalks made our gums bleed and we drooled sweet blood-water on grid paper. Like it won't hurt when the sugar dries up, when she doesn't wake up. Unfelt sores and private scars. My mother holding her older sister one last time while the cemetery men kick stones at the road. A final moment before placing her ashes in the ossuary beside their father and grandfather. Her hands are on the box, her eyes are on the lid, and her voice cracks, splinters, pierced and piercing. "No one," she says, "can call you names now, *Chiqui*." A girl, dropped off after a visit to the dentist, opening her mouth so wide we can hear the sides crack as we stick our heads in like lion tamers. A single-file line of staples above the gum line while the Novocain wears off.

**AGUA QUE SALE DEL RIO,
NUNCA A SU CAUCE REGRESA**

or

Water that come out of river, never to its banks return.

or

Water ~~that~~ [*which*] ~~come out~~ [*leaves*] ~~of~~ [*the*] river, never to ~~its banks~~ [*it*] ~~return~~ [*returns*].

or

What's gone is gone.

or

"Still waters run deep."

CID–LAX–BOG

Any minute now a message from the Offices of International Students and Scholars Services will appear in my inbox.

Please read this email carefully.

And I will. Though, of course, I don't have to.

It is the same email I've read dozens of times before, and like every time before I will find—listed at the very top—my full name. Official, personalized. With the strange precision and familiarity of automated bureaucracy.

My name. Long and unpronounceable. Too many *R*s, "So many *R*s! Am I saying this right? *Fuh-ruh-rah*?" But the name is Portuguese, so technically, I'm not saying it right either. *Feh-rrrrr-eee-rah.*

Dear Lina Maria Ferreira Cabeza-Vanegas.

Like my mother would say when I'd made her truly mad. "Lina Maria," number of names directly proportional to the heat of her rage. "Ferreira Cabeza-Vanegas." Personal, precise. Though the email itself will be pocked with the generalities of mass-generated messages.

Some students may not need to respond. Your legal status may be impacted.

A list of self-selecting *ifs* cascading down the page like an immigration Choose Your Own Adventure.

If you plan to apply for an extension . . .
If you plan to change your legal status . . .
If you believe you have received this message in error . . .

227

I don't. I can't. I haven't.

The eleventh of May is my last day here. Then sixty courtesy days to exit the country, during which—the email informs me—I'm not allowed to work or drive.

If you fail to apply for a necessary extension . . .

Though I most certainly will do both. Sixty days. *Tick-tock.*

So I hit refresh. MLA, NWP, HigherEd Jobs, the Higher Education Recruitment Consortium. *Click-click, tick-tick.* I send out letters and emails like braids down tower walls and corked bottles into high tide. Like that kid in grade school who would catch beetles and ladybugs to write his name across their shells with marker, in case they ever came back. "This way I'll know they're mine."

Reinstatement requires approval, a minimum of $290 in fees, several months of processing, and does not have guaranteed approval.

I feel sweat stream down my back as the summer presses itself up against the windows. I listen to the ambulances driving past my apartment and a sound I can't quite make out inside the walls. Something shifting between rooms, like the creaking of wet ropes, or the turning of a crumbling wind wheel, as if I were living inside the rotting belly of whaling shipwreck.

By following these instructions, you will avoid that difficulty.

Hickory Moby Dickory Dock. *Tick-tick, tock-tock.*

You are responsible for your own legal status.

∎

A man sees a woman across the plains. He notices her hair streaming down her shoulders like black cracks down a mountainside. He notices how she walks so softly through the mist, as if there were birds fluttering inside her bones. And then he falls in love.

This is the most famous legend Colombia has to offer. And it leaves a lot unsaid. Which is mostly fine. We've all heard it before. Except, I think about it more and more lately. It does not say what he saw in her, what made him stop, and stare, and want her so decisively that he ran full speed across the plains to reach her. And it does no say "love" either.

∎

"Welcome to the Unmmm. . . . Of. . . . Ammrr. . . . May I please have you Immm . . . frmmmm . . . ?" The second time I entered the United States on my own I was greeted by an exhausted, middle-aged immigration officer with a three-fingered hand. He slurred his words like a drunk priest through mass and thumbed through my passport pages before looking at the blue immigration form I'd filled while flying over Mexico, and then he sighed. "Wrrrng."

"I'm sorry?"

He cleared his throat. "Wrong. Got to do it over."

I stand at a barely rollercoaster permissible five feet two inches. Three inches below average and scarcely three above the Atlanta airport immigration counter. Eight hours on a plane, a sleepless night before, and a desperate need to rest my head on the sticky counter beside the immigration officer's hand. So it was hard to concentrate. A counter whispering promises of primordial sleep. But then, that hand. Bull's-eye center counter. A thumb, an index, a middle finger, and two sprawling knuckle-knot scars like a tarp lain over copper pipes.

If I could have only laid my head down for a second, I thought, everything would have faded into a self-solving haze. "Got to do it over. Understand?" But it would not move. His hand would not give an inch. It sat firmly on the counter, unmoving and unmovable. Skin and scar and anchor, full of bones, full of stones. "Hey!" So I tried to picture it in motion. A finger can-can, then a hermit crab shuffle, and finally one long sweep across the surface of the counter, fingers and knuckles striking my forehead and nose, brushing me off as if he were sweeping crumbs from a table. "You listening?"

It's not complicated. Not really, not at all. A dozen little fill-in-the-blank boxes. I went through them quietly in my head, trying to find my error. *Name*, right, *birthdate*, right, *address*, right. "Which," I started, while the officer began waving the next person over, "part?"

"What?"

"Which . . ." Three fingered hand on a lovely flat counter. "Which is the wrong one? Where's the one . . . the not right one?"

He looked down at me and I looked up at him. He had a reddish white face and eyebrows like prickly patches of gray grass. I remember hearing knuckle bones turning like gears inside his hand, but that memory can't be right. "Residence."

Below the blue eagle inside the blue circle at the top left corner. About three inches down. Question number seven: *Country of residence*. So, *right*, I thought, *right*.

Country of residence, in turbulence-shaky penmanship. *USA. Country*, I thought. *Residence*, I thought. Rolodex bilingual brain loop. *To reside, to live, to inhabit, to dwell, to settle, to occupy. To nest, endure, sojourn.* Re-side. Re-sident. *Where do I settle-dwell-nest-endure? Where do I lay down my head?*

So, *right*, I thought. *That's right, right?* So, "That's right," I told him. "Right?"

The immigration officer straightened his back, spine like the string in a trap. "Like, what's the wrong part of it?" Thinking, perhaps, that I should have written out the whole thing, *The United States of . . .*

"The," he said, taking a breath as if he were loading a gun, "the part that says 'Country of Residence.'" Then he lifted that three-fingered hand from the counter. I stared at the ghost mark of condensation it left behind, thinking of how vast it really was, that short distance between my head and the counter. "Do it," words, lead-heavy and lead-slow, "over." He said pointing at a table against the very back wall of the room.

"But. . . ." I tried again.

"Please." Taut spine-trap snap and a tower-of-Babel tall immigration officer bending low to meet my eye. "Do it over."

"But, what's the right answer?"

∎

What it actually says is this: he saw her and wanted her immediately. Which could be the same thing as love, but isn't. So I imagine her hair, and the color of her eyes. Black, like Huitaca's eyes, like scorch marks and the inside of a wolf's belly.

Right or wrong. This is it. All that is given.

He sees her and he wants her. Desperately, furiously. As if he had been born with that longing, always wanting her from the beginning of all wanting.

He sees her and feels the need to press his hand against her hip bone, to press himself against her rib cage. To push her down against the earth and the rock edge of a cliff, and feel those birds fluttering against his thighs, against his knees, against his own bones laid out over hers like wood for a bonfire.

But this man is not just any of many. He is the Cacique of Guatavita, a prince of the Muisca nation. Rulers of the *altiplano cundiboyacense*, where gods once trod, once drank *chicha* and wove labyrinthine patterns onto blankets, once flooded the valley to make a point. Where invading Europeans set down shackles and both intentional and unintentional roots, where I was born with a European last name and paleness which burns, blisters, and peels under my native sky.

This prince, however, does not burn. He was born clad in sun and divine intent. Born full of holy, royal blood which is, this instant, boiling and stirring and leaping up to meet the woman drawing terracotta snakes down her arms and legs.

And his wanting is hallowed breath through clay nostrils. It is decree and revelation, and there is nothing he cannot want which he will not also have instantly.

Likely, I think, she is honored by this attention. So she leans when he pushes, and follows when he pulls. She takes the blanket her mother made her from around her shoulders and raises it to his lips when he wishes to spit, so that no part of him is ever made to touch the dust of the earth he was born to rule. And she becomes the Cacica of Guatavita.

Possibly she is happy. Happiness is such a strange, sharp-beaked thing—it is possible. Happiness may be implied in how she receives him nightly and prays for him daily. How she runs her fingers through his long hair when he stumbles drunkenly into her bed, spilling holy tears and saliva on her lap as he mumbles about the burdens of blood and land and how it's all just red mud in the end. Though perhaps there is no choice to feel or to want, only to concede.

The legend says little of her wanting, so maybe it is less important. Maybe it is not important at all.

Regardless, heartbreak need not be implied. One night, he runs his finger down her neck, between her collarbones and ribs, finds a taut belly quickly swelling, and she thinks it is only the beginning. A billowing out in every direction and a wooden click of pieces snapping together. But, of course, she is wrong.

■

I visit a friend's apartment and look at all the shiny surfaces and uphol-stered things in her home. I lay my hand on an end table and it feels elec-trified, charged and sticky with days and dust. I dream of shapes falling into place and rooms full of sundried amulets to ward off impermanence.

I set aside some books I don't want part with: my great-grandfather's dictionaries, a green book with a dedication, and a tower-of-Babel stack of Colombian mythology. In the morning I pack all these things along with my passport and computer in a duct-taped canvas bag and go out. I drive around town with the windows down. I buy apples and kimchi and oat-meal in a corner store, and none I meet so much as suspect. I could have kept driving, leapt onto a train or the back of someone's pickup truck. I walk in and out of bookshops and Seven Elevens, I fall asleep in some-one's front yard, and I stay out until a cloud of frenzied insects descends on me as if I'm covered in blood and sugar and neon light. And then, because there's nowhere else to go, I go back home.

■

This is not wanted, or rather it makes the Cacica unwanted.

A woman heavy with sleep and heavier with child, and the Cacique cannot be expected to make his wantings wait for a woman, any woman. Even a Cacica of the holy Cacicazgo of Guatavita.

So she is left alone. Beside him but not with him. A woman on her back, then on the ground, with a child in her womb and then on her breast. The Cacica pinned down by weightless love and the cacique's choice, while she rubs the little girl's back until she falls asleep and soaks her mother's blanket with drool.

Long empty days spent walking alone around the lake, once and twice and three times over, until her child begins to walk beside her.

The Cacica watches the little girl leap up and try to catch clouds of black butterflies drifting on ribbons of gray mist, and that is when she sees him.

Across the shore, a shaved-head güecha warrior. And she knows instantly—desperately, furiously—she wants to press him down onto the wet sand like a finger into a wound. She wants to cut him down, wants to leave him in pieces, kneecaps and fingertips and nothing at all except his longing for her to come back and give him breath again.

Maybe this warrior wants the Cacica, too. Maybe he has wanted her for a very long time in silence and it is like coming home and going away all at once.

Or maybe she is the Cacica of Guatavita, and she is not quite the law but she is close enough to it, so there is no choice to feel or to want, only to concede.

The legend says little of his wanting anyway, so maybe it is less important. Maybe it is not important at all.

He exists as the object of the Cacica's wanting, and as the reason for the banquet that follows.

■

Hi Lina,

Tabs and digits and scrolling advertisements, and the sound of me clicking away on a hundred-dollar computer I bought in a garage sale two months ago.

You are due for the Imaging study here in Psychiatry.

Two years ago I responded to a mass-generated email sent out by the University of Iowa Hospital and Clinics.

You will need to do a 0.5 hour brain scan and 1.5–2 hours of cognitive testing.

A week later I rode my bike to the hospital through sprinklers and joggers and puffy brown birds mimicking the sound of speeding ambulances. I made my way past well-lit lobbies and waiting rooms and hallways, and I got lost twice before finally finding the wing reserved for researchers and their research subjects.

Payment is $120. Scanning times are generally between 8:30–3:30.
I will contact you closer to the time to set up an appointment.

A woman in white sneakers holding a clipboard met me by the elevators and explained that before the initial brain scan some tests needed to be administered. So, "Of course," I said, and, "Makes sense," I said, as she led me into a small room where two more women sat waiting for me. I tried to fix my posture and smile like those charming people in sport-themed airport bars, swiping their cards and checking their watches. But the woman in the sneakers was already gone and the two new women were clicking their pens and scribbling notes. *Come in, sit down.* The younger of the two explained that the other was only there to attest to the scientific standards of the evaluation. So, "Of course," I said, "Makes sense" I said, and sat down. I glanced over at the older woman who called herself the monitor, and who instructed me to ignore her completely because she was not important. Only there to observe the observer, whom she then instructed to begin the study, and who in turn instructed me to pay close attention because this was important, this was the point. "Find your way through," she said, handing me a pencil and placing a piece of paper on the table. "Nothing too complicated. Just a maze. Easy, right?"

I looked at the monitor whom I was not supposed to look at and then back at the grad student. "Easy."

"Do you have any questions for me?"

Sometimes the tests start before the test have started. The study that you are taking part in is not the study you thought you were taking part in. So, "Is there," I asked, turning to the woman who wasn't important, "anything I should be asking?"

"Oh," the younger woman seemed confused. She turned to the monitor, "Is . . . is there something? I'm just supposed to ask. People don't usually ask anything."

And then we both waited for the woman who wasn't important to shake her head and tell us it was ok to keep going.

■

The cacique sits in the very center, the Cacica by his side. It is the first time in a long time that it has been so, and this alone should have given her pause. Which perhaps it does. But they are both surrounded by throngs of subjects, and the cacique does not utter a single word. So she waits—they all wait—until the soldiers and priests burst into the circle, dragging behind them, tied to a pole, the main course.

The man is beaten, swollen, and bruised, but she recognizes him immediately, and I imagine this is the moment the Muisca prince decides to speak. To explain the price of betrayal, that there are oaths you cannot break and things you cannot stop being—no matter whom or what you may think you love. I imagine this is also the moment when the Cacica has stopped listening, stopped hearing anything but the screams of the man tied firmly to the pole now set before them. Now it is she who does not utter a word.

Though maybe she says nothing because there is nothing to say.

■

"Ok, then. Ready?" The younger woman asked.

"Ready."

And she clicked the start buttons on the chronometer hanging from her neck. *Ready.* Six two-dimensional tunnels, through which my pencil sprinted. Beginning to end within five or so seconds. "Done!"

"Ok, now this one." She laid out the next sheet with a maze about twice the size of the previous one, and I fought the urge to start from the heart of it and draw the line back out because it always seems easier to find your way back than to find your way in. "Ready?"

"Ready." I dug the lead into the page like a knife. My full weight against the pencil and I feared it might snap. Feared it would burst into splinters, lightning-split and wooden sparks. Partly to mask my overeagerness for the first maze—which maybe I had thought would be the only maze—*What? This is how I always do mazes. Do mazes all the time, me.* And partly because this is a rare definite problem I can rarely definitely solve.

One, two, three. Each maze doubling in size from the last. Four, five. A wild-rabbit pencil leaping and crashing through printer-ink tunnels, searching desperately for a way through. "How many more?"

"This'll be the last one.

■

Sometimes, in the legend, it is his heart, and sometimes it is his penis. Depending, I imagine, on the interpretation of her sin.

Sometimes they pull out the member from between his legs and sometimes from between coals, singed and blistered and still raw in the middle. Sometimes it is pulled taut like a thread, then hacked clean and tossed before the Cacica while the real work begins.

Because a heart is not an easy thing to cut out. A man is a hard thing to hold down, and a sternum is a harder thing to crack open and pry apart. A heart is a beating knot of red ivy, and it is very difficult to get one's hand around it, to get a grip, to hold and pull and rip clean out of a screaming man's chest.

Every time in the legend, however, they do. And I can't help pressing my fingers down on my sternum as I imagine fingernails digging into his ventricles. A finless, red-fish heart, flapping in their grip.

■

Iowa City is a quasi-transient town. Of seventy thousand residents nearly thirty thousand are students who come and go as they please.

From house to house, and state to state, counties and countries, study-abroads and jobs and stupors and fogs, like semi-domesticated animals, the tumbleweed people in tumbleweed towns.

I sit on my doorstep and watch them pack the trunks of their cars with coolers and grills, sometimes for tailgating, sometimes for barbeques, sometimes for nearby lakes full of golden fish and black-green frogs. Drive out, drive back. I watch them pack backpacks and purses and clutch bags full of loose pens and change and lip gloss. Sometimes for class, sometimes for fun. Go out, come back. Watch them pack large Penske trucks full of Hawkeye memorabilia and sidewalk furniture. Drive out—always, eventually—never come back. And I like the summer solitude of half-deserted college towns. I like walking at three in the morning when the earth has finally cooled and nothing awake can speak any language I can understand. I like watching them drive away. And I like that they don't come back.

■

Sometimes he is a man—any of so very many—and sometimes he is a warrior.

This is not his story. Not the point of it. The legend barely mentions him.

But I prefer to think of him as a warrior. Not because it is romantic, but because it is more likely. A jealous cacique with a beautiful but neglected bride, it's only logical.

Regardless of who or what he is, he must always die. His must be cut open. Must be served before the Cacica of Guatavita in literal and symbolic pieces. And she must be made to feel that it is her heart being cut out, too.

It is possible that she loved him, just as it is possible that their affair was pure reaction and opportunity.

Possible, surely, that the sight alone, and nothing else, would warrant the Cacica's trembling. Her skin turning pale gray as she leans over her knees and vomits in convulsive fits as the Muisca soldiers pry her lover's chest open with their fingertips.

She needn't even have known him to react to the sight. Sitting there beside the holy cacique of Guatavita while a man's chest is split open with a hatchet like lightning striking a rotten tree. And what else is she supposed to do but scream, as the cacique orders that she be lifted up from the ground where she has fallen and be made to watch. Be made to stick her head into a wide-mouth chest like a lion tamer, between rib-cage fangs and pulsing gums to feel the scarlet breath of organs grinding to a halt.

So maybe she loved him, or maybe she actually loved the cacique, and maybe she would have loved the anguish of having a choice between them.

Or maybe it's simpler than that. And after the cacique's scorn all she wanted to do was go back home. To the plains where she drew terracotta snakes down her arms and legs, down her sister's arms and legs and on the ground where Huitaca and Nemqueteba once walked and talked, and where she last felt she belonged. And maybe the man hanging his head and spilling into the unholy dirt beneath simply had the right accent to remind her of what she might have been had she never left.

But who would turn down a king?

■

"So where are ya off to now? PhD? Home? Vacation?" Some days it seems like I know every single one of the remaining forty thousand people left in Iowa City. And it's always the same question.

"Not that much of a choice," I say, in the middle of the Iowa City Public Library, waiting for my next tutoring job to start. "Government says I gotta go—so I gotta go."

"Oh, right. That." The woman turns her head in a sympathetic angle, and she really does seem sincere, "Tough. Well you can always . . ."

"I'm thinking about having a deportation party," I cut her off before she has a chance to finish her sentence.

When I was a kid, my father's sister—who worked as a nanny for rich people in the U.S.—sent us Betamax tapes of recorded U.S. television. *Frosty the Snowman*, *A Pink Panther Christmas*, *The Dark Crystal*, and *The Blue Lagoon*, like whole rotisserie chickens, skin and bones, magnetic-strip static and seasonal Sears's commercials.

"Oh yeah?"

And though neither Paula nor I spoke English, we watched them on a loop on my family's brand-new, twelve-inch, color TV.

"Sure. People could come dressed to fit the theme. It could be great." I see the woman shuffling and know she has somewhere to go, something to do, she works here—of course she does. But I don't stop talking either. "It really could be, you should come." Though *The Blue Lagoon* proved disappointingly boring and *The Dark Crystal* was our instant favorite, I loved one commercial above all else. A man driving through the white howl of a winter storm, which neither of us could even imagine back then. He sat in his car for a second and then pressed a single-red-button remote and watched as the garage door raised itself like Lazarus from his grave. "I've never thrown a theme party before . . . or a party. But how hard can it be?"

I remember rewinding the tape and watching the commercial over and over and over again. My parents said winter was brutal, *Up there? Brutal. En los Estados Unidos.* That we couldn't begin to imagine. *They pay to make their buildings feel like our weather.* The man pressed the button, the wind howled. *Bogotá isn't cold. We don't know real cold. We're so lucky like that.* The door raised itself—all on its own, miraculous-mechanical. *We went there once. We took our galoshes. Useless. Cold that stays with you your whole life.* The man drives in, single-red-button push, the door closes behind him. *But it's like Star Trek, too. You can't imagine. Doors open all on their own.* And when they said my father's sister might come back to Colombia, I couldn't imagine it either. Who would turn down *Star Trek?*

"And the theme?"

"Deportation."

The woman in the library raises an eyebrow and turns her head a little. "Like," a pause, "immigration officers?"

"No. Well, I don't know. Could be." I have not thought this through. I hear automatic doors sliding open and the AC fighting the Iowa heat. "More like, get a baby, tie an anchor it. Wet your back, bring a bouquet made of green cards. Maybe something to do with Home Depot?"

"Oh my!" She is smiling but she straightens her spine like someone has just dropped an ice cube down the back of her shirt. "That could be fun."

"And everyone can take something on their way out. Like a lamp, or a chair, or a book, or my TV. That way I don't have to drive that stuff to the Goodwill. Right?"

"Do you mean . . ." She plays with her nametag. "Like a baby doll, or a real baby?"

■

It is too late for the Cacica.

Too late for her and too late for the legend to explain more than it has. Too late to reverse the European invasion and recover the legend as it was once told and understood.

The Cacica runs to her bed chamber with specks of her former lover's blood on her cheeks. She falls to her knees at the sight of her child, this little girl with black eyes, covered in dirt and blisters from braiding long roots and swinging from tree branches, and the Cacica wraps her arms around her daughter.

She must say something to her, as she picks her up and begins running toward the lakeshore. The legend does not specify, but I am certain she does. Something incomprehensible, perhaps. Even to herself, "It's all red mud in the end," because the cacique's men are already coming for her and there's no time left.

So she picks up the girl and she runs.

To the lake and into it.

She does not wade; she does not stumble. She leaps in. Sand and stones and bare feet and a bottomless lake high atop Andean peaks. She lets the blankets wrapped around her shoulder float away. She holds the child tight to her chest and she dives into the water. She plunges in—she swims down.

The story is about heartbreak. I've heard it a million times, and I've asked. "It's about heartbreak," a tour guide in Guatavita told me.

"But why does she go into the lake? What's there for her? What does she think she will find?"

"Nothing."

"It can't be nothing."

"Nothing."

"There must be something. She seems so sure, and there are so many ways to die."

"It's about heartbreak. She is not thinking, and she doesn't swim—she sinks."

It's not that I can't understand, or disregard the authority of official tour guides.

It's just that I think she swims.

I've read it a million times, and sometimes she definitely swims.

I see her through streaks of stolen light streaming through the shattered surface of an Andean lake. Suspended for a second while soldiers race to the shore. She's cut her foot with the sharp edge of a rock, and thin red threads slip out like whispers as she swims, one handed, clutching her daughter tightly to her breast.

∎

Are you feeling healthy and well today?
Are you currently taking any antibiotics?

I walk through the empty hallways of the normally undergrad-filled plasma center, and it's like a cracked maraca. The normal noise of the rolling crowds, shaking donors and grumbling phlebotomists is now reduced to a few hollow *plicks* and *placks* inside a nearly empty building. I alone stand before the row of touch-screen computers, halfheartedly answering the prescreening questionnaire.

Have you been pregnant in the last 12 months or are you pregnant now?

"Black Dynamite" plays in the background, and a frat boy in grey sweatpants falls asleep in a chair, while an older man in a grease-stained coat rocks back and forth on a folding chair, whispering into a paper cup as if it's a tin-can telephone.

In the past 8 weeks have you had any vaccinations?

The frat boy catches himself right before falling off his chair and on to a freshly disinfected tile floor, but then he stumbles to his feet, pulls his sweatpants up and his t-shirt sleeves down, while the older man taps the side of his cup gently as if to keep the heavier words from pooling at the bottom, and I try to hear what he whispers. The frat boy manages only two or so steps before a beautiful blonde phlebotomist walks past us, and he pull his pants back down and his sleeves back up, exposing a pair of black and gold basketball shorts and a pink Band-Aid on his shoulder.

*In the past 12 **months** were you the recipient of a transplant
such as organ, tissue, or bone marrow?*

On-screen, Black Dynamite finds out his murdered brother had been working undercover for the CIA, and off-screen the frat boy goes into one of the screening rooms. As he walks by he flashes his pink Band-Aid one more time and I immediately know that floating in his bloodstream, like backwash in a can of Coke, are traces of the rabies virus.

*In the past 12 **months** have you come into contact with someone else's blood?*

I know, because I have them, too. A couple of shots a week and more than double the money for each "donation." Two shots, seven times, and one cheap, pink fluorescent Band-Aid that always fell of within the hour and left a sticky outline around a swollen patch of skin.

I touch my shoulder where the Band-Aid used to be as the next question flashes on the screen.

*In the past 12 **months** have you had a tattoo?*

■

"And then?"
"What do you mean?"
"She dives into the lake, ok. She sinks. The end?"
"No."
"So then what?"
"Then . . . he follows."

But the cacique does not follow.
Not really. He cannot be expected to baptize his hallowed limbs for the sake of this woman. And yet, he cannot, also, be expected to do nothing.
To let them slip through divine grasp and watch his only daughter sink to the bottom of a bottomless lake.
So he orders his priests to go down and bring the child back.

The legend implies love. Implies an unripped heart still beating inside the cacique's chest for this little girl, his only one little, dark-eyed girl.

It implies a man whose feet have never touch the ground suddenly falling to his knees on the shore. Unholy sand and dirt and stones touching sun-anointed skin as he trembles and watches soaked priests crawl out of the lake, breathless and childless.

It may imply guilt, even. Fistfuls of gray sand like he is trying to dig out the shore's own heart. Rage, maybe, envy. Childish fury at being cheated out of his party. And maybe he howls. He weeps and rubs sand down his face, covering himself in black dirt and red mud as he mumbles to himself, *What have I done? What have I done?* Maybe he really did love them.

But likely it is not just one thing. Because it very rarely is.

■

"You kinda have to sign it here while I watch. It's weird, I know. But, you know. Just to make sure, you know?" The Phys Sub pointed at a line that read *I understand the risks involved in participating in this study.* Which I didn't, because I barely glanced at the document before signing above the dotted line. What I did know was this: first, you were paid four times a month; second, reporting "adverse reactions" would get you booted from the program. And what's a little headache, dizziness, muscle pain, nausea, stomach pain, vomiting, diarrhea, lightheadedness, and fainting, anyway?

The Phys Sub rubbed my left shoulder with a cotton swab soaked in alcohol and asked me where I was from, "*Fu-ruh-rah?* Am I pronouncing that right?" The question implies only one correct pronunciation; it implies authority and authenticity I may not have.

"Oh, it's a Portuguese name. I'm not pronouncing it right either."

She took out a small glass vial of clear liquid and shook it like a kid with a soda can. "So, Portugal then?"

"Oh. No. Colombia. The Portuguese just got around. Colonial thing."

She ripped a new syringe out from its packaging and pulled off the plastic cap. "And your family is still out there?" I nodded. "I bet you miss them tons." I smiled. "You gonna go back after this? Or they gonna follow you up here?"

My aunt Chiqui is not long for this world and she knows it. She sits on her bed all day, staring out at Bogotá from her window. What cancer didn't take, chemo wrecked. She can barely see, barely walk, and she never leaves her apartment. She holds the oxygen mask to her face and feels a deep crumbling rot, which the doctors cannot account for, spreading through her back, so she turns to my mother and says, "Vilma, please don't go." She knows my mother has not seen her daughters all together in well over a decade, and I believe she empathizes, but she also does not want to die alone. Not in her country, not in her bedroom. Not anywhere. The rot feels deep and ancient. Like wooden beams made into moldy peach meat by fat, white worms chewing holes in her muscles and filling them back up with squirming egg sacks. The pain holds my aunt tight, and she holds my mother tighter still, but she promises that she will die soon and my mother won't have to take care of her anymore. "But please don't leave me yet."

"Probably not," I said, watching the Phys Sub stick the needle in the vial's plastic cap, a white-hot knife into a tub of vanilla ice cream.
"So," she said, "how do *you* say it then?" What does staying imply? What does going back?
"Oh, um. *Ferreira.*" I rolled my tongue, overenunciating as I held up my sleeve and watched her stick the needle into my shoulder.
"Oh, wow," she said, pushing on the plunger head and pumping me full of iced rabies. Then she winked. "That's sexy." And asked, "What do you miss the most from back home?"

∎

He paces on the beach, and he yells at the wet priests coughing algae and little silver fish until he falls once more to the ground and holds his head between his hands. Likely he cannot hear the shivering priest explain to him that the lake is a deep kingdom of ravenous life. That though they have crowned the Cacica their queen and placed her on a throne made of the long bones of an unrecognizable animal, it is too late for the child.

∎

The second I stepped out of the air-conditioned plasma center I felt it. I scratched around the Band-Aid and felt the swollen vaccine-knot growing under my skin. Then three steps into the wafting curtains of heat and humidity of an Iowa City summer and the sky began to flicker. A white-blister sun and lemon-juice light suddenly dimmed and watered down. Translucent rabies termites crawled through my rotten-wood veins, and I made it three blocks before stumbling onto a bench and fainting. And I sank, I did not swim. Something held me tight and pulled under.

∎

"Why too late? How too late?"
"Unrecoverable."
"How? Why?"
"Because."
"Because?"
"Some things you can't get back."
"She's dead."
"No."
"Little girl is dead, has to be."
"No."

"What then?"
"Her eyes."
"What about them?"
"Gone."

■

I scratch at the scab on my left arm while I wait to be called in for my intake interview. Scar tissue has built up like grime, like barnacles, like gold flakes in a pan over the years. Sometimes enough builds up that when a phlebotomist pierces the scab, it crumbles like a sugar cookie, warm blood drips down my forearm and pools in my palm while a man or woman in a white lab coat frantically dabs it with cotton and gauze as if trying to plug a dam with Q-Tips.

A young phlebotomist tries to calm the man speaking into his paper cup. He tries to place his hand on the man's shoulder, but the man shakes it off and his whispers suddenly become audible. "I'm not going anywhere," the man says, pacing and shaking his head. "Not going anywhere. Can't make me. Can't make me. Stay right here, I'll stay right here." Sometimes speaking into his paper cup and sometimes directly at me and the young phlebotomist. "I'm staying right here."

As a thin thread of blood drips down my forearm, I picture my veins like great cylindrical halls lined with all the willing and unwilling participants of my mixed heritage, while the rabies virus floats soggily between them like too few Cheerios in too much milk.

■

The lake is a kingdom of ravenous things.

This is what I imagine the Cacica whispers into the child's ear before plunging into the lake. *The lake is a kingdom of ravenous things.* Softly and calmly, there is no point in alarming her. *So close your eyes, child. Close your eyes and don't look back.* Because the water is full of tiny, needle-toothed dragons, and they cannot be blamed for pecking at a young girl's wide, white eyeballs as her mother swims them both back to the beginning. Like Bachué swam back, like Nemqueteba said he'd come back. Like two black birds into a black night throat, down into the belly of an ancient god. Like looking up at a blue-gleam planet from the dark bottom of the universe's abyss.

Close your eyes and don't look back.

But a child cannot be expected to wait. She cannot be expected to not look back at the only home she's ever known and knows, even now, she will never see again.

"This legend is about heartbreak. It's a love story."

■

I sit in the Iowa City Public Library across from Sung Ho as he pulls out torn pieces of paper from a bag.

"I was watching a commercial Monday and in it they said . . . the man said . . . the voice . . . *it* said: 'Come down and test drive one . . .' Wait." He is a man of constant reiterations and interruptions. "Let me find it. I have it somewhere." I feel my neck like a rusted hinge as I watch Sung Ho pull out torn scraps of paper as if he's been gathering breadcrumbs all night and now lays them out on the table so I can draw him a map of the woods. "Right. Here. 'Come on down and test drive the new Toyota Camry.'"

He turns his head and places the piece of paper between us like the last hand of the night. We've talked about this before.

"Why test drive, 'The'?" He says, "You are only driving one car. You said 'an' is an old spelling for 'one.' One car. Right?"

"Right."

"And there are so many Camrys in so many of these car shops . . . malls . . . lots?"

"Lots."

"So why, 'The'? Why not, 'Come test drive *a* Toyota Camry?'"

We've been talking about this for weeks upon weeks for eighteen dollars an hour, but it doesn't seem to matter how many times I tell him that it doesn't *really* matter. "You *could* test drive *a* Toyota Camry too." That it's all about exposure. That if you are in the tropics you develop a tan, and if you're in Iowa you learn to drive in the snow, and you can't help it. It'll seep into you and, *You'll know like they know, eventually—you'll be like them.* It doesn't matter. He wants to know now. So, I repeat, "It's mostly usage, Sung Ho," and I watch him sigh and pull out more indefinite-definite sentences from his bag.

"Does that make sense, Sung Ho?"

He nods, "Yes." Then he shakes his head. "Sort of. Not yet. I . . ." he scribbles in English with tiny Hangul notes between words. "I will think on it." And as he's pulling out another scrap of paper, his phone rings.

"Sorry, sorry," he says, "it's my wife," and he begins speaking in a fast-paced, whispered Korean. He holds the blue flip-phone to his ear and cups his hands around his mouth as if he is afraid the words might spill out and soak the carpet.

■

Guatavita doesn't exist anymore. Not really.

In 1963 they decided to build a damn, and by 1967 the lake-adjacent town of Guatavita was completely submerged. Nothing left but the sacred lake and a sunken queen beneath.

The newspapers of the time are riddled with stories of the Guatavas refusing to leave their houses until new ones were built and readied for them in a new location. There is no mention in the reports, however, of any sense of tragedy, nostalgia, or ancestral loss. There are no grandiloquent odes for the place that had been theirs since long before there were colonies and church-sanctioned massacres, because the Guatavas are not a sentimental people, a town is just a town, and a new house is better than an old one.

So the government built houses with red-shingled roofs and white-painted walls. They built a plaza and a large church with a white bell tower beside a bullfighting ring of blood-soaked sand and red-mud clay. And then they placed a great, gray stone statue of the Cacica by the gates of the fake colonial town, and they did not call it *'Un' pueblo de Guatavita,* not 'A town of Guatavita,' but *'El' pueblo de Guatavita.* 'The' town of Guatavita.

This is what we call it, so this is what it is. And maybe it's that simple. They share the same name; they have the same blood.

"This story is not about heartbreak. It's not a love story."

∎

"Hey, Sung Ho?" I say as he hangs up. "You are almost done, right?"
"Yes, only a few more questions."
"No," I rub my eyes and lean forward. "I mean with school."
He looks up for a brief moment and returns to the pages of commercial snippets and overheard bus conversations. "Yes, a year."
"A year is nothing," I say, and I mumble to myself that I could hold my breath for a year, if need be. "When you are done," I start again, "will you go back?"
Sung Ho straightens his spine and narrows his eyes. He looks confused. Like I should know better, and I wish I did. *What is this story about?*
"I have a son," he says unsentimentally. "There is nothing to go back for." South Korea underwater, like a sunken city and a heartbroken queen, and then he pulls out another piece of paper. "'The McRib.'"

∎

This is a story about gold, really.
At least, that is why it's famous—the way the Spaniards made it famous after they heard it from the Muiscas and started telling it to others and themselves.
Because, usually, it doesn't start with the Cacica drawing terracotta snakes.
It starts here: there is a young man on a raft floating on the olive green water of the Guatavita Lake. He has not seen sunlight, known the touch of a woman, or tasted salt for weeks in preparation for this precise moment.

His arms are outstretched as if he were waiting for rain or revelation. As if he were too hot to let his arms touch his own burning skin. And quietly, as the priests around him mix plant pulp, gold dust, and spit in small bowls, the prince thinks of the Cacica and her kingdom of ravenous life.

She is the spirit of the Guatavita Lake, of whom he has heard all his life, to whom he has directed sacred words so many nights, and for whom he always searches in the early morning, hoping one day to see her wrapped in mist and gray light as she moves softly over the waters. Because sometimes she unfurls prophecies and warnings to those who will listen—floods, illness, dead cats, and bearded men in white-sailed boats. And now, as the raft floats on the surface of the water, the young prince feels as close to her as the child she pressed against her breast when she first plunged into the lake.

So he takes a deep breath and imagines eyes like emerald dust mixed with ash watching him from below, as she holds a holy staff and sits on a sacred throne. Then he hears the priests begin to pray, rhythmic pleas for the queen beneath the waters to anoint this Muisca prince, starved of daylight and women and salt, to reign true and just over this sacred patch of earth.

As smoke from burnt offerings rises from the shore, the priests dip their fingers into their bowls and they cover the young prince in gold dust. *El Dorado*, "The Golden Man." They lick their thumbs and press gold scales unto the prince's skin, then they all rise on the raft, standing close together shoulder to shoulder as if fencing in a wild hare, and they all call out her name in unison. *Cacica de Guatavita, Cacica de Guatavita! Oh Cacica hear our prayer!* Throwing emeralds, gold nuggets, golden carved snakes, two-headed turtles, nose rings, breastplates, bracelets, and masks, until there is nothing left but for the prince himself to dive into the lake.

And all the while the Cacica will be listening. Sitting on a sunken throne deciding whether to extend or withhold her blessing, as she watches her blind child twirl beneath a golden deluge.

∎

When Juan Rodriguez Freyle, the chronicler of the Bogotá "conquest," described the coronation ritual in 1638—long after it had stopped— he wrote that it was a "sacrifice to the demon which they worshipped as their god." The Cacica is not important; she's not the point. It's not her story anymore. Though few really focused on the satanic accusation, concentrating, rather, on the golden frogs and piles of emeralds below the water with the drowned queen.

How many times did they try to drain the lake? How many men? How many months filling up buckets with water and sand? How many

Spaniards traveling and dying through jungles and mountains to reach this dream place of naked emeralds and wild gold that would tell them exactly what their stories were about, that would make everything they suffered meaningful and all they did to find this place justifiable?

That *it* would make *them* meaningful and justifiable.

Heroes on their way back home.

El Dorado. El-Dorado. ElDorado. Eldorado.

■

"There are other ways, you know," a friend tells me at a local bar while I scratch under the adhesive gauze wrapped around my elbow. "We can go do it first thing in the morning." Whatever Iowa City summer heat the night dispels we summon back with bodies and shouting and music and alcohol and anxiety. "Just say the word."

I laugh. There is something to be said about the kindness of inebriation that so often leads to offers of immigration fraud. "Done! I'll meet you at the courthouse, I'll be the one wearing a Colombian flag."

A pound of fries is set down on the table, and I begin to pull off the neon-colored, plasma-center gauze as if I'm unraveling myself by a thread. I check my inbox on my phone. *Please read this email carefully.*

"My sister married a U.S. Marine, you know?" I say while scrolling through emails and job postings.

■

The first time my sister went back to Colombia as a U.S. citizen, she was greeted by a blond immigration officer sitting at a folding-table desk.

She stood in line feeling the communal sweat rising and mixing in the air while sweat-stained maps sprawled across tucked-in polo shirts and white linen blouses, until, finally, the immigration officer waved her over. *Documentos y pasaportes.* "Documents and passports."

Claro. "Of course," she responded in her flat Bogotá accent, and she sets down three identical blue U.S. passports—Paula, husband, and daughter. The officer picked up each one and flipped through them like an animated flip-book while heavy white foundation dripped down her forehead and down the sides of her face. She read through one and picked up the next while all the other crumpled-uniform officers repeated the same motions beside her.

But then she broke from the rest.

"And your passport?" she asked, looking up at my older sister. "What do you mean?" Paula asked. "Right there." But instead of a quick *oh-right-so-sorry-of-course-right-here!* The immigration officer sighed. She was a woman whose sole job was to meet travelers from all across the blue-speck world and who surely would have met other Colombians married to other foreigners by then—surely. And yet.

A sigh like steam from a pressure cooker. And she said, "No," with that mix of annoyance and disappointment usually reserved for children and dirty-pawed animals on white sofas. "You are *Colombian*. Where is your *Colombian* passport? Don't you know you can't travel without a passport?"

■

"Really?" My friend orders another drink. "Did she do the . . . what's it called? The swearing-in thing?"

I put my phone on the table and take an ice cube from my glass. "Yeah." I hold it between my index finger and thumb until they feel numb. "Whole thing. She even renounced her allegiance to Colombia."

"Hm. Must be true love then." My friend raises her glass as if to make a toast.

"Must be."

"So how does that work then?"

"Which part?" I scratch the terracotta skin ruts on my arm that the tight gauze left behind.

"The whole forsaking your country thing." Handfuls of fries and mouthfuls of alcohol, and the sound of billiard balls and ice striking the edges of tables and glasses. "How does it work?"

"Oh. I don't know."

■

"But I have a passport," Paula replied, "It's a U.S. passport because I am U.S. citizen. And it's right there."

Documents and credentials lay scattered on the officer's table like breadcrumbs. Paula changed her hair color, changed her haircut, and—much worse, for the officer—she changed her last names to match her husband's. Switched her maternal "Cabeza-Vanegas" and her paternal "Ferreira," for a single all-encompassing name, which Colombians generally don't do. So what was the officer to do? "Where is your passport?"

"Right there!" Paula points.

"No," the officer responds, "*your* passport."

"That one, that's *mine*."

"No. You are Colombian." But that is not what Paula calls herself any longer, or not what the U.S. government calls her, and maybe not what this story is about anyway. "So why don't you just give me your *Colombian* passport?"

I wonder, if that is the moment when it occurred to Paula that all her shiny new documents were in English, and that the immigration officer with strands of bleach-burnt blond hair may not have been able to read any of it. Maybe, this was the moment the officer became acutely aware of more than mere location inscribed in my sister's accent, because all houses stand divided, and there is privilege, education, and colonial heritage locked inside our voices and drawn on our skins. Maybe Paula changed her name to hold her child more tightly to her chest, because this U.S.-born child would only have one last name and Paula wanted to share it. More likely, that's when both my sister and the officer felt the crowd growing around them, pushing in on them, inhaling the air others exhaled and exhaling it right back into their nostrils, until the room was a mist of continuous breath and sweat and human heat. And in the end, there is no more compelling argument than that.

"I really shouldn't let you in, but . . ." said the woman who had likely never left her own country, never flown, and never had much of a choice to leave or to stay. "If you don't get a new passport," she continued as she stamped, and typed, and finally let the woman before her into the country where they were both born, "you won't be able to leave again," while white beads of makeup and sweat dripped off her dark Muisca skin. *You are Colombian.*

■

"Maybe," I tell my friend as the waitress sets a drink down before her, "you just say the words, 'I renounce my allegiance, I renounce my allegiance . . .' and it's done. Like that whole saying 'I divorce you' three times thing."

She raises an eyebrow. "I don't know." And tilts her head. "I've never renounced anything."

"Me either," I say, though it can't be as simple as that.

"What is there to renounce anyway?" She laughs and takes a sip from her drink. Half the fries are gone and more rounds are ordered.

"Don't know," I say, flipping through emails and looking for jobs. "Satan and Colombia."

■

Sir Walter Raleigh's son died in Colombia trying to find El Dorado.

After founding Bogotá, Gonzalo Jimenez de Quesada embarked on the most expensive expedition to date, only to waste nearly all his fortune and return defeated to live a few more years and then die of leprosy, skin washing off like flakes of gold and emerald dust.

Gonzalo Pizarro tried to match his brother's Incan conquest by setting down the Amazon River to find the lost city of gold. Famine, disease, violent attacks, and his ultimate failure to find a figment of collective European imagination foiled him.

In 1545 they tried to drain the lake and managed to lower the water level enough to find hundreds of golden pieces scattered across the shores, but not enough to justify the further costs of draining the entire basin.

■

"So," a man across the table asks, "you actually leaving?"

"Looks like it," I say, suddenly remembering that there is a Colombian waitress in this bar. One of whom I often think as more sincerely Colombian than I'm capable of being. "Unless a job comes through last minute." Reasoning that it's because she lived there longer, or lived there better, or at more important ages. Maybe she has more cousins—she cooks, she dances, she drinks *aguardiente* and goes to mass. "But that seems kinda unlikely right now." Though it might be as simple as her long black hair and dark eyes. Because I am no descendant of Huitaca, or Bachué, or any drowned queen of any sacred lake. I am no true daughter of the Muisca nation, but I've no interest in moving to Europe either.

"Bummer," the person across the table says. "Do you know when you'll leave?"

"Soon," I say, still looking for the Colombian waitress. "I just gave away my books. I've only to pack up and hand my car over."

"You sold it already?"

"Mm-hm, yesterday." I look behind the pillar, behind the bar, by the pool tables.

"Have you then . . ." the friend beside me interrupts, "have you already bought the ticket back?"

I pause. "No . . . my father," I say, and clear my throat because it suddenly feels like I have lake water in my lungs. "He insisted on buying the ticket himself." And I leave out the bit about how he cannot really afford it and hasn't been able to afford it for a good long while now, and how sometimes I pay his credit cards. "I think maybe it's symbolic, or something." And how I'll be moving in with my parents into their one bedroom apartment in Bogotá after nearly eight years of education in this foreign country of Star Trek and plenty.

"It'll be good though," she says nonchalantly, "to see them again. Right?"

I think I see the Colombian waitress coming down from a wooden staircase with a tray under her arm, and I want to speak Spanish again. I want to hear that history-heavy accent, speak in that slang. Feel like I *don't* have an "accent," and just as she turns the corner I feel myself turn, too. Away from the staircase, away from her, sliding down on my chair and pulling up my hood, because I want to say something in Spanish, but I also realize I don't have much to say.

■

On October 3rd, 1823, captain Cochrane wrote that after venturing into the hills surrounding the lake, a Spaniard spotted the sepulcher of two deceased caciques and the entrance of a cave flanked on either side by two life-size golden statues of native soldiers. He wrote that the Spanish soldier, seemingly unable to help himself, attempted to slice off the statues fingers when two indigenous men fell upon him, and—I imagine—tried to repay him in kind.

By the time Cochrane's men returned, the cave's entrance had been sealed off, and the golden sentinels with the once-whole hands had been sunk to the bottom of the lake, in part to spite the Spaniards, in part a last offering to the drowned queen.

■

The position has been filled thank you for your interest . . .
We received an unexpectedly large number of applications this year . . .
Please read this carefully.

Walking out of the bar is like sticking your head into an open chest cavity. Stagnant air and pulsing heat, and I miss the snake-jaw-snap chill of Andean nights. I miss the rain. I brush my hair behind my ear and imagine that in the bottom of a sacred lake a drowned queen brushes her blind daughter's hair with a gold comb while she whispers prayers into her ear. Miles away in Bogotá, my dark-skinned aunt Chiqui feels a crumbling rot inside her back and my grandmother loses the last of her memories. I think of them both in that small apartment. How my grandmother ranked her daughters and granddaughters according to the paleness of their skin. "No, Lina, you are wrong. Paula is whiter than you!" And how my aunt ranked last, and how she was the one who stayed with her all her life.

I think about talking to my mother on the phone earlier in the week.

"I don't think," I stumbled, "it's just . . . I don't think anyone is gonna hire me."

I walk through crowds of wailing undergrads and short-skirted girls sitting on the curb and vomiting in convulsive fits. "I know, Lina. I know," my mother said.

"It's just . . . I don't think." I picture the Cacica's daughter screaming underwater-screams as little fine-toothed dragons nibble on her eyeballs.

"Just consider," my mother said, "just consider . . . just staying."

The Cacica does not sink, she swims.

"Just . . ." I paused. My mother is a woman who believes in laws and fairness and holy lands and divine intent. "What do you mean?"

"Just," she said and I could hear my grandmother's nurses shuffling in the background and my aunt moan in pain. *Some things you can't get back.* "Lina," my mother on the other end, "don't come back."

■

Three months after that night in the bar, a plane lands in the El Dorado airport runway in Bogotá, Colombia, and I am on it.

It lands on time but then neither docks nor moves toward any gate or walkway, as if it is struggling with indecision. Instead it veers into a far-off corner of the strip, where it sits quietly in darkness as if at the bottom of a lake, while I stare out the window at the red lights flashing through a black-fog night like the eyes of sacred snakes swimming in the deep.

Inside the cabin people wearing various assortments of Disneyland memorabilia begin to wake up tangled in cables and drool-soaked blankets. A woman tries to wake up her little girl; a man tries to look up her skirt; and my father rushes for the aisle with a return ticket in my name in his breast pocket. Because, "You'll be back in no time," he says. *Del ahogado el sombrero, de tripas corazón, donde uno menos piensa salta la liebre.* "When God closes a door . . ." *That's what this story is about,* he tells me. But I'm not sure. I look out a window and try to see the drowned queen through the mist.

"It's ok," my mother says, sitting beside me, trying to console me as she clutches my forearm. "It's ok." Though I can tell she is on the verge of tears and my return marks her failure to keep me away from a country she is convinced is a kingdom of ravenous things which will either blow me up, or shun me, or "much worse"—she says—"turn you into me."

But now she holds the tears back. I should tell her that that is not what I am afraid of, but instead I say nothing, and I feel her pat me on the arm and say. *Ya llegamos, Linita,* "We're back, now. We're home."